The Relativity of
Continuous Improvement

Dr. Klaus Blache

RELIABILITY®
WEB.COM

The Relativity of Continuous Improvement

Dr. Klaus Blache

ISBN 978-1-941872-37-6
HF022021

©2015-2021, Reliabilityweb, Inc.
All rights reserved.

Printed in the United States of America.

This book, or any parts thereof, may not be reproduced, stored in a retrieval system, or transmitted in any form without the permission of the Publisher.

Opinions expressed in this book are solely the author's and do not necessarily reflect the views of the Publisher.

Publisher: Reliabilityweb, Inc.
Design and Layout: Jocelyn Brown

For information: Reliabilityweb.com
www.reliabilityweb.com
8991 Daniels Center Drive, Suite 105, Ft. Myers, FL 33912
Toll Free: 888-575-1245 | Phone: 239-333-2500
E-mail: crm@reliabilityweb.com

20 19 18 17 16 15 14 13 12 11 10

Contents

Foreword vii

Permissions. xvi

Dedication xvii

Acknowledgments. xix

Preface xxi

Introduction. xxv

Chapter 1 - Continuous Improvement and Change Management 1

1.1 The Current State of Continuous Improvement – A Personal Viewpoint 1

1.2 Observations and Lessons Learned 5

1.3 Employee Involvement and Enthusiasm. 7

1.4 Continuous Improvement and Standardized Work 11

1.5 Operations in Chaos and Crisis 14

1.6 Continuous Improvement for Business Excellence. 16

Chapter 2 - Change Implementation Concepts and Models 21

2.1 Back to the Basics with Current Issues 21

2.2 PDCA Cycle 22

2.3 Lewin's Model. 27

    2.3.1 Force Field Analysis 27

    2.3.2 Current State – Unfreeze – Change – Refreeze - Future State 29

2.4 Gleicher, Beckhard and Harris Change Equation 30

2.5 Kotter's Eight-Step Model. 33

2.6 Implementation and Expectations 34

Contents

Chapter 3 - Using Lean Tools and Other Techniques for Continuous Improvement 39

3.1 Lean Thinking 39

3.2 Total Systems Thinking 43

3.3 Nominal Improvement Hierarchy 44

3.4 Select Tools and Techniques as Related to Continuous Improvement... 45

    3.4.1 5S.. 48

    3.4.2 5 Whys 49

    3.4.3 Cause and Effect (Fishbone) Diagram 53

    3.4.4 Root Cause Analysis.................................. 54

    3.4.5 Seven Wastes... 57

    3.4.6 Overall Equipment Effectiveness 58

    3.4.7 Visual Aids/Controls.................................. 59

        3.4.7.1 Mistake Proofing 60

    3.4.8 Reliability Centered Maintenance...................... 61

        3.4.8.1 Failure Mode and Effects Analysis.............. 61

    3.4.9 Learning Curve 63

    3.4.10 Total Productive Maintenance 64

    3.4.11 Six Sigma 66

    3.4.12 Simplify and Reduce Complexity 66

    3.4.13 Ergonomics 67

    3.4.14 Safety.. 69

        3.4.14.1 Safety Process (Contextual Risk Assessment Tool) 70

3.5 Kaizen 79

    3.5.1 Grasp the Situation................................... 81

	3.5.2 Value Stream Mapping	82
3.6	Practical Problem Solving and A3s	83

Chapter 4 - Enablers for Successful Change and Sustainable Continuous Improvement ... 87

4.1	Core Enablers	87
	4.1.1 People As the Center	88
	4.1.2 Quality As the Driving Force	90
	4.1.3 Engaging Management Style	90
	4.1.4 Small Team Continuous Improvement	91
4.2	Individuals and Teams	94
4.3	Leaders	97
4.4	Followers	102

Chapter 5 - Model for Sustainable Change ... 107

5.1	Dysfunctional Activity Costs	107
5.2	What the Best of the Best Companies Do	109
5.3	Simplified Sustainable Change Model	113
5.4	Managing Complex Change	115
5.5	Assessing Readiness for Change Scorecard	116

Chapter 6 - Sustaining Change ... 119

6.1	Change the Thinking Process	119
6.2	Big Picture Thinking	121
6.3	Organizational Learning	122
6.4	Flexibility	123
6.5	Business Plan Deployment	124
	6.5.1 Business Performance and Continuous Improvement	126

6.5.2 Balanced Scorecard Metrics 127

6.5.3 Coach and Calibrate 128

6.6 Choice Map. 128

Chapter 7 - It's Up to You 133

7.1 Making It Work for You 133

7.2 Do Something 136

7.3 Ya Gotta Wanna. 138

Appendix 139

A. Blank Force Field Diagram. 139

B. Blank Cause and Effect (Fishbone) Diagram 140

C. Blank Risk Assessment Worksheet. 141

Foreword

The competitive benefits of a thriving *continuous improvement process* and understanding the people side of the business that drives it transcend all industry types and will stand the test of time. Properly engaging the workforce was an issue over 25 years ago and will most likely still be a challenge for another 25 years (because sustaining competitive advantage is a continual effort). The journey of continuous improvement never ends, but we can get better at getting better – enabling all employees to make a difference.

Terry L. Jarrett, CMRP, CRL, CPMM
Global Reliability Director
Operations Excellence
Koch Industries, Inc.

Continuous improvement (CI) is one of those business buzzwords/acronyms that has been thrown around operations meetings, boardrooms, personnel review discussions and consultant "value-added" sessions often with little to zero accountability for results. Human nature makes us very eager to engage in or approve CI initiatives because most results driven leaders are looking for the next "game changer." However, often when we speak about CI, we are talking about incremental change and even worse often companies do not follow up to "validate" the anticipated value creation. These incremental improvement initiatives may have been enough to stay in business prior to the globalization of competition when there were few competitors who were all using the same raw materials, equipment asset base, processes, and pool of similar cost human resources. However, for companies to **excel** in a free market today, CI needs to include "step change" improvements as well. Furthermore, if it is not faster than your competition, you may not remain in business for long.

Many companies have formal CI processes, such as those imbedded in lean manufacturing where eliminating "muda" is THE continuous improvement effort. Other companies have pretty work process flows with RASI charts to show how people and systems work together to continuously improve operational performance and cost. However, few have a strong enough focus on step change improvement in today's rapidly changing global marketplace. In addition, even fewer truly realize that all CI initiatives require empowered and engaged employees who have a real sense of ownership, understand how their behaviors impact success, and are encouraged to experiment with new ideas with the proper coaching and incentives.

Klaus has focused on many of the areas in this book that I have found to be strong predictors of successful CI endeavors. He begins with personal "lessons learned" examples, which often "connect" with the reader better than anything else does that can be communicated in writing. He follows this with a chapter on various change models and change

Foreword

implementation processes. I stumbled into a strong change management methodology about 15 years ago and have found this to be a tremendous way to increase the probability of success for CI efforts in the past. In Chapter 3, Dr. Blache provides an overview for lean manufacturing processes that have been successful when the right culture, decision rights, and virtues and talents are in place. In the next two chapters, he discusses probably one of the single most important aspects of success in this arena…people being engaged in the process and understanding how their role connects to the improvements as well as what the expectations are for them personally to assist in the value creation. Chapter 6 also touches on one of the frequently forgotten areas for successful CI….the right incentives being in place in order for people to change their behaviors so that the "new way" of working becomes the "normal way" for sustainability. Klaus ends with a great human action model anecdote with a challenge for the reader to become a leader in any CI process. If a leader does not establish a clear and shared vision for the CI with their people and if the employees do not act like owners instead of renters, your efforts will either fail completely or realize much less value than anticipated.

Jim Serafin, PE, PMP
Computational Facilities Complex Manager
Oak Ridge National Laboratory

Continuous improvement is integral to our business of maintaining and operating, data center infrastructure at Oak Ridge National Laboratory (ORNL). Adapting our power and cooling systems and use of data center space to evolving trends in computing technology is one of our biggest challenges. High performance computing technology is constantly evolving – the very nature of the multi-mission data center design is wrought with technical challenges. To this end, we must have effective improvement and change management processes to adapt to new computing requirements. At any point in time, our team is implementing improvement projects in all areas of our business: power and cooling infrastructure, power and water savings, operations & maintenance/equipment reliability, network/communications, SCADA (supervisory control and data acquisition), and security.

Why continuous improvement? It's simple: if we fail to meet the requirements of our customers and the lab, we jeopardize our ability to secure future business. While ORNL utilizes a landlord-tenant model of providing space and support services to its researchers, data center users are more like business travelers – they show up with their gear and nothing else, and they only plan to stay for a short duration (technology inherently has a short lifecycle). We cannot afford to "fix it as it breaks." Our main challenge is identifying and managing risk in a timely manner in an environment that is constantly changing. We want our data center infrastructure team to have a high reliability mind-set – to arrive at work each day worrying about what can go wrong and where we need to improve. This type of cultural change does not happen overnight. It takes a commitment to continuous improvement from leadership to enforce and drive this mind-set.

Foreword

On a routine basis, our data center team utilizes some very basic best practices to identify improvement areas (customer feedback, field work observations, independent assessments, and self-assessments). Moreover, our relationship with the University of Tennessee-Knoxville Reliability and Maintainability Center (UTK-RMC) has been invaluable, as we have recently optimized every preventive maintenance (PM) work order in our system ("PM Optimization" is now in our vernacular!). One thing we have come to appreciate over time is that every failure is a learning opportunity. We scrutinize all failures to identify the root cause, but we especially appreciate those that do not negatively impact our workers or customers, as those also offer learning opportunities (in data centers, human error is the largest factor in causing downtime). We value these "safe events" like gold, as they are an excellent test of a system's components and people, and their response to an event. For example, if a sensor fails in one of our chiller plants, our team determines root cause of the failure (we often send failed components to the manufacturer for their input). We also explore questions like: Did our notification systems work as designed? Did the operators respond properly? Does the computerized maintenance management system data provide information on latest inspections? Do our PMs need to be modified?

Our approach to continuous improvement has led to many successes. However, one lesson learned is that some change initiatives necessitate a change in the behaviors of the organization more than others. A couple of years ago, we initiated a project to develop arc flash and electrical coordination studies for our medium and low voltage electrical distribution equipment. This was a huge endeavor that took many hours of data collection and analysis. We were very successful at assigning safety boundaries and improving coordination of our electrical distribution system. What we underestimated in the planning phase was the amount of effort it takes to maintain such a process. We needed to shift the mind-set of our staff (supervisors, engineers, electricians, and contractors) to emphasize the importance of identifying and communicating configuration changes in an accurate and timely manner. We are finally turning the corner on this. It took a while to recognize this project was as much an organizational/cultural challenge as it was technical. We had primarily focused on the technical because we understood it.

If change is your normal, as it is in our world of maintaining and operating data centers, adopting continuous improvement principles like those described in "The Relativity of Continuous Improvement" is essential, unless you decide it's best to just "fix it if it's broke."

Rick Petito, CMRP
Col (r), U.S. Air Force
25 year - Aviation Maintenance Manager

I agree with Henry Ellmann (*Founder, Chairman and CEO of Ellmann, Sueiro y Asociados, Management and Industrial Engineering Consultants, in Europe and America - North and South*) that continuous improvement is one of five key functions of any maintenance organization. It is equal to, if not more important than, any other primary function (improving reliability, planning and scheduling, executing the plan, recording and documenting). During my more than 25 years as a Reliability and Maintenance Leader, I have had the privilege of leading organizations as small as 100 and as large as 2500. Although the names used to describe the continuous improvement effort have been different, every one of those organizations attempted to create or leverage a culture that improved continuously. I have never experienced dissent regarding the value of continuous improvement. However, I have seen the unrecognized, slight nuances of the embedding mechanisms of continuous improvement having drastic influence on whether an organization succeeded or failed in its quest. In my experience, there are three critical components to embedding a successful culture of continuous improvement: empowerment, risk tolerance and competence to make changes stick. In my opinion, all three are absolutely necessary to flourish.

A culture of empowerment and risk tolerance does not start with continuous improvement. That culture must be manifested in the behavioral norms of its leaders and followers. Edgar Henry Schein, a former professor at the MIT Sloan School of Management, would say any culture is embedded by the very things the leaders: pay attention to, put resources to, reward people for, disenfranchise people for, and how its leaders react in a crisis. For example, if an organization is unwilling to tolerate mistakes, that organization will never have personnel willing to take risks and therefore, will not have a risk tolerant culture. A risk tolerant culture HAS to embrace mistakes. The same is true with empowerment. To achieve a culture of empowerment goes deeper than continuous improvement, but a lack of empowerment will have an absolute effect on any organization's ability to achieve continuous improvement nirvana. Arguably, these two components are the hardest to achieve of the three.

The easiest component to achieve is the organizational competence to make changes stick. The competency can be easily institutionalized by policy, procedures, and training. Although these things do require work and a level of discipline and redundancy, establishing repeatable standard work is easier than establishing cultural norms of behavior.

I would like to share one process that worked extremely well. It was called A Suggestion About Processes (ASAP). The concept was simple: any employee could suggest any idea. Any supervisor or manager in the organization's hierarchy could "approve and implement it." However, only the organization's Director could disapprove. As the idea moved up the hierarchy, supervision would either implement or comment on it until the Director made the final decision. If disapproved, the Director would go to the employee's work area and explain why face-to-face. This program produced hundreds of ideas and embedded empowerment AND risk tolerance.

I'm a believer. Continuous improvement is a key function of R&M and the components that define success are empowerment, risk tolerance and the competence to make changes stick.

Foreword

―――――――――――――∽⃝⃟―――――――――――――

Alan Costlow
Asset Maintenance Leader for a Global Petrochemicals Company

As a maintenance professional in the chemical and steel industries, my experience has been that sustainable improvement is rarely the result of a single defining event, but is rather the result of having a clear vision, a defined process which includes a feedback loop, appropriate key performance indicators to guide follow-up actions, and finally, leadership that can effectively influence desired behaviors. With these elements in place, continuous improvement can be realized and sustained.

The vision and process are formalized through accurate documentation. It is very difficult to drive sustainable improvement in a process that is not well documented. An example of this can be seen in asset maintenance strategies. Upon commissioning of an asset, the reliability team must define and document the maintenance strategy. This strategy must not remain stagnant over the life of the asset however, but rather must become a living document which is continually reviewed and improved based on asset performance under the existing operating conditions. Without the existence of the documented strategy, there is no opportunity to drive continuous, sustainable improvement.

The key to an effective feedback loop is the ability to engage experts to review performance and recommend appropriate updates based on data and experience. In the case of asset maintenance strategies, the seasoned craftsmen who maintain, troubleshoot and repair the assets are an extremely valuable source of this knowledge and experience. The work process must provide an effective method for craftsmen to provide feedback and the use of this feedback process must be strongly encouraged. The leaders must then ensure the feedback is given consideration and recommendations are implemented as appropriate. In my experience, most craftsmen have a high degree of ownership for the performance of the equipment which they maintain and they are therefore willing to provide expert feedback provided leadership has demonstrated that the input will be applied to improve equipment performance.

Key performance indicators are used to monitor performance and drive improvement. Lagging indicators measure a desired result which is typically influenced by multiple factors. Leading indicators are used to drive specific behaviors that impact the lagging indicators. Typical lagging indicators in a maintenance organization are equipment availability and maintenance cost as a percent of replacement asset value. Typical leading indicators would include such things as PM ratio, PM compliance and percent emergency work. It is important to not only select the right combination of performance indicators to drive the right behaviors, but to also have flexibility to adjust these indicators as the process matures.

So to enable continuous improvement we must define the vision, develop and document the process, provide a means for effective feedback, identify and monitor key performance indicators and provide effective leadership to influence behavior. It's not always easy, but if we are not driving continuous improvement, we will quickly fall behind in our pursuit of world-class performance.

Foreword

---ೞರೞ---

Barry Cross
Drilling & Measurements Segment
Global Operations Support Manager
Schlumberger Technology Corp

In the oil and gas well drilling service industry, it is an ongoing, almost daily challenge to look for incremental improvements that can be made to increase the competiveness of the company and/or the impact on customer results. These activities must also be conducted in an ever changing business environment, with the inevitable up and down cycles with the price of oil and natural gas.

One thing to be avoided with any continuous improvement activity is the "initiative of the month" type of management. It cannot simply be the latest buzzword or program that appears literally overnight and then stops when management discovers the true cost of such a campaign. You must have a clear, concise education/communication program to ensure there is full understanding at all levels of the organization and that the amount of time, effort and costs to be effective be understood as well.

Any continuous improvement program must look "outside the box," i.e. not only at what your top competitors are doing, but "world class" companies operating outside your industry. Some of the better projects have resulted from best practices used in other industries totally disassociated from oil and gas well drilling operations. Being the "first to market" with a new process or better widget can drive financial results.

In the rather new business environment whereby employees tend to move between jobs and careers, we are faced with the inevitable fact of training people again and again; not just re-training the existing population but all the newcomers as well. Numerous continuous improvement tracking or monitoring tools are available and no one group of employees use all these tools. The key is to have the right tool used at the right time. This is partially related to training and also to capturing lessons learned and communicating these lessons over time.

Last, but not least, continuous improvement efforts have to be related to the business, with clear deliverables, all focused on a business reason. Too many projects get sidetracked with interesting, but unnecessary tasks. A clear business focus helps keep the team and the project on track.

---ೞರೞ---

Joseph Park
Global Director of Reliability
Novelis, Inc

Several years ago when I left my plant reliability role to join the Continuous Improvement group within our company, I initially saw it as a move in a completely different direction. However, when asked to lead a corporate reliability program a few years later, I realized I was coming back equipped with a much stronger skill set for the work ahead. One of the most valuable aspects of the continuous improvement tool kit is that it can be applied to virtually every aspect of a business from manufacturing to office based transactional processes. From the beginning, we interwove continuous improvement approaches into the fabric of our reliability improvement strategy. We design our plant maintenance management work flows through the use of mapping, documenting current state and future state as a road map for improvement. 5S is the foundation for all focused equipment improvement activities. We teach PM optimization using a 5S approach. Recently one of the sites virtually eliminated the number one downtime issue by bringing a cross functional team together in a kaizen event. The solution they found was simple, yet elegant, and has proven over time to be sustainable. The employment of A3 thinking is integral to all projects and it is rare when a group comes together to tackle a reliability problem without using root cause analysis approaches, such as fishbone diagramming and fault tree analysis.

From the Six Sigma side, one of our plants employed the DMAIC process under the leadership of a Lean Six Sigma Black Belt to completely revamp its maintenance planning program. Through the use of statistical tools, we have demonstrated the relationship between reduced downtime and improved safety within our maintenance organization. We have also successfully driven improvement in PM completion rates by showing the direct correlation to mean time between failure. Data visualization and analysis are an indispensable part of ensuring we are focusing our time and resources in the areas which will provide the greatest benefit to the business. Without a doubt, the application of Lean and Six Sigma tools in our Reliability program has yielded the best and most sustainable results we have achieved.

Our motto "Reliability Is Not Just Maintenance" is intended to emphasize the cross functional nature of reliability. The team facilitation skills and rapid improvement focus of lean, combined with the data analysis and DMAIC discipline of Six Sigma, together provide a solid foundation to bring a diverse team of people together for a common solution. In my opinion, any company not employing CI tools and approaches in reliability improvement efforts is missing a tremendous opportunity.

Emily Rawlings, PE
Manager of Reliability – Engineering Services
Columbia Pipeline Group

For Columbia Pipeline Group to meet the demands of an extremely competitive industry, we must operate safely and efficiently with a high degree of reliability. For CPG, reliability refers to an avoidance of downtime or negative events of our assets, mainly compressor stations. We ensure peak performance through the application of cornerstone programs, including: preventative maintenance work, root cause analysis, and real time monitoring of our system. The common thread in our programs is continuous improve-

Foreword

ment. An organization maintains excellence with constant mindfulness of opportunities to further the success of the work and modifications to process to advance achievements.

Continuous improvement is observed within our organization on a persistent basis. It can be as simple as a lessons learned debrief following the completion of a project or as in-depth as a kaizen event to better a current process. Every organization that outperforms their competitors does so through continuous improvement and positive change efforts.

Awareness of the importance of organizational acceptance to change and a strong change management plan will help to ensure the success of your initiative. In reality, possessing the best technical solution is only half of the equation. The solution can fail without capturing the hearts and minds of your people and the individuals driving the change within our organization understood that. They started with a best-in-class reliability framework and then drove to integrate it into the company's culture. Numerous hours were spent crafting the communication message and plan to ensure the cornerstone programs' success. Today, we have a program that is highly integrated into the company culture.

Finally, it's important to understand that change has to be sustained and a need will always exist for continuous improvement. The organization must maintain awareness of opportunities and constantly challenge themselves to improve to ensure continued success and competitive advantage.

Larry Bryant
Director of Reliability
Domtar Paper Company

Continuous improvement: two words that are at the front of many corporate discussions today where the need for improved performance is a reality. What's interesting is that these two words have been part of the "need to change" discussion for quite some time. As employees work hard to improve the way things are done, many times those changes are seen as "onetime" improvements. Many continuous improvement projects bring about things that we will do differently than we used to, but once we make the "project" changes, we've reached our goal. This leads to long-term results not matching the effort applied to change the way we do business, which then brings frustration to our team members.

Real continuous improvement has to come from all employees seeing that they are part of the process and what they do affects the success, or failure, of our long-term improvement needs. Questioning everything we do and the value those things bring to the bottom-line results has to occur, but many times we only see others need to change, not ours.

Having a resource that helps us understand why past initiatives have failed and what needs to be done differently to implement true continuous improvement is needed. We all have to understand that no matter what level of the organization we work in, we can and should become champions in the continuous improvement process. Never being satisfied that our performance today was the best it could be can be the catalyst for others to become a part of the continuous improvement change. Sustaining a continuous improvement culture is a much bigger challenge than making one time changes. Our history of "program of the day" improvement projects has trained our employees that continuous improvement has just been words we say, not the reality of what we become.

We have to break the quick fix program of the day improvement cycle and get on the path of long-term success. We have a lot of history to overcome in making continuous improvement the reality of the way we do business.

With an experienced career in making continuous improvement a reality, Klaus Blache has proven his ability in bringing successful solutions to what has often times been unsuccessful improvement attempts – this book should bring those who read it success in implementing continuous improvement and making it a reality.

Permission

Copyrights

The excerpts used in the book are credited in the Reference section at the end of each chapter. Larger items, like charts, were used with permission. My best effort was made to give credit. If any errors or omissions are found, please bring them to my attention for correction in future updates.

Dedication

In memory of my parents, who risked everything to give their family a better life. What they endured and overcame will always inspire me.

Acknowledgments

When thinking about who impacted me the most, the first thoughts go to the early days. There were many influential people that I had the opportunity to interact with, like W. Edwards Deming, Eliyahu Goldratt, and John Moubray. Their teachings influenced much of the initial foundation of my early thinking. Then, it's an accumulation of learnings from experiences and hundreds of individuals who were willing to risk criticism to make a difference. Like continuous improvement, most new things developed come from ongoing small adjustments and corrections and the input of many. Numerous people test, debate and improve on an idea, but someone eventually puts it on paper or organizes it in a logical manner so it's more easily understood. So even if a single person eventually gets credited for an item, it was most likely constructed by a myriad of influences. Similarly, as I tried to think about influential individuals, I ended up with two groups. 1. Three individuals, each for a different reason, but all had several common characteristics and 2. Hundreds of people (at all levels of the organization) who were willing to take risk toward making things better, sharing their thoughts, taking a first step and staying the course. I will thank the three to explain the characteristics that warranted me to focus on them. These same positive traits are also at the core of what is needed for moving your workforce towards continuous improvement.

The characteristics that I most remember are trust, integrity, positive outlook, easy to engage in open and direct discussions, did what they said they were going to do, staying on course/consistent message, able to discuss tough issues and look for win-win outcomes and providing support when the going got tough/had my back. What's unique is that all three of these individuals had very different jobs. When I first worked with them, one headed up Corporate Industrial Engineering, one was my UAW partner in rolling out the Corporate Reliability and Maintenance processes across North America and the other had production responsibility and provided lean process mentorship for the new Cadillac CTS plant. Thanks Jim Rucker, Larry Gontko and Ken Knight. Also, note that you must demonstrate the same characteristics or it doesn't work. Successful large change projects and sustainable improvement requires a robust process and consistent leadership support. There were also numerous people at all levels that were willing to share their knowledge, use their skills and engage to make improvements. So, I humbly submit this book knowing that what I know was influenced by many.

Thanks also go to Reliabilityweb.com support, including from Tori Bobbs, Maryellen Cicione and Deborah Linville for the editing and improvements.

My greatest thanks go to my wife and best friend, Michele, who supports me in all things. She typed the first draft of the book, helped with the charts and endured the many updates and changes. Her smile, patience and love make this journey of life a pleasure and something that I look forward to every day.

Preface

Change has always been present in our business and personal lives. But it's when a specific change actually impacts us in some way that we pay more attention, try to understand, and support or resist it. This happens to be a time of turbulent change (Ongoing pressures from global competition, financial and political instability, knowledge loss and lack of skilled resources as much of the workforce can retire, data storage and related knowledge increasing at an exponential rate, continual competition for the same internal resources, and so on). For some people, that's very stressful. For others, it's a time for retrenching, new thinking and risk-taking. They enjoy the challenge of change and have instilled core values and priorities that lead to results.

Companies, like people, aren't any different. Some thrive in this unpredictable environment and others fall apart. Being able to adapt and improve is paramount to any successful team and business initiative. Understanding this and being able to implement and sustain a continuous improvement culture requires a deeper insight regarding change and continuous improvement. This ongoing improvement mind-set also is a cornerstone for instilling processes, such as lean thinking, reliability and maintainability, total productive maintenance and sustaining the never-ending journey of business excellence. It also enables becoming a learning organization, where, fueled by employee enthusiasm, it is able to adapt to ongoing challenges. This book is focused on contributing toward this understanding, developing pathways toward cultural readiness with business improving action items and, most importantly, how to sustain it for long-term viability.

If you've heard my presentations at any time, you've probably listened to the hot dog story. I was almost five years old and we had just gotten off the boat in New York from Germany. My parents had arranged for a friend to pick us up and he was running a little late. We were getting hungry and noticed a street vendor. None of us spoke any English, but his cart stated "hot dog." So while I was handed the food, my father got out his German to English dictionary and looked up "hot." About the time I was ready to take my first bite, he had looked up the second word separately and yelled, "No hot dog, no hot dog!" The pastry in the window appeared safer and tasted good. I like this story because it is similar to what I encounter in most facilities implementing lean concepts, total productive maintenance (TPM), reliability processes, design for maintainability and various practices to support key process metrics and goals. A typical scenario goes like this. I walk into a room of executives, managers, and/or reliability and maintainability (R&M) leaders after being invited to help them with improving lean or an R&M process. When I ask these individuals to write down their definition of what lean/R&M is and their expectations, I get mostly different answers. People respond based on what their experiences have taught them.

So, this is usually where we start, by grasping the situation and getting everyone on the same page. To some people, lean equates to reducing manpower, so they have already

Preface

taken a no lean position, even if they don't verbalize it. Others are hoping it will reduce head count. Some focus on removing waste with kaizen events. This scenario has been similar, whether it's TPM, lean medical, office or engineering process changes, ergonomics, standardized work, or problem-solving and implementing other business plan initiatives. What I don't hear often is what is being done to change behavior or, in other words, the thinking process, how continuous improvement teams can address the issues and how to foster systems level thinking. Just like the hot dog story, people react to what they think they know, especially once they have some data that support their concerns, issues and fears, even if the data is being misinterpreted or incorrect.

For example, the term "dog" has been used in place of sausage since the mid-1800s. Also, accusations of dog meat being used have been around just as long, according to David Wilton[1]. The American Heritage Dictionary (Second College Edition) defines hot dog as "a hot frankfurter, usually served in a long, soft roll." Frankfurter is defined as "a smoked sausage of beef or beef and pork made in long reddish links." Wikipedia[2] defines hot dog as "a type of fully cooked, cured and/or smoked moist sausage with even texture and flavor. It is usually placed hot in a soft sliced hot dog bun of approximately the same length as the sausage and optionally garnished with condiments and toppings," or more simply, a combination of sausage and bun. Did you know in the 1800s, buyers of hot dogs sold on the streets of St. Louis, Missouri, and Chicago, Illinois, were given white gloves to avoid burning their hands? Buns and rolls were later used to keep the white gloves from disappearing as souvenirs.

I heard Dr. W. Edwards Deming often say in training sessions, "knowing what you know and knowing what you don't know – that is true knowledge."[3] In the hot dog story, my father acted on what he viewed as profound knowledge, his translating dictionary. It's also possible he knew more, since the frankfurter was named for the city of Frankfurt, Germany, where sausage in a bun originated and near where we lived. It's a good ending to the story as we've since learned to enjoy a grilled hot dog on a summer day.

I've spent most of my career working on continuous improvement and changing cultures, both on the plant floor and with engineering/business processes or medical department processes. I've had the opportunity to design plants, open new plants, change the culture and processes of plants, and close plants. I say opportunity because it is not so much about what I did, but rather what I learned from the people involved regarding what worked, what didn't work and understanding why. Regardless of the type of facility (e.g., medical /ergonomics, assembly, process, energy, manufacturing, etc.), hourly or salary, union or nonunion, level in the organization, factory floor or administrative, almost all solutions required two fundamental things for success. After grasping the situation:

1. **Change or improve the culture.** Being able to successfully change the thinking process and transition to an engaged, supportive culture moving toward the desired change.
2. **Instill or improve the reliability of a process, product or practice.** This may involve establishing a standardized process to follow; adding visual controls and mistake proofing; aligning the goals of all organizational levels; using process mapping tools

and techniques to prioritize and focus efforts; rolling out a common, practical problem-solving process; and more. Reliability also includes human reliability. What's important is improving with a detailed plan and toward a clear and well communicated end result.

The word "improve" is a verb, an action word meaning such things as, "to raise to a more desirable condition, to increase in productivity, to put to good use and to use profitably."[4]

To instill sustainable change, you can't just talk about it. As Philip Crosby stated, "There comes a time when someone has to actually get the job done."[5] Until you demonstrate your support and continue to demonstrate it, you are not going to get lasting change. It also means you need to tie the change to something that is visible to the workforce and requires stakeholders to make decisions or offer opportunities to show support. Any lasting improvements can only happen and continue if there is buy-in to the tools, methods and overall process. The enabling concepts to sustainable continuous improvement are common to any issue that you will encounter. Being able to understand the basics required for change and knowing what to do to enable long-term continuous improvement are the basis for this book.

Even Einstein spent a lot of time reworking his concepts and was unable to see past some intuitional roadblocks.

"Einstein's equation is only partially correct (it needs a + and − sign). The correct equation is actually $E = \pm MC^2$."[6]

"Not only did the Dirac equation predict the existence of antimatter; it also predicted the 'spin' of the electron. The spin of the electron, in turn, is crucial to understanding the flow of electrons in transistors and semiconductors, which form the basis of modern electronics."[7]

"Einstein was a rather good mathematician, though in mathematical technique he was not the towering figure that he was in physical insight."[8]

"Einstein made clear and unequivocal his rejection of his own intellectual legacy: the black holes that his general relativistic laws of gravity seemed to be predicting."[9] His opposition to the existence of black holes prevented him from realizing that implosion was the answer to their understanding.

Although a genius, Einstein went through a lot of recalculations and corrections to continuously improve on his theories. Relative to continuous improvement, some key things to point out from the Einstein legacy are:

- Someone has to first accept some risk and take a stand to start the process of ongoing improvement.
- It is new and revealing insights that give direction and purpose to the supporting mathematics and theories.
- Without controversy, conflict and competition, continuous improvement would be much slower.
- Believe the data and stay open to understanding what it's telling you. View the facts using your insights, but also be open to those of others to fully "grasp the situation."

Preface

If Thomas Edison was more open to others' opinions and supported alternating current (AC), then maybe he would have invented additional things. Edison's generating stations with direct current (DC) were only good for about half a mile. So, Westinghouse and Thomson-Houston built more effective AC generating stations. The irony is that today's household electronic devices (e.g., televisions, laptop computers, coffeemakers, etc.) run on DC, requiring AC to DC conversion.[10]

Basically, change is about successfully instilling the culture and an understanding of how continuous improvement can be nurtured, performed and maintained in any circumstance. This book uses lean and reliability-based examples and explanations that can work in any business and/or team environment, such as insurance, hotels, assembly, hospitals, government, manufacturing, etc. The focus is on the implementation of business critical processes, as supported and driven by a robust continuous improvement process.

If you have the support of the people, even a mediocre process, machine, or practice can be made to work. But if you don't have the support of the people, the best process, machine, or practice will not work that well or even fail. Establishing the proper culture is not all that you need. It's everything that you need.

Dr. Klaus Blache
Knoxville, TN

REFERENCES

1. Wilton, David. Word Myths: Debunking Linguistic Urban Legends. Oxford: Oxford University Press, 2004.
2. http://en.wikipedia.org/wiki/Hot_dog
3. Deming, W. Edwards. Heard firsthand in several presentations at General Motors.
4. http://www.thefreedictionary.com/improve
5. Crosby, Philip B. Quality is Free. New York City: McGraw-Hill Companies, 1979.
6. Kaku, Michio. Physics of the Impossible. New York City: Doubleday, 2008.
7. Ibid.
8. Thorne, Kip S. Black Holes and Time Warps. New York City: W.W. Norton & Company, Inc., 1994.
9. Ibid.
10. Knapp, Alex. "Nikola Tesla Wasn't God And Thomas Edison Wasn't The Devil." Forbes 18 May 2012 <http://www.forbes.com/sites/alexknapp/2012/05/18/nikola-tesla-wasnt-god-and-thomas-edison-wasnt-the-devil/>.

Introduction

To be excellent in business, you need a vision with a clearly defined purpose. By successfully managing the cultural changes and continuous improvement, you are transitioning your organization's vision into reality. How well you are able to do this will largely determine your level of success. It's about steady continuous improvement – lots of little changes and some big ones. Learning how to change and sustain the behavior of the individual and, collectively, the team is the foundation of ongoing improvement and striving to be the best.

Change issues have been around for as long as there have been people. It has caused disagreements, stalled or stopped improvements, and has even caused the failure of companies.

In 1988, I researched and wrote about success factors for implementing change (*Success Factors For Implementing Change: A Manufacturing Viewpoint*). At that time, I was fortunate to be entrenched in sessions with W. Edwards Deming, including direct meetings and projects. As a result, my writings at that time reflected that. Also at that time, I had not yet been exposed to the Toyota Production System (TPS) in any meaningful way. The GM-Toyota joint venture agreement was signed in 1983, with the first Chevrolet Nova produced in December 1984. In the early 1990s, as I moved from a plant position back to corporate, my involvement with New United Motor Manufacturing, Inc. (NUMMI) and TPS began. Being able to work on the production line and interacting with their employees was always great for learning. Prior to that, my initial insights on continuous improvement and change management came from personal experiences in global projects and benchmarking numerous companies. The year 1990 was also when the book, *The Machine That Changed The World* by James P. Womack, Daniel T. Jones, and Daniel Roos, was published. It taught the world about lean production systems and strategies. Although I had been involved in numerous earlier change implementation and process improvement efforts, my in-depth study of production systems, and the related cultural change to support them, started at about the same time. The foundation, learning and associated success factors of the original concepts I proposed in 1988 appear to have held the test of time. After many additional years of worldwide change implementation and learning, it's now time to revisit and expand those original concepts. Furthermore, the cumulative findings can be integrated into a model for sustainable continuous improvement.

Even extremely large and well-planned efforts can result in marginal benefits without a systems-thinking (i.e., comprehensive) approach. The challenge is technical and social, and must be understood and addressed from all aspects together. Many past change efforts have been minimally, if at all, successful because we continue to change the content without changing the context in which the new content has to function. As stated by the authors of *Thoughtware*, "Change the thinking and the organization will change itself.

Introduction

Thinking is what dictates decisions and actions, and if the action is wrong, then it stands to reason that the thinking behind the action is wrong, too."[1] Furthermore, "Thought is the ancestor of all action. People's thinking is the basis for everything they do – all behavior is rooted in thought. The sum of all people's thinking and then collective interaction is the mastermind of the organization's performance on which every organization operates."[2]

Competitive position, operational excellence and the workplace empowerment structure have never been more intertwined and critical in enabling successful operations. Improvements will be required in technology strategies (e.g., robotics, expert systems), technical strategies (e.g., lean production, computer integrated manufacturing) and social system strategies (e.g., empowerment, involvement). However, it is not new information that social system strategies have a more significant positive impact on business results, including quality, cost, profitability, employee skills and knowledge. "Many studies have shown that high levels of workforce engagement have a significant, positive impact on organizational performance."[3]

Understanding this and how to integrate and implement in any work environment are paramount in successful change and attaining excellence. Standardized work (i.e., established flow to perform a job) will only be successful if team members act with discipline. Kanban (a visual scheduling system) will only work if everyone does their part. The Andon system (an informational tool, typically a lighted board triggered by a team member pulling a cord, which provides immediate response to an abnormality) will only work if both team members and team leaders know what to do and are willing to do it. Eventually, it's the cumulative benefit from dynamic teams thinking ahead, problem-solving and improving that is at the heart of a well-working system.

Even if we don't change, things will continually change around us. Most have seen the two rules of change:

1. The only constant is change.
2. Rule #1 can change at any time.

Actually, the changes are becoming less predictable, are happening more quickly and are of greater magnitude and consequence than ever before.

- "Our intuition about the future is linear, but the reality of information technology is exponential, and that makes a profound difference. If I take 30 steps linearly, I get 30 steps. If I take 30 steps exponentially, I get a billion."[4]
- "A century later, we are living through another transition. The way we connect with one another and the institutions in our lives is evolving. There is an erosion of trust in authority, a decentralizing of power and, at the same time, perhaps a greater faith in one another."[5]
- "Of the 500 companies that appeared on the first Fortune 500 list in 1955, only 71 hold a place on the list today."[6] It should be noted that the Fortune 500 list changed for a lot of reasons beyond just performance, including mergers, acquisitions and com-

panies going public. Service companies were not included on the list at the start and there are more entries and exits by service companies (e.g., health care, banks, utilities, insurance and retail) as compared to industrial companies.[7] So, interpreting what that means for historical learning is not so clear. However, it has been shown that "the pace of company turnover has quickened."[8]

- "Within 30 years, we will have the means to create superhuman intelligence, shortly after, the human era will be ended."[9]
- "Singularity is defined as the moment when technological change becomes so rapid and profound, it represents a rupture in the fabric of human history."[10]
- "A few years ago, physicists would have said that sending or beaming an object from one point to another violated the laws of quantum physics. Today, because of a recent breakthrough, physicists can teleport atoms across a room or photons under the Danube River."[11]
- "In February 2013, Cisco Systems, Inc., released a study predicting that $144 trillion of value (net profit) in the private sector is at stake globally over the next decade, driven by connecting the unconnected people-to-people (P2P), machine-to-people (M2P) and machine-to-machine (M2M) via the Internet of Everything."[12]
- The University of Tennessee's supercomputer, Kraken, "can crunch a thousand trillion (or quadrillion) calculations per second, with a peak performance of 1.03 petaflops."[13] A petaflop (PF) is a quadrillion (thousand trillion) floating point operations per second (FLOPS). Breaking the petaflop barrier is having significant effects on the future of science. Titan, the ORNL supercomputer, operates at 17.59 petaflops and has a theoretical peak of 27 petaflops[14,15].

Exponentially expanding information technology, Facebook's relationship mapping, and computers that can quickly solve highly complex and large calculations are all with us now and, yet, we still struggle to accomplish sustainable continuous improvement. Combining human relations/interactions with any method or technology makes the outcome less sure. For enabling sustainable change, these concepts need to be better understood. For example, with small and mobile technology, many computerized maintenance management tasks can be done in the field. I had asked at a facility that had this technology for several years why it's not used more. The reply was that the older technicians, which was most of them, could not read the small screens well.

The change management and continuous improvement concepts that will be discussed in this book are applicable to all types of companies. However, to best convey concepts and ideas, the examples and discussions will be around three general themes:

1. Industrial, such as manufacturing, assembly, aerospace, process, military and energy;
2. Medical, such as hospital, insurance and pharmaceutical;
3. Everyday, such as travel, restaurants and driving your car.

This will help clarify the continuous improvement/change management concepts and demonstrate that they can be universally applied. Many of the concepts also have a

Introduction

basis in lean processes. Similarly, reliability processes need the same level of continuous improvement understanding. A reliable plant is a safe and effective plant. It all comes together at the operational level. Notably, the lean medical practices are emulating automotive and aerospace industry best practices. For example, Robert Chalice compared the best in his 2007 book, *Improving Healthcare Using Toyota Lean Production Methods*. He used leading assembly plants of major automakers, including the General Motors Lansing Grand River Assembly (LGA) Plant as one of the benchmarks. Similarly, the University of Michigan medical teams visited the LGA plant to learn lean concepts, as have military groups and many others. Since I was the manufacturing engineering director during the design, build and operation stages of this world-class facility, I can provide unique insights regarding success factors and lessons learned. The plant had a highly active continuous improvement process that contributed to many successes, such as the J.D. Power Gold Plant Quality Award in 2004 and awards in productivity, manufacturing, maintenance reliability, energy, environmental and many more. Another large change effort that I managed involved working jointly with the United Automobile Workers (UAW) union to develop a manufacturing maintenance and reliability process and rolling it out across North America. This could not have been done without a willing and capable joint union partner, skilled trades and engineering team members.

- "Plant leadership must set the example for implementation and provide resources to ensure success. The end result is for the plants to have autonomous problem-solving teams in maintenance capable of addressing opportunities in the maintenance process."[16]

The initiative required a major emphasis on cultural change at many levels of the organization, especially on the factory floor. Earlier in my career, I was part of a small team that developed and initiated the General Motors Ergonomic Process, which was coordinated between engineering and medical, and also jointly implemented with the UAW. I was also assigned to develop a medical visit record keeping and analysis system using standard reliability tools, data mining and root cause analysis. It resulted in a forty percent reduction in occupational medical visits over an average of twenty plants. I have been involved and responsible for numerous other related efforts, such as process benchmarking, implementing new technologies, changing work practices and processes, and launching new facilities and will draw on these experiences as they are relevant and align with the focus of this book.

The need for continuous improvement and more robust reliable processes are all around us. Let's look at three totally different examples of the *lack of reliability*.

Example 1 – Everyday

You drive up to the order speaker of a fast-food restaurant and place your order. You drive to the first window and pay. Then you proceed to the second window for your food. First, a person gives you your milkshake. You have to wait a few minutes and a second person gives you the bag of food. You look into the bag and the straw and napkin are missing. Or sometimes, it's an incomplete or incorrect food order. So, what happened? Did one person assume the other person had already placed those items in the bag? Did both just forget? Were roles unclear? Was there no standardized process or did they not follow it because they were busy? Was one of them simply trying to help and confused the situation? What role did increased order choices (complexity) have in potential human error? Should there have been more mistake-proofing? Regardless of the reason, it was a lack of reliability from the viewpoint of the customer. Reliability is not just about machinery and equipment. It's also about repeatable processes and capable people knowing what to do and willing to do it all the time.

Example 2 – Medical

Similar to other industries, equipment and the treatment of disease have greatly increased in capability and complexity. However, with all these modern tools, technologies and knowledge, why do so many people die from infection? As mentioned in the March 2009 *AARP Bulletin*:

- "Hospital infections kill 90,000 Americans per year.
- Many of these deaths are preventable."[17]

We all know someone, whether a friend or relative, who went into a hospital and following surgery recovery at home needed to go back due to an infection. I went to www.hospitalcompare.hhs.gov and looked up ten hospitals in my area. The question I selected was, "Patients who reported that their room and bathroom were 'Always' clean." Only one was at eighty percent. Eight others ranged from seventy percent to seventy-nine percent and one was at sixty-one percent. You're probably wondering how that could be possible, given the high cost of hospital stays. It was stated in the aforementioned *AARP Bulletin* that the government recommends twelve hundred separate practices to prevent infection in hospitals, with five hundred strongly recommended. Again there was a *lack of reliability* in process and/or practices.

Example 3 – Industrial

As reported in the December 8, 2008, *Wall Street Journal*,[18] a marine pilot takes off from an aircraft carrier. A few minutes into the flight, the pilot noticed low oil pressure in one of the two engines. Next, low fuel is indicated in the other engine. En route to an emergency landing discussed with traffic control, the second engine flames out and the electrical system is gone. The pilot aims his plane at a canyon and ejects safely. Unfortunately, the plane crashed into a neighborhood, killing four people. Why did this happen? The assistant wing commander reported that the crash was due to wrong decisions and was avoidable. Problems in the jet's fuel transfer system were known for about six months, but the plane was not removed from service and repaired. Also, the young pilot did not go through the safety checklist (lack of standardized work). Furthermore, the pilot decided to go to an airport he was more familiar with, but further away, eating up time and fuel (lack of knowledge and discipline).

Introduction

These kinds of activities and decisions go on every day at most industries and businesses with a wide range of risk and outcomes. So why, with all the knowledge, processes, tools and technologies available today, do we still experience so many daily performance, process and equipment failures of all levels of consequence. The answer to understanding how to enable sustainable change, instill reliability thinking in people, processes and machines, and promote ongoing and continuous improvement is at the core of achieving business excellence and success. This book is aimed at helping you achieve a working knowledge of continuous improvement and how to use it for a competitive advantage.

Chapter 1 on Continuous Improvement and Change Management begins with my personal viewpoints on the current state of continuous improvement. With some observations and lessons learned, the importance of workforce culture and process is discussed. It finishes with several sections on the impacts and benefits of continuous improvement toward attaining and sustaining business excellence. Chapter 2, Change Implementation Concepts and Models, reviews select basic historical models used for implementations of change. Stages of change and continuous improvement from my experiences are aligned and presented. Chapter 3, Using Lean Tools and Other Techniques for Continuous Improvement, is an overview of multiple methods utilized to make improvements. To be able to support ongoing improvement, it's necessary to be familiar with the many tools and techniques available. Numerous books cover each of these topics in detail. My purpose is mainly to raise enough awareness so you know what some of the possible choices are. Chapter 4, Enablers for Successful Change and Sustainable Continuous Improvement, focuses on the success factors for implementing change. It also discusses the need for understanding the value and roles of individuals, teams, leaders and followers. Chapter 5, Model for Sustainable Change, elaborates on what happens when employees are and are not engaged. A model for sustainable change is depicted, along with a brief discussion on several past models. The chapter concludes with a readiness for change scoring sheet. Chapter 6, Sustaining Change, hones in on changing the thinking process to enable, deploy and support ongoing change. It closes with a model for how you view choices. Chapter 7, It's Up to You, is all about doing something to get the change process started and making a positive difference.

Companies and individuals can benefit greatly by leading at all levels, from team leaders to project leaders to chief executive officers, and understanding and applying the change implementation and continuous improvement concepts presented in this book.

REFERENCES

1. Kirby, J. Philip and Hughes, David. *Thoughtware*. New York City: Productivity Press, 1997.
2. Ibid.
3. The Baldrige National Quality Program. *2009-2010 Criteria for Performance Excellence*. The National Institute of Standards and Technology, Gaithersburg, Maryland. <http://www.nist.gov/baldrige/publications/upload/2009_2010_Business_Nonprofit_Criteria.pdf >
4. Kurzweil, Ray. "10 Questions for Ray Kurzweil." *Time* 6, Dec. 2010: p. 8.
5. Grossman, Lev. "Person of the Year 2010 - Mark Zuckerberg." *Time* 15, Dec. 2010: p. 43.

6. Collins, Jim. "The Secret of Enduring Greatness." *Jim Collins*. May 2008. <http://www.jimcollins.com/article_topics/articles/secret-of-enduring-greatness.html>
7. Strangler, Dane and Arbesman, Sam. "What Does Fortune 500 Turnover Mean?" *Ewing Marion Kauffman Foundation*, June 2012. <http://www.kauffman.org/~/media/kauffman_org/research%20reports%20and%20covers/2012/06/fortune_500_turnover.pdf>
8. Ibid.
9. Grossman, Lev. "The Singularity Is Near." *Time* 21 Feb. 2011: pp. 43-44.
10. Ibid.
11. Kaku, Michio. *Physics of the Impossible*. New York City: Doubleday, 2008.
12. Grubb, Jim. "An Innovative Infrastructure to Capture the Value of the Internet of Everything." *Cisco Blogs* 12 Dec. 2013 <http://blogs.cisco.com/news/an-innovative-infrastructure-to-capture-the-value-of-the-internet-of-everything>
13. Freeman, Katie. "Kraken: University Supercomputer Gets Faster, Reaches Petascale." *The Daily Beacon* 14 Oct. 2009, Issue 39, Vol. 112, p. 1.
14. Oak Ridge National Laboratory. <http://www.ornl.gov/science-discovery/supercomputing-and-computation/facilities-and-capabilities>
15. https://en.wikipedia.org/wiki/Titan_%28supercomputer%29
16. Creedon, Betsy Reid, Weekley, Thomas L. and Wilber, Jay C. *United We Stand*. New York City: McGraw-Hill, 1996.
17. Greider, Katharine. "Fending Off Hospital Superbugs." *AARP Bulletin* 2 March 2009: p. 12.
18. Noonan Peggy. "A Tragedy of Errors, and an Accounting." *Wall Street Journal* 6 March 2009: p. A11.

CHAPTER 1

Continuous Improvement and Change Management

> *"It is not necessary to change. Survival is not mandatory."*
> — W. Edwards Deming

> *"I walk slowly, but I never walk backward."*
> — Abraham Lincoln

1.1 The Current State of Continuous Improvement – A Personal Viewpoint

The future success of any company is more than just chasing global competition. It's about learning how to apply what's being learned. This is equally true for manufacturing, chemical, pharmaceutical, oil and gas, utilities, military, medical, and most other company offices and factories. Business practices and processes all can be improved, and many are in need of significant improvement. Although appearing simple, many existing methods used to improve performance have a high degree of complexity attached to them, such as social norms, work that is not standardized, unclear roles and responsibilities, perceptions of a level of fairness and more. So without a comprehensive systems-thinking approach, even very comprehensive change efforts often provide only marginal benefits.

The challenge is organizational, technical and social, and must be understood and addressed from all aspects together. Even if your initial change effort is successful, sustaining it is even more questionable. Why do so many systems and processes fail? The answer encompasses such things as large and small changes, safety, quality, reliability, productivity, cost, long-term implementations and kaizen events. The following examples are of failed change efforts and failed systems of varying magnitude and consequences. Yet, they all could have been avoided or greatly improved upon if a robust, continuous improvement process (CIP) and a sustainment plan had been in place.

As you read through each item, think about whether it was an issue regarding machinery and equipment, operational process, product, people's behavior, or any combination of them. The failures from these items have a wide range of consequences, yet they share similar underlying weaknesses.

Chapter 1

- Many companies cut cost as a strategy. Yet, research found that only ten percent of cost reduction programs show sustained results three years later.[1]
- I stopped at a truck stop to gas up and get coffee. Numerous packets of sugar were barely filled or empty. I did a check of twenty and half were unopened and empty. The sugar company obviously had a problem with production reliability.
- Studies of IT projects in the U.S. have shown that, in any given year, roughly twenty-five percent are done on time, on budget and met stakeholders' specifications. Roughly twenty-five percent have to be abandoned before completion and an estimated fifty percent of these projects are expected late or over budget. In other words, the success rate is twenty-five percent.[2]
- The North American electrical grid is experiencing many more incidents of outages and quality problems not caused by weather events. An energy plan that fails to address energy reliability is incomplete and under-resourced.[3]
- I'm making a non-refundable hotel reservation online and everything works until the final step. A message states that it could not complete the reservation process and to try again or call the nearest agent. I repeated the process thirty minutes later and it worked this time, providing a confirmation number. Being suspicious of these events, I called the hotel to check if I now had two reservations. It turns out the system did, indeed, book two reservations.
- "It's not easy for manufacturers to ensure their medical devices are reliable. For example, upon examination, seemingly identical lead wires in a random sample were found to have up to ten times variation in durability."[4]
- "Farmers in Hebei province (China) say in interviews that 'protein powder' of often uncertain origin has been employed for years as a cheap way to help the milk of undernourished cows fool dairy companies' quality checks. When the big companies caught on, some additive makers switched to toxic melamine – which mimics protein in lab tests and can cause severe kidney damage – to evade detection."[5]
- I drive into a gas station that has a big advertising sign reading, "Full Service Gas Station." When going to the restroom, there is a sign on the door that reads, "Sorry, out of paper towels." Interesting to note is that the convenience store in the gas station sold paper towels.
- Two months after the daylight savings time change, a major airport hotel still had the incorrect time posted on its lobby information screen and TV bulletin displaying hotel events. This was next to where they posted flight times.
- An aircraft started dropping seven thousand feet while the captain was away on a toilet break. It was caused by a copilot accidentally pushing a button while performing a seat adjustment. None of the one hundred and thirteen passengers on the flight were injured.[6]
- Periodically, I receive cell phone messages several days after being sent.
- "The Deepwater Horizon had a series of blackouts, seized up computers and other maintenance problems in the months before the drilling rig exploded in the Gulf of Mexico, the rig's chief engineer told investigators."[7]

Continuous Improvement and Change Management

- I approached the entrance to a Florida turnpike and put in a quarter, but the light did not turn green. I repeated the process with no success, so I drove on. I called the Florida Department of Transportation to explain what happened, but they were insistent that their system does not make mistakes. I sent them a check for twenty-five cents.
- In regards to human reliability and safe driving, "Nearly nine in ten teenage drivers engage in distracted driving behaviors, such as texting or talking on a cell phone."[8]
- I had an old wet/dry vacuum that I used for general cleanup. It worked well, except it was "on" when plugged in because the on-off switch was broken for as long as I can remember. After ten years, I bought a new one, the same brand. I returned it the next day. The on-off switch did not work.
- One brand of water softener salt is a few cents cheaper. It just has cut out handles to carry the forty pound bags. Three out of four handles ripped through, while moving them from the car to the back of the house. The better brand, with reinforced handles, is a few pennies more, but proved to be better very quickly.
- When checking out of my hotel, I pointed out that the bill was two cents higher on the printout than what my credit card was charged (my room was prepaid). I asked if this would cause an issue. They said no. It was probably automated, but the hotel charged two cents to my American Express card later. One has to wonder, at what expense?
- "Two hundred and forty thousand water main breaks per year occur in the U.S." The infrastructure is old and not reliable.[9]
- I purchased a new desk stapler, with the packaging claiming it comes with four hundred staples. There were twelve included.
- It was time to renew my cell phone contract. With a new phone, I needed a new carrying case for my belt. The salesperson recommended a hard plastic one that rotates on the belt clip and said it's "very durable." I put my new cell phone in it, clipped it on my belt and went to my car. Upon getting in the first time, the belt clip cracked and broke off. I went back to the store and asked if they had something better than "very durable."
- The current system allows bad nurses to skip to other states and continue working. Multistate licenses don't always update issues across state lines and let nurses avoid consequences of misconduct. A twenty-four state compact was created to help get good nurses to where they are needed. "When a compact state is slow to act or fails to share information, nurses suspected of negligence or misconduct remain free to work across nearly half the country."[10]
- When I renewed my passport, the government's passport website clearly states to not attach the second photo to the application, but to insert it inside the envelope with the application. When I went to the post office's passport center to mail it, I was informed that they don't want the second picture anymore.
- A crosswalk near a Manhattan school misspelled school as 'shcool.' This was a crossing sign, with large letters printed on the sign on the street outside a preparatory school, yet no one noticed it. A utility crew dug up the road leading to the issue.[11]
- An IBM study showed that about sixty percent of business change projects do not fully attain their objectives.[12]

Chapter 1

The risks and consequences of all these situations vary greatly, but the underlying reasons are similar.

These projects, programs, products and initiatives failed because of such things as:
- Insufficient understanding of the degree of impact on the people affected.
- Lack of employee engagement.
- Poor change management strategies and tools.
- Lack of standardized work.
- Resistance from norms and existing values.
- Change management is viewed as a project or something done while implementing a project, rather than an ongoing process.
- Supervisors and employees in supporting departments are not prepared enough to deal with the people issues that arise during a change implementation.
- Lack of a follow-up or sustainment plan.

After reading all the things that can and are going wrong, you may start to not trust any system. Now, combine that with issues of corporate governance, global recession and tomorrow's unknowns. Yet, you are still responsible for leading ongoing continuous improvement and, at times, complex and large change efforts. I fully agree with Ralph Shrader, chairman of the board of Booz Allen Hamilton, Inc., when he discussed taking risks.

"We need to take them more than ever. But we must make a better job of deciding which risks to take, managing the consequences of those decisions and becoming resilient to the risks that we cannot control."[13]

In this age of computing, there is often an abundance of data. Yet, many companies are data rich and information poor. I am referring to available information and data at all levels of the organization. Good data-driven decisions at the top will steer you in the correct direction. However, good data for problem-solving at the operator level will help you attain or sustain business excellence.

If you want to attain a desired state, such as business excellence, you must operate as if you are already there – the future context. At the Lansing Grand River Assembly Plant, there were several core values, such as teamwork, standardization and continuous improvement. At every staff meeting, which was conducted with the union, a core value was displayed and read. Then, a few stories were shared on how the specific core value was positively demonstrated. Next, examples of how the core value could have been better supported were also shared using specific examples. The process was repeated with the next core value at the following meeting, until they were all discussed. This was an ongoing process, continually repeating the list. By openly discussing good examples and examples needing improvement, fellow team members were learning how to ask the right questions on the plant floor. Changing the thinking process improves all areas of operation.

1.2. Observations and Lessons Learned

Get the culture right first and implementing a robust continuous improvement process will be more beneficial. When implementing large-scale lean processes, there is a sequence of many items that need to be implemented for each sub-system (e.g., quality, continuous improvement, production, etc.). Each of these systems has numerous items attached to it that need to be established. For example, the continuous improvement system is made up of items, such as standardized work, 5S, error proofing, kaizen events and attitudes/behavior. From my discussions with lean subject matter experts and my observations of over twenty implementations around the world, attitude demonstrated by leadership and workforce culture were repeatedly brought to the forefront in the sequence of implementation of the numerous lean elements. Items related to culture need to be implemented first for best results.

Understanding how to engage in meaningful, results-oriented improvement is critical to the ongoing success of every business. From numerous implementations requiring significant change, I have found that:

1. When you focus on changing the thinking process of the people, the organizational change will follow.
2. The rate at which we change behavior will determine the rate of business process success.
3. The level of capability and willingness of your employees to perform problem-solving/continuous improvement will determine the flexibility and robustness in achieving and sustaining competitive practices.
4. The current and desired states are usually well-defined in business plans. What's typically missing is a detailed transition plan, which enables the desired state.
5. Existing methods of optimizing performance have reached a state of diminishing returns. Many improvement efforts overlap areas and compete for the same resources.
6. For most issues, long-term strategic thinking leads to better decisions.
7. Many organizations need a better process to capture global learning and redistribute knowledge.
8. Companies, when implementing best practices, have local variations that need to be better understood. For example, in a given team, how is conflict resolved? What is the absentee coverage policy? Are team leaders elected by the team or appointed? A few variations can be the difference between success and failure in performance outcome differences.
9. Implementation usually slows down or fails at the putting it into practice stage. This happens even after many weeks of training and involvement in developing standardized work. This indicates that the required behavioral change has not occurred.
10. Kaizen events are good, but make sure they don't overshadow the desired long-term team culture. For example, team members involved in the kaizen previously waited many months or longer to get their suggestions heard and hopefully implemented. What message is that sending to your plant floor team? Why are they getting support now?

Chapter 1

11. A focus on safety and ergonomics is a key enabler toward positive attitudes. The workforce must know that you care.
12. The role of leadership is critical in promoting and rewarding the sharing of data and facts to enhance continuous improvement behavior.
13. Leadership, both hourly and salary, must be prepared to answer the numerous questions they will get from the workforce. They need to be able to ask the right questions to foster learning and answer tough people issues with sufficient understanding. Otherwise, you can lose control of the process if support capabilities don't match stated expectations. Most of the tough questions will be people related.
14. Implementing change, such as lean systems, will not make people do things differently. It only works if people want it to.
15. Roles and responsibilities for everyone need to be clear, including the boundaries for change/continuous improvement.
16. You must create a logical, desired and understandable need for change.
17. Following standardized work is a fundamental step in continuous improvement.
18. If your workforce is not disciplined enough to do 5S/6S, don't even think about implementing a lean process.
19. It is necessary to take the time needed to change the behavior of your people. Don't put a time limit on it.
20. The establishment of a problem resolution process for teams to use is necessary. It needs to be able to handle a high volume of problems and provide a way to address questions/issues that the teams can't answer/resolve.
21. The closer your problem-solving process is to the persons actually doing the work, the more robust and meaningful the improvement will be.
22. You must provide the needed information for decision-making to team members. Make sure the information is useful. Don't be data rich and information poor.
23. Better integration at the boundaries of groups and departments is where many of the big potential gains are.
24. The continuous improvement process should be monitored and done as much as possible with a total systems viewpoint to balance the interaction between materials, machines, people and task time, and their impact on safety/ergonomics, quality, throughput and cost.
25. You can only talk about changing behavior for so long until it's time to do something. Only implementation of a change on a real issue will show your current tolerance/ability to change behavior.

Albert Einstein stated that "doing the same thing over and over again and expecting different results" is the definition of insanity. How many things do you repeat every day at work hoping for a better outcome?

After reading the rest of this book, you should have a better and more in-depth understanding about each of these statements. Establishing a healthy and robust continuous improvement process requires putting several fundamental elements in place. Getting the techniques and technologies in place, like standardized work and 5S, allow you to compete (see Figure 1.1). Getting the enabling success factors in place, like proper levels of complexity and demonstrating respect for employees, define your limits of competitiveness. Finally, instilling employee enthusiasm allows you to win.

The elements in Figure 1.1 are only a partial list of tools, techniques and enablers. Moving to the right in Figure 1.1 increases your level of continuous improvement, which supports more business success evidenced by improved safety, quality, throughput and cost, all driven by positive employee attitudes.

1.3 Employee Involvement and Enthusiasm

At the heart of any organization are knowledgeable and capable employees wanting to make a difference. It reminds me of a sign I saw in a production facility that read: "Ya Gotta Wanna." That says it all. Stephen Covey[14] defines a habit as the intersection of knowledge (understanding what to do and why to do it), skill (knowing how to do it) and desire (wanting to do it). Furthermore, I support replacing the word empowerment with "allowment," as proposed in the book, *Thoughtware*, because it recognizes that employees must first be entitled before they reach allowment. It's about employees reaching a level of understanding by taking on the information, skills and authority needed for ongoing improvement and being accountable for results. "The worst thing you can do is empower the organization that is not entitled to be empowered."[15] According to the definition from the Baldrige Criteria for Performance Excellence, workforce engagement:

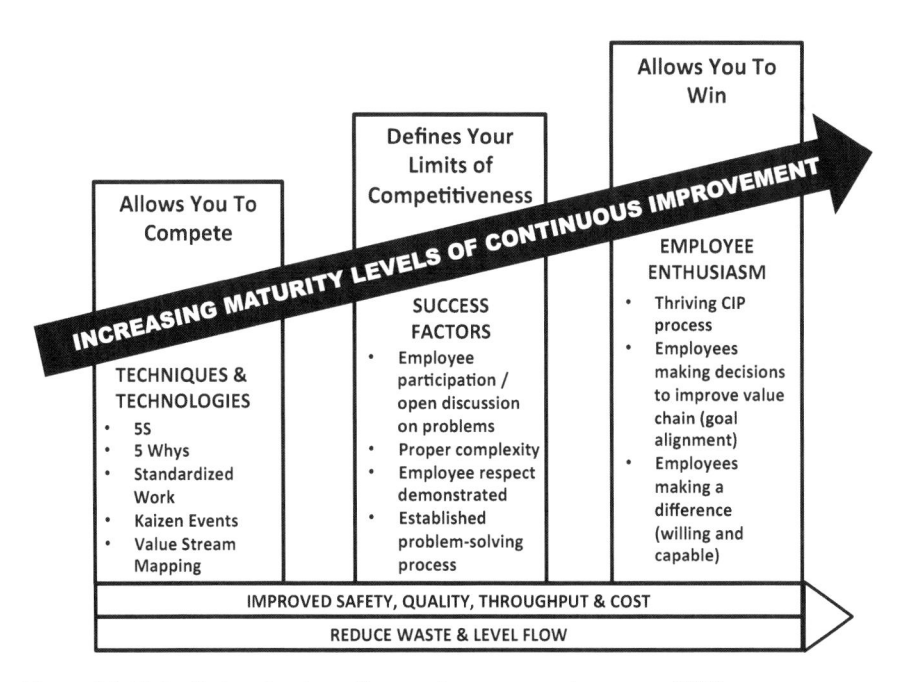

Figure 1.1: Maturity levels of continuous improvement process (CIP)

Chapter 1

"...refers to the extent of workforce commitment, both emotional and intellectual, to accomplishing the work, mission, and vision of the organization. Organizations with high levels of workforce engagement are often characterized by high-performing work environments in which people are motivated to do their utmost for the benefit of their customers and for the success of the organization.

"In general, members of the workforce feel engaged when they find personal meaning and motivation in their work and when they receive positive interpersonal and workplace support. An engaged workforce benefits from trusting relationships, a safe and cooperative environment, good communication and information flow, empowerment, and performance accountability."[16]

A few years ago, I attended a workshop by the Disney Institute on Disney's approach to business excellence. It was stated that areas with the strongest ratings in cast member satisfaction also had the highest customer results and the highest leadership ratings. It's all related and starts with supportive leadership that walks the talk.

It is not surprising then, that institutionalizing a change process is, at best, extremely difficult. This simplistic, yet often difficult to implement, concept and the improvement power behind it is finally being more fully acknowledged. The behavior of the individual in performing the continuous improvement process is at the center of the term kaizen (Japanese word referring to the constant, incremental improvement of processes and work practices by reducing waste and increasing value). Kaizen will be discussed further in Chapter 3.

Workers generally do not resist change. They resist how it impacts their lives (at work or home) or the perception of what they think might happen (e.g., implementing lean and losing their job). Change seldom looks the same to the initiating person and the recipient. It requires trust and respect for the individual. We've all heard the expression that we should treat others the way we would like to be treated. It sounds simple enough. Yet, have you had experiences similar to the following?

You're at a leadership presentation where it was enthusiastically stated that "people are your most important asset." However, within a week, you start hearing things about the same leader, such as he wanted to use a specific conference room and rudely told the people in it to be out in five minutes.

An executive overseeing a group of plants told the IT manager that he wanted his group of plants to get the new software installed first. Furthermore, he told the IT manager that the discussion never happened.

The executive presentation may be a motivating vision, but the discussion around the coffee machine will define your reality or culture. The same holds true for small teams or one-on-one interactions. Early in my career, I was asked to meet with a seasoned union leader who was upset about an issue. Meeting for the first time, he looked at me and said,

Continuous Improvement and Change Management

"All that I've heard about you, I thought you would be older." He probably thought I didn't have enough experience to handle the situation, or was it an indirect compliment? I walked up to him and replied, "Everything I've heard about you, I thought you would be uglier." He stared at me for awhile and then stated, "I think we will do just fine together." The lesson here is: Give respect, but also expect to have it given back to you.

New thinking is needed. As Albert Einstein said, "The thinking process used to get us into a situation cannot be the same process we use to get out of that situation." When looking at what separates the leading productive plants from the others, it's the people working in them that's making the difference. Mainly, it's the level of involvement and enthusiasm toward adding value to the product and process. That's not new information, yet many still struggle on how to capture that genuine enthusiasm that defines the best operating businesses and facilities of all types. I've witnessed it in hospitals, steel manufacturing, aerospace, engineering management, plant floor employees, etc. For example, when I observed and analyzed various world-class operations, I noticed they all still had daily problems to resolve. The difference was that the people knew what had to be done, were willing to do what was required and had support structures in place to help enable the corrections in process to keep things in order. There is a heightened level of discipline and enthusiasm that makes the difference. The enthusiasm gives you the desire to do what it takes. However, discipline to do the right thing by following a standardized process results in a stable process. When everyone does this, it allows you to get the job done on good and bad days. In addition, the system variability is minimized, and production and operational uptime/throughput are maximized.

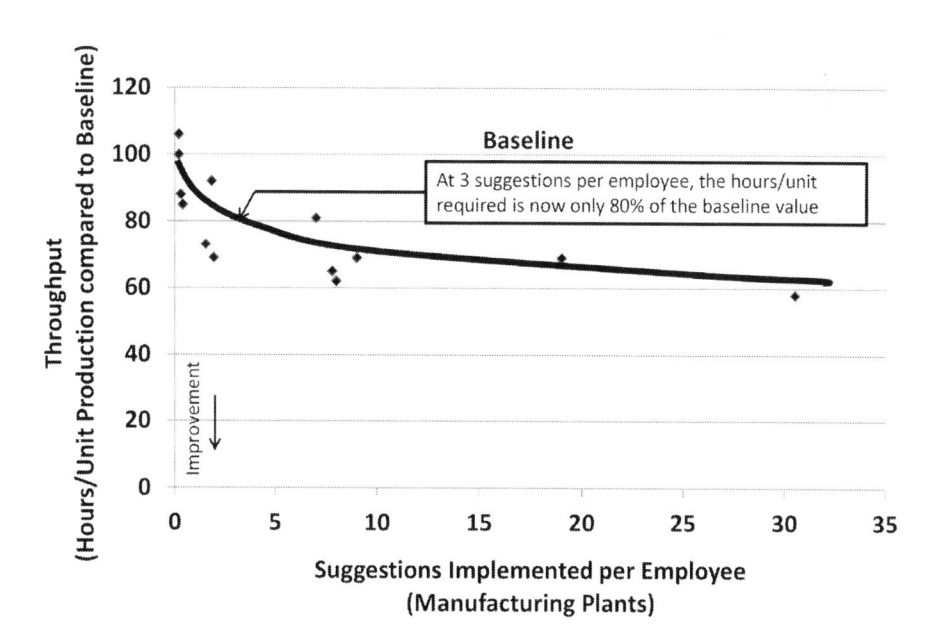

Figure 1.2: Impact of employee participation on productivity

Chapter 1

(Team influence index = Level of problem-solving and personnel issues handled at team level)

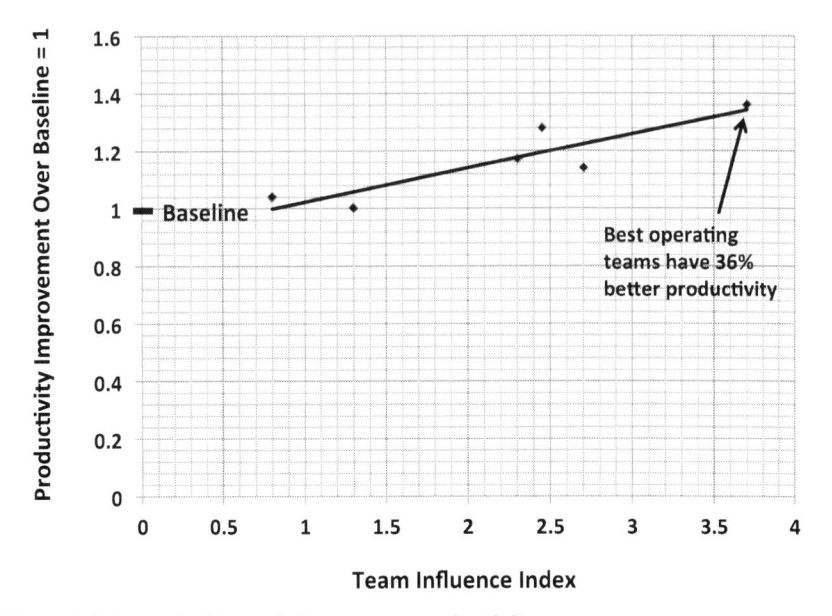

Figure 1.3: Impact of team influence on productivity

Enthusiasm can come from a number of things, such as sense of mission, team competition, personal satisfaction, shared benefits and profits, and job interest. Genuine enthusiasm, however, is built on trust. How fair the reward system is, as perceived by the employees, and answers to "what's in it for me" if I change my behavior, will largely determine the level of enthusiasm. This directly impacts the rate of continuous improvement.

Figure 1.2 shows the results of a study regarding the impact of employee participation on productivity. Companies that counted all the small, incremental plant floor improvements were getting thirty to forty suggestions per employee, per year, with productivity values in the better half of Figure 1.2. Note that much of the improvement benefits came early, with few suggestions implemented per employee. At three suggestions per employee, there is already about a fifty percent increase in productivity. At six suggestions per employee, about two-thirds of the productivity benefit has been achieved. Additional suggestions help, but at a diminished rate of productivity improvement. Facilities with greater employee suggestions implemented per employee had lower production times per unit, (higher throughput). This supports the thinking that employee participation does, indeed, make a quantifiable difference toward improving bottom line results.

Figure 1.3 displays a similar trend by comparing the impact of team influence. The team influence index is based on several plant floor involvement indices: such as level of problem-solving, within team absenteeism coverage and extent of conflict resolution handled by the team. A higher team influence index resulted in better productivity.

Continuous Improvement and Change Management

	Low → willing or capable → willing and capable → High
Organizational Engagement High	Moderate Improvement · High Improvement
Low	Low Improvement · Moderate Improvement

Continuous Improvement Process Maturity

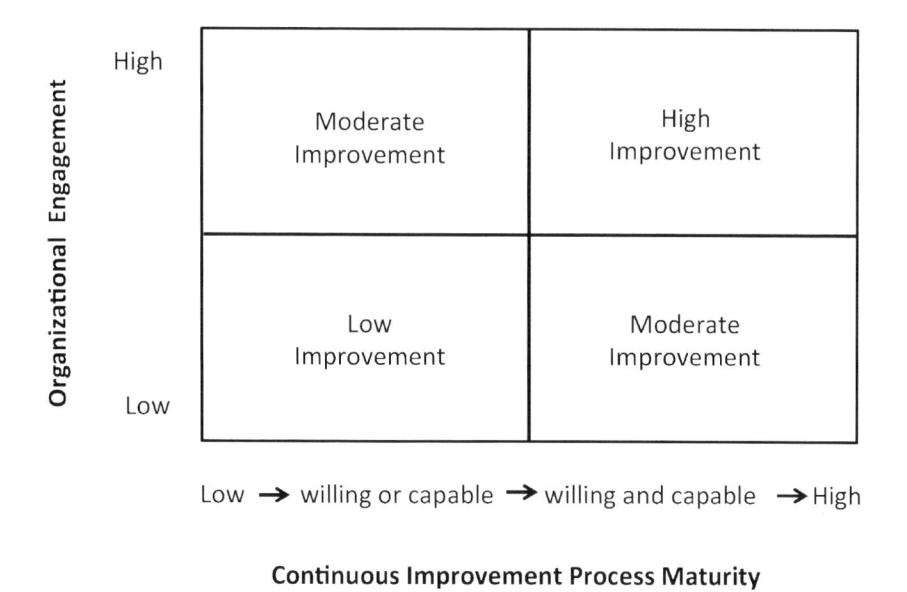

Figure 1.4: Relationship between organizational allowment and CIP maturity

To get high improvement, you need both high organizational engagement and high continuous improvement process maturity, as shown in Figure 1.4. Increasing levels of CIP maturity were illustrated in Figure 1.1. Get the workforce engaged (i.e., allowment) and support the continuous improvement process. People who enthusiastically support continuous improvement can usually overcome most daily issues that arise, or at least improve on current work processes and practices.

In an ongoing study started in 2009 and completed in 2013 using data from over two hundred company project results, it was determined that when employees are engaged (i.e., buy-in is attained), *"there is a seven times greater likelihood of success."* Based on an earlier study of more than two hundred facilities, Figure 1.5 shows that when operators had greater involvement in such things as using visual aids, preventive maintenance (PM) checks and the minor use of tools if the plant culture allowed it, the maintenance expenditures, as a percent of the original investment in machinery and improvement had improved.

1.4. Continuous Improvement and Standardized Work

On August 28, 2012, three days after American astronaut Neil Armstrong died, I listened to a radio interview that described him as "disciplined and calm in the face of disaster." An example used was Armstrong cruising just above the moon's surface and landing with just sixteen seconds of fuel left. Our consequences may not be as severe, but standardized processes and disciplined execution, when it matters, are at the heart of continuous improvement.

Chapter 1

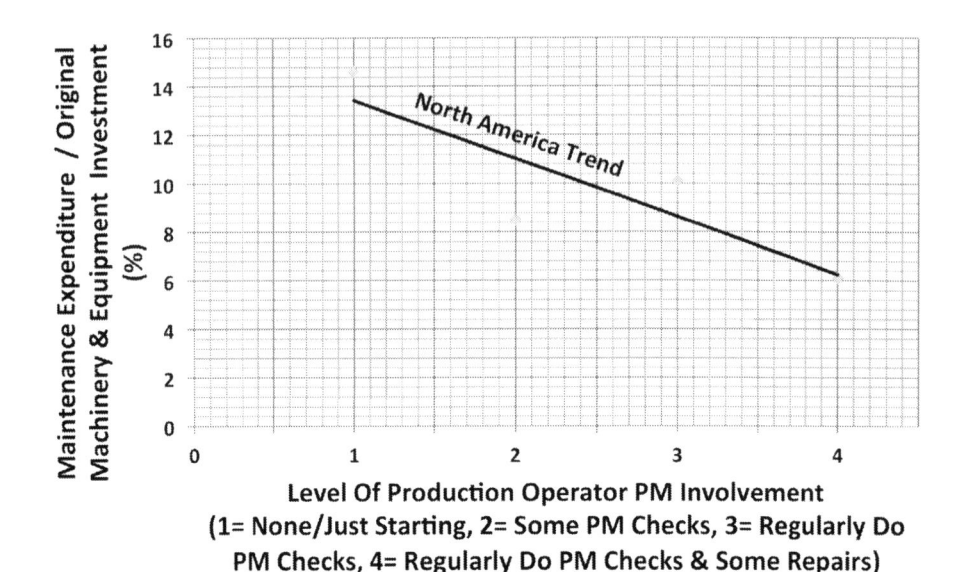

Figure 1.5: Positive impact of production operator PM involvement on maintenance expenditure

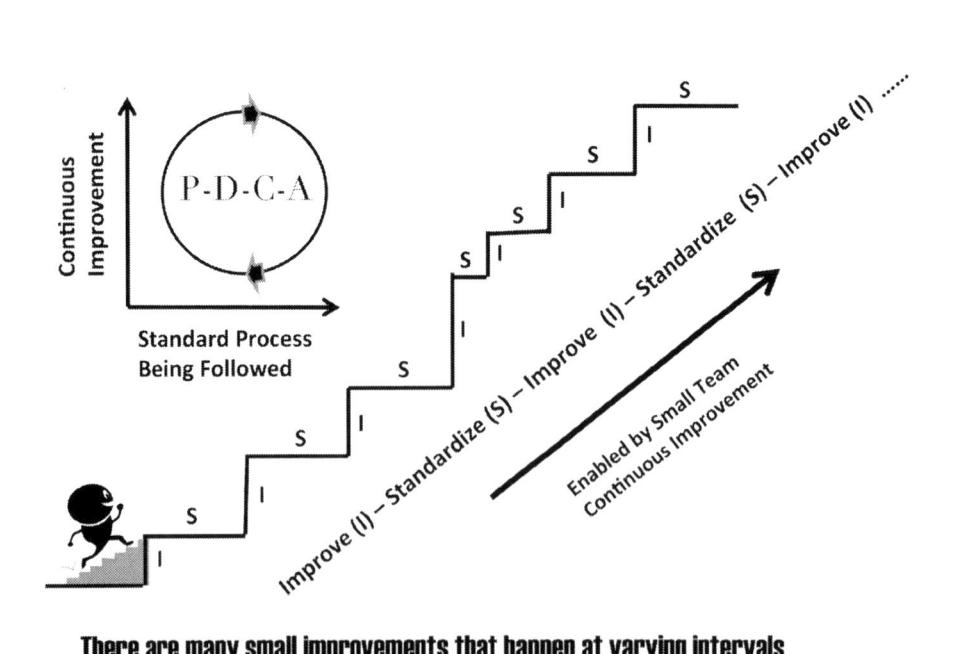

There are many small improvements that happen at varying intervals

Figure 1.6: Improve and standardize steps of improvement

The first step in making an improvement is to understand the current process and related standardized work. This defines the baseline from which all improvement begins. Figure 1.6 illustrates incremental steps of improvement. Standardized work refers to having every job done the same way in both sequence and procedure so it's always performed in the most efficient manner, regardless of who does the job. The recommended improvement should be clarified and understood by those who will be most impacted (Plan). The new idea or improvement is then ready to be tried for a designated period of time (Do). Next, results should be compared to the baseline, which is the current standardized work (Check). If the proposed method is better, then it should be communicated to all those impacted and it becomes the new standardized work (Act). This process, called PDCA,(P-D-C-A) should be ongoing by individuals and teams throughout the company. The standardized process should be regularly checked for consistency. This process also introduces numerous small improvements, always building on the previous standardized work. As it was taught to me: 1.) Make Rule; 2.) Teach Rule; 3.) Follow Rule and include the check to assure process integrity.

One example of standardized work instructions is a standard operating procedure (SOP). It is a list of established procedures to follow when carrying out a given operation, regardless of who performs the task. It is the step-by-step instruction to be routinely performed. Standardized work also enables doing things right as team members change on the plant floor and in the office. In many operations, numerous employees are getting their job done based on what they learned over time, on-the-job training and, too frequently, who they know in the organization (e.g., plant floor friends, supporting departments and working through the informal network that gets things done). Even though there are organizational charts, success is too dependent on position in the organization and the relative positioning of other team members. If you have an engaged workforce following standardized work processes, you still have all the same team members. But now, an action (i.e., best practice standardized work) is only done in a single manner with a known outcome.

Not following standardized work can negatively impact anyone, even the company that created the model for lean manufacturing. "Toyota deviated from its own system by responding too late to customer concerns and focusing too much on growth….Toyota had become far less lean as its inventory turns went from 22 in the 1990s to 10 in 2008."[17] Without the proper continuous improvement culture, operational excellence cannot be sustained.

People not wanting to follow standardized processes also cause issues to their personal health. "Too many patients, when they are diagnosed with an illness or an injury, do not follow through with their treatment. They don't take their medications conscientiously and don't change their habits as recommended."[18]

By regularly following a standardized routine, you can quickly teach a common process to others. When I first came to the University of Tennessee, I lived on campus, so three nights per week, I ran up one thousand steps around school and then went to Subway. I would order a Number 27. At first, the sandwich artists would look at me and say, "What's that?" I replied, "It's my Subway the way I like it." (It's a particular sub

Chapter 1

with select toppings and some salt, pepper and honey mustard.) Every running day for several weeks, I would order Number 27 and give very specific instructions. It took about three weeks before the sandwich artists knew what a Number 27 was and the assembly instructions were no longer needed. As people changed jobs/shifts, I needed to start over, but it always worked and was a fun experiment.

The United States Postal Service has an online process for temporarily changing your mail delivery address, which I used. However, after checking why no mail was showing up, it was determined that the postal delivery person saw a for sale sign on the front yard and assumed no one was home. He didn't' follow the standardized process of leaving a delivery notification card. Even after deviating from the process, he could have knocked on the door or called the phone number on the change request. So, two weeks of mail went full circle twice, from Tennessee to Michigan!

When a group, department, or company does not have standardized work processes, common traits are typically evident.

- There is no basis or foundation on which to build continuous improvement.
- Variability increases.
- When things go wrong, people are blamed instead of focusing on improving the process.
- It's more difficult to make decisions based on data.
- What's important changes from week to week or daily.
- Goals and targets change frequently.
- Goals and targets are mandated without methods to attain them.
- Employees find individual ways that best complement their needs and style to attain the targets, but efficiency and cost usually suffer.
- There is high stress in the organization.
- Many things don't make sense to the workforce because they don't make sense.
- Employees do not contribute openly to ongoing continuous improvement.
- There is more arbitrary cost cutting than ongoing improvement.

In general, places of business that do a better job performing the check (C) in PDCA PDCA are more likely to be one of the best.

1.5 Operations in Chaos and Crisis

In good financial times and when business is strong, it's much easier to do things right. However, it's when times are tough that the true character of your team, company and leaders come forward. I've found that in times of extreme chaos or crisis, most companies start to behave in a similar manner, regardless of the type of company.

- If you don't have a robust improvement process working in stable times, how can you expect reasonable results in times of crisis?

- If you don't have standardized work, when you test/measure improvement ideas, how do you know what works? This is further compounded as more and more ideas – at this time usually mandated from up high – and quick fixes are expected.
- There is a lack of transparency in improvement idea implementation. Typically, it's something like, "Give me all your ideas by the end of the week." Once in a while, you may hear something back, but more often there is no feedback. Then a few days later, a list of ideas gets handed down, with little or no data supporting the ideas and no comments on your previous ideas.

With regards to managing people, it's always easier to do the right thing when the business is profitable and things are going well. However, the true nature of your organizational values are better revealed when things get tough. Organizations without standardized processes and work will have a more difficult time performing and sustaining continuous improvement. Employees will experience high frustration, inconsistent direction and more people-related issues, and are less likely to enjoy their place of work, even though they may like what they do as a career. It is just a matter of time before even the most optimistic employee is worn down and just shows up. These types of organizations and companies will merely operate at a fraction of their potential toward business excellence, if they continue to operate at all in the long run.

Figure 1.7 shows the positive impact of lean on continuous improvement over time. After five years of lean implementation, more than seventy percent of two hundred companies still only achieve a low or medium positive impact of lean on continuous

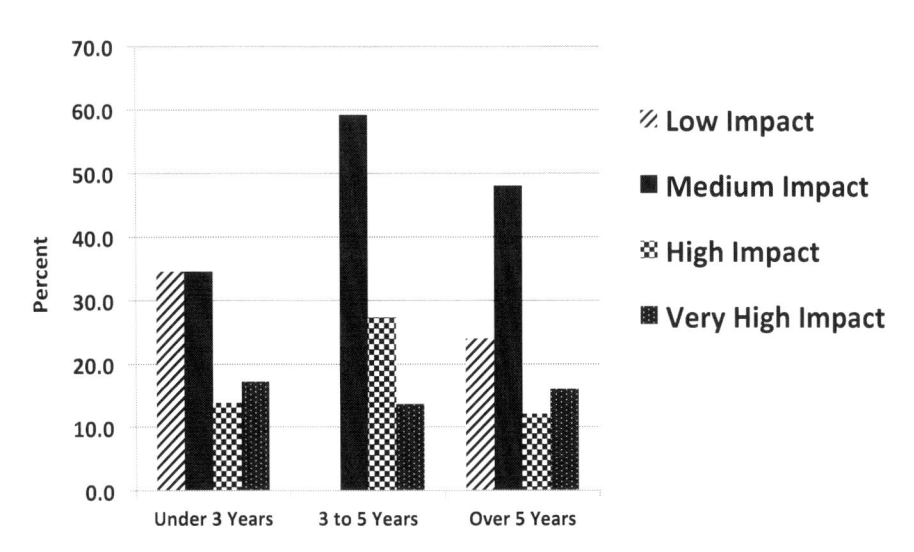

Most Lean Implementations Fail (fall short of expectations)

Figure 1.7: Positive impact of lean on continuous improvement as related to years of implementation

improvement. I've seen many facilities that are rolling out a lean process, but at best do a mediocre job of implementing 5S. When I visit plants, I usually observe varying levels of 5S implementation, not just between plants, but within the same facility. I may notice someone not following 5S visuals and ask why. The response is usually something like, "Bob doesn't like to do it exactly that way, but he's been here a long time, so he's okay." Before long, I've found numerous other exceptions for one reason or another. I would ask if they are implementing a lean process and, typically, they are. My concern is, if there is not enough discipline in the workforce to follow standardized work at its simplest level (i.e., 5S), how can they expect to be successful in a full lean implementation, which is an order of magnitude more complex and challenging?

A working and sustainable lean process is doable in typically two cultures:

1. Where the workforce is required to follow specific instructions (e.g., military) or is highly regulated (e.g., airlines).
2. Where the workforce is engaged performing standardized work and willing to correct daily issues back to proper standardized work practices and perform continuous improvement.

When a workforce does things out of fear (e.g., losing their job and/or business is failing), success can be sustained only for a limited time. This, however, is neither desirable nor sustainable.

The team discipline practiced to perform and sustain 5S or 6S implementation is a good leading indicator of eventual success in implementing lean practices. Analyzing the data from the same two hundred plants in Figure 1.6, but aligning them by years of 5S, showed that by properly implementing 5S first, the likelihood of a positive outcome in lean implementation doubles. Without the discipline and standardized work being followed by an engaged workforce, the many lean implementation failures will continue. If you can't do this in good times, how will it ever support your company in tougher times?

1.6 Continuous Improvement for Business Excellence

Operational excellence can be made sustainable only by instilling an enabling culture. Having said that, what are the current definitions of excellence?

"-… the quality of excelling; possessing good qualities in high degree.

-… an outstanding feature; something in which something or someone excels; a center of manufacturing excellence.

-… the use of herbs in one of the Excellencies of French cuisine."[19]

- "The quality of being excellent; state of possessing food qualities in an eminent degree; exalted merit; superiority in virtue."[20]

Continuous Improvement and Change Management

One of the early things taught in grade school is never define a word using the same word that you are defining in the definition. So, let's move to a more business-focused definition.

One well-known model for performance excellence is the Baldrige criteria. This framework takes a systems perspective and refers to an integrated approach to organizational performance management utilizing seven categories. Figure 1.8 displays the flow of information between the seven categories:

1. Leadership;
2. Strategic Planning;
3. Customer and Market Focus;
4. Measurement, Analysis and Knowledge Management;
5. Workforce Focus;
6. Process Management;
7. Results.

The seven categories are further divided into eighteen items that consist of one or more areas to address. "The term 'performance excellence' refers to an integrated approach to organizational performance management that results in (1) delivery of ever-improving value to customers and stakeholders, contributing to organizational sustainability; (2) improvement of overall organizational effectiveness and capabilities; and (3) organizational and personal learning."[21]

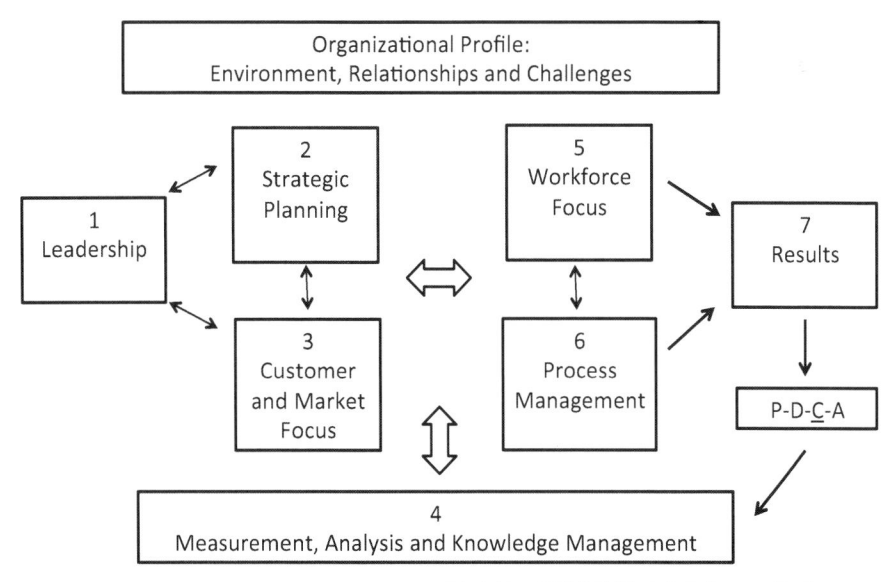

Adapted from 2009-2010 Criteria for Performance Excellence, Baldrige National Quality Program at NIST, Gaithersburg, MD, p. iv

Figure 1.8: Baldrige criteria for performance excellence framework

17

Chapter 1

Similarly, the European Foundation for Quality Management (EFQM) initiated an excellence model in 1988 and revised it in 1999. The EFQM model has nine criteria and thirty-two sub-criteria organized under the overall headings of enablers leading to results and improvements coming from innovations and learning.

"In the Netherlands, many health care organizations apply the EFQM model. In addition to improvement projects, peer review of professional practices, accreditation and certification, the EFQM approach is used mainly as a framework for quality management and as a conceptualization for organizational excellence."[22]

The nine EFQM criteria are:
1. Leadership;
2. Policy and strategy;
3. People;
4. Partnerships and resources;
5. Processes;
6. Customer results;
7. People results;
8. Society results;
9. Key performance results.

Figure 1.9 displays a combined Baldrige and EFQM approach. Both the Baldrige and EFQM models, although quality models, can be used to do a general self-assessment and help guide your continuous improvement effort.

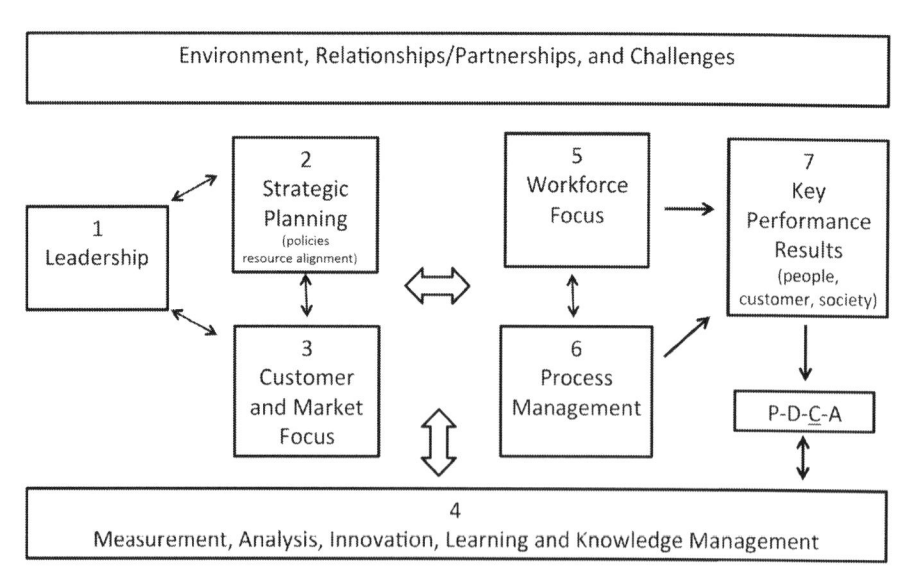

Adapted from 2009-2010 Criteria for Performance Excellence Baldrige National Quality Program at NIST, Gaithersburg, MD, p. iv and European foundation for Quality Management (EFQM) Model

Figure 1.9: Systems framework for performance excellence

Both models can provide the framework you need. The EFQM model appears a little more change management oriented as "…it relates to theories on organizational change and knowledge management and innovation, rather than theories on engineering structure of organizations."[23]

Both the Baldrige and EFQM models have a continuous improvement focus to enable the ongoing journey toward business excellence. Most users of both award criteria do so for the initial self-assessment, which drives significant continuous improvement. Others use it for performance measurement, benchmarking, or a model for corporate culture. My experiences have shown that instilling sustainable cultural change through such a process takes about five years to accomplish.

It is also mentioned in the *Baldrige Criteria for Performance Excellence* that, "many studies have shown high levels of workforce engagement have a significant, positive impact on organizational performance."[24]

The main benefit is the journey, which typically leads to increased business excellence maturity.

REFERENCES

1. McKinsey Quarterly. "*How to Make Cost Cuts Last.*" Chart Focus Newsletter, October 2010, p. 1.
2. Dalcher, D., and Genus, A. "*Avoiding IS/IT Implementation Failure.*" Technology Analysis and Strategic Management, December 2003, pp. 403-407.
3. Garforth, Peter. "*The Costs of Poor Energy Management.*" Plant Services, November 2010, http://www.plantservices.com/.
4. Medical Design. "*Virtual Life Management for Medical Implant Wires.*" *Medical Design*, February 12, 2010, http://medicaldesign.com/news/virtual-life-management-medical-implant-wires.
5. Fairclough, Gordon. "*Dairymen Routinely Spiked Milk In China.*" Wall Street Journal, 3 Nov. 2008, p. A1.
6. Turgis, Chloe. "Clumsy Co-Pilot Caused Plane to Dive." Yahoo Travel UK, December 28, 2010.
7. Casselman, Ben. "*Rig Engineer Details Problems Before Blast.*" Wall Street Journal 19 July 2010.
8. Copeland, Larry. "*Most Teens Still Driving While Distracted.*" USA Today 2 Aug. 2010, p.7A.
9. Simeonova, Meda. "Deferring Maintenance." *Water & Wastes Digest*, July 2010.
10. Weber, Tracey and Ornstein, Charles. "Problem Nurses Fall Through the Cracks." *USA Today* 15 July 2010, p. 2A.
11. Eyewitness News ABC 7. *Crosswalk Near Manhattan School Misspells 'School.*' WABC-TV New York, January 24, 2012, http://7online.com/archive/8516656/.
12. IBM. *IBM Global Study: Majority of Organizational Change Projects Fail.* Armonk: October 14, 2008, https://www-03.ibm.com/press/us/en/pressrelease/25492.wss.
13. Shrader, Ralph. "Risk Taking in a Tentative World. *Global Agenda* 2004, p. 120, http://www.boozallen.com/media/file/138088.pdf.
14. Covey, Stephen R. *The 7 Habits of Highly Effective People.* New York City: Simon & Schuster, Inc.'s Free Press, 2004.
15. Kirby, Philip J.; Kirby, J. Philip; and Hughes, David. *Thoughtware: Change the Thinking and the Organization Will Change Itself.* New York City: Productivity Press, 1997.
16. Baldrige National Quality Program. *2009-2010 Criteria for Performance Excellence.* Gaithersburg: National Institute of Standards and Technology, p. 64, http://www.nist.gov/baldrige/publications/upload/2009_2010_Business_Nonprofit_Criteria.pdf.

Chapter 1

17. Shanley, Agnes. "Toyota's Meltdown: and Lessons for Pharma on Its Lean Journey." *Pharmaceutical Manufacturing*, June 2010, p. 23, http://www.pharmamanufacturing.com/articles/2010/091/.
18. Roth, William F. *Comprehensive Healthcare for the U.S: An Idealized Model*. Boca Raton: CRC Press, 2010.
19. http://www.webster-dictionary.net/definition/excellence
20. Ibid, *2009-2010 Criteria for Performance Excellence*, p. iv.
21. Nabitz, Udo; Klazinga, Niek; and Walburg, Jan. *The EFQM Excellence Model: European and Dutch Experiences with the EFQM Approach in Health Care*. Oxford: Oxford University Press, International Journal for Quality in Health Care, 2000, p.191, http://intqhc.oxfordjournals.org/content/12/3/191.
22. Ibid, p. 129.
23. Ibid, *2009-2010 Criteria for Performance Excellence*, p. 43.

Chapter 2
Change Implementation Concepts and Models

"Bad systems can make good people behave badly."
— Robert Wright, Systems Thinking

"It makes no sense to show them what heaven looks like, when they can't even see the greener grass on the other side of the street."
— German Proverb (translated)

2.1 Back to the Basics with Current Issues

Over the years, I have had the opportunity to try many of the numerous models available for change management, both in small and large change projects and under various situations. Although there are many approaches and variations of models that could be discussed, I am going to focus on select ones that will adequately make the points I would like to emphasize. The models I have selected are the plan-do-check-act (PDCA) cycle, Lewin's freeze-unfreeze phases, Gleicher's formula and Kotter's eight-step model.

I have found the underlying concepts in these change models to be very helpful. These earlier models have stood the test of time, are familiar to many individuals, and adequately encompass all the fundamental elements of a change process that I have encountered. So, when looking at numerous implementations of lean, reliability, ergonomics, engineering process improvements and many other change efforts, why is it that the long-term results have been disappointing?

- In discussing Kaizen event success and sustainability, "Some organizations seem to be able to sustain improved levels of performance. Many, however, find that within six months to one year, work area performance has degraded, sometimes even to pre-event performance levels."[1]
- "Most companies will have difficulty sustaining even half of the results from a given event."[2]
- In a June 2004 Aberdeen Group report, the top item listed among the top five concerns/challenges that potentially represent a barrier to adoption/expansion of lean strategies was "significant culture change required," at just under seventy percent.[3]

Chapter 2

- "Companies today are no more effective at delivery on large-scale change initiatives than they were twenty years ago. In a recent Bain & Company survey, seventy percent of the companies said their change management initiatives did not deliver the expected results."[4] They stated similar results were obtained in the 1980s and 1990s.
- "There's no shortage of headlines or analyst reports citing enterprise resource planning (ERP) implementation debacles and a chilling industry implementation failure rate. Analysts from Gartner estimate that fifty-five percent to seventy-five percent of all projects fail to meet their obligations.[5]
- An IBM Consulting Group survey of 790 executives from the United States, United Kingdom, Germany, Brazil, and Mexico found that "resistance to change" was most often named as the greatest obstacle to productivity.[6]
- "Many techniques have been used to 'change the work culture' in older plants and facilities. In many equipment-intensive operations, these culture changing activities are rarely sustainable when little attention is paid to the day-to-day equipment and machine frustrations that people have to deal with."[7]
- A 2014 study by Klaus Blache on reliability modeling and analytics usage showed that only about one in one hundred companies are seriously doing it. The number one roadblock was organizational culture.[8]
- Change management is also a key factor in healthcare and related costs. "Doctors and other healthcare professionals are not equipped to solve the problems of patients not taking care of themselves."[9] More specifically, in 2004, "healthcare spending amounted to $1,525 for every vehicle GM produced in the U.S. and analysis of health cost details suggests obesity is costing GM at least $286 million dollars a year."[10] In 2004, General Motors paid more for healthcare costs than it did for steel ($5.2 billion).

Whether it is organizations going through changes toward healthcare reform, lean manufacturing implementations, reliability centered maintenance, office/administrative process improvements, or like change initiatives, they all go through similar stages and have the same underlying needs for success.

Historical models based on extensive research and real-world data are fundamentally still applicable. However, in implementation and especially sustaining a change, I would like to add my perspectives in the spirit of continuous improvement. I believe in using models for change. Keep it simple – the best tool or model is the simplest one that works. Tools or models may not always work exactly as planned, but they provide a basis for organizing and visualizing what is working, what is not, and conceptualizing what to do next.

2.2 PDCA Cycle

PDCA gained much of its popularity from Dr. W. Edwards Deming. It also is referred to as the Shewhart cycle and plan-do-study-act (PDSA), which Deming felt was closer to Shewhart's intent. In Six Sigma programs, define, measure, analyze, improve, and control (DMAIC) is a similar cycle if it is viewed with iterative cycles in mind. The power of

Change Implementation Concepts and Models

PDCA is its simplicity and cumulative improvement possibilities by continually repeating the cycle, done either by the same team or other teams.

PLAN: Start with the expected results in mind. Establish the objectives and processes required to attain the expected results.

DO: Implement the new process. Start small at first to test the new idea.

CHECK: Measure the new process relative to the expected results.

ACT: Analyze the differences and root causes by comparing current best practice versus new idea to understand specific opportunities. Each cause should be the beginning of another PDCA, resulting in further improvement.

The intent is to always further refine the PDCA cycle so there is always an improvement. One can see why the word study better explains what should be happening. PDCA originally came from Deming when he was teaching in Japan in the 1950s. So, PDCA or PDSA is repeatedly applied with improvements being implemented until the expected results are achieved.

Figure 2.1 depicts a schematic of the plan-do-check/study-act cyclone. Through ongoing improvement and building on current best practices, every iteration increases clarification and improves on the current best practice. Listening and implementing the many plant floor suggestions increase plant floor buy-in and relevance at the operational level of the organization. In Figure 2.1, note that the black arrows designate plan-do-check/study and only if a change is worthy of testing do you go further down the cyclone, as indicated with the white arrows.

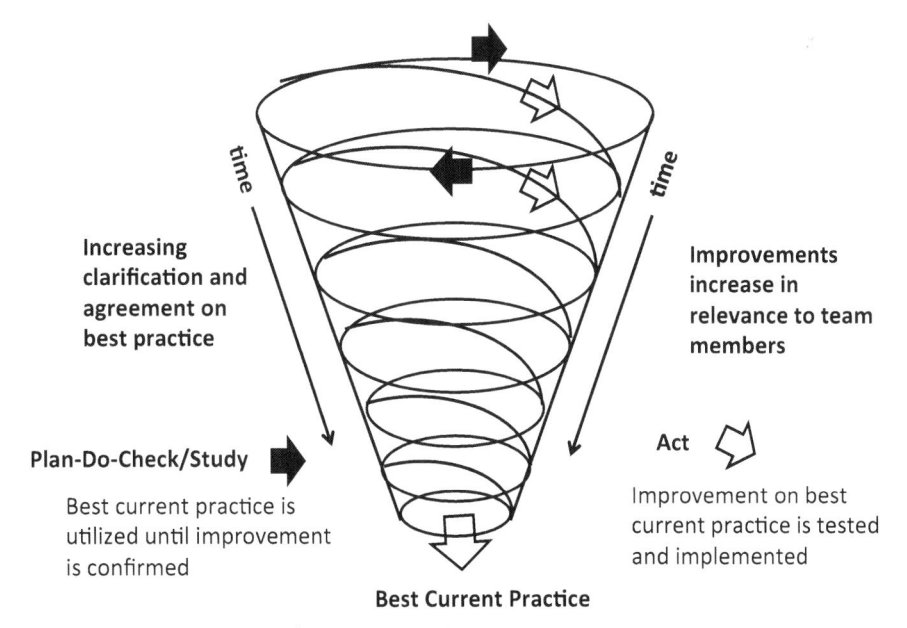

Figure 2.1: Plan-do-check/study-act cyclone

Chapter 2

In the United States, the focus has been more often on large impact suggestions, large projects and expecting large rewards. In Japan, reports show that employees were doing over thirty suggestions per employee per year. These were the number of suggestions implemented. More companies are better understanding the importance of small team continuous improvement. If you understand the PDCA cycle and its many small improvements, it is easy to see how such high suggestion numbers are possible.

In the U.S., this was, and in many workplaces still is, a time when most companies struggled to get at least one suggestion from every employee. Many companies only counted larger suggestions because the thinking process is not the same. Small and frequent continuous improvement must be supported and understood as important and the path to gaining the ultimate competitive advantage.

Let's say Plant A and Plant B both have one thousand employees. However, Plant A gets one large suggestion per employee and Plant B gets thirty small suggestions per employee. If the focus is on mainly large ideas to get large rewards, much energy is expended in justifying or trying to justify them for approval. Furthermore, if they are not approved, employees are often more disappointed, feel like they have missed an opportunity, or are being taken advantage of by the company. At one plant I visited, a skilled trade's employee was getting his second maximum monetary award. Management was making a brief presentation and congratulating him while a newsletter photographer was taking his picture. I walked over to several of his coworkers who looked disgruntled and discreetly asked why. They said, "He's getting a major reward for the second time and all he does is spend most of his day writing suggestions while we're doing our job."

Meanwhile, Plant B is getting thirty small ideas from one person, which are incrementally improving work practices and processes. Wouldn't thirty small improvements on a process be cumulatively as good, or most likely better, than one large improvement? Also, wouldn't the learning and buy-in of many small improvements be much greater? Now, do this for ten years and you have three hundred thousand improvements, and most likely several big improvement ideas that resulted, as well as learning, buy-in and plant floor understanding. That's the path to gaining a competitive advantage.

The continuous improvement process model in Figure 2.2 encompasses the Shewhart PDCA cycle. As supported, I agree that the check step is better represented by the study term. However, the acronym PDCA is deeply ingrained everywhere, so I will use PDCA, PDSA and PDC/SA interchangeably.

When doing continuous improvement:
1. Grasp the situation by clearly defining the problem.
2. Use the small team continuous improvement process for iterative improvements, going through P-D-C/S-A as many times as needed.
3. Use the short- or long-term tools when needed for a specific task or to support a special initiative.
4. Use the experience to focus on changing the thinking process toward ongoing problem-solving and following standardized work. In other words, engage the workforce.
5. Align the plant floor goals with higher level goals for business plan deployment. Make

Change Implementation Concepts and Models

sure everyone knows what they are allowed to do (i.e., differently, more/less of, how much money can they spend on improvement without other approvals, etc.) to have a positive impact on the desired outcome. Share the learnings with other areas.

First, it's important to point out that the focus always should be continuous improvement (CI) and removing waste. Applying myriad of improvement tools is something that should be done when daily activities or standardized work to keep processes in balance aren't working, or to accelerate a desired result. Most companies that I speak with are quick to point out how many 5S, Kaizen, value stream maps, etc., they have done. I would ask:

1. Do you have standardized work and is it being followed?
2. Do you have individual/small team continuous process improvement and is it working?
3. Do you have a methodology to improve and sustain the thinking process to one of ongoing improvement and is it working?

If the answer is not "yes" to all three of these questions, then the first priority should be to establish a robust process to support this needed foundation. It's also rare to hear

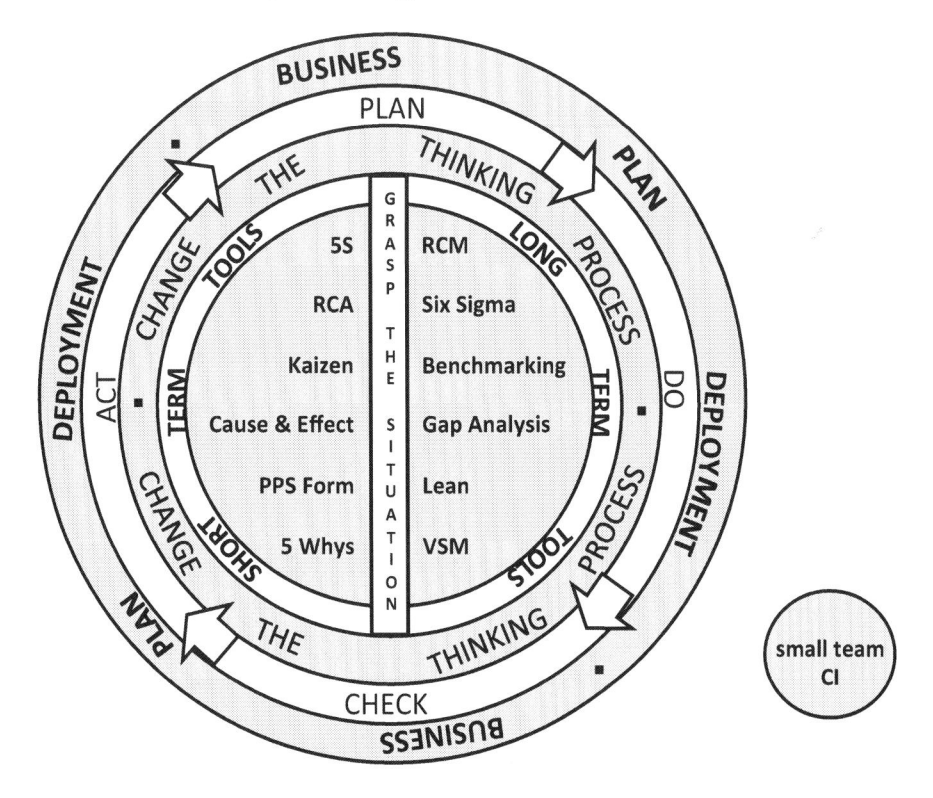

Figure 2.2: Continuous improvement process model

Chapter 2

someone say, "We are maintaining balanced flow through current standardized work and daily continuous improvement." Let me explain. Improving flow should be a systems-wide approach that keeps everything in balance. If everyone does what they are supposed to do according to their standardized work and all processes and equipment perform to specification and production output is equal to the plan, their flow is level. If you're an automotive assembly plant that both plans for and produces four hundred quality vehicles per day, your flow is good. If you're a medical insurance claim issues resolution department and planned claim responses per week equal actual output, your flow is good. Note that doing less or doing more can result in problems. Managers often request more to raise output goals without addressing the processes and standardized work needed to support that request. This is just as much an issue in office processes as it is in industrial energy production, hospitals, pharmaceutical, manufacturing and most other processes.

Figure 2.3 displays how to use Figure 2.2 in a flowchart format. This generalized schematic will satisfy most situations. If you need to accelerate your continuous improvement, teach a skill, have a chronic problem, or an issue in an area too large for your daily CI process to handle, this is when you should consider using the short- and long-term improvement tools to remove additional waste in the process. Think of them as methods to use to reduce variations in standardized work when your small team CI process needs support. Remember, the small team continuous improvement process is your engine powering your success. As you continue to change the thinking process, the workforce becomes more resilient to daily issues. Make sure your cumulative small changes or large changes are aligned at all levels of the organization to support your business strategies and goals.

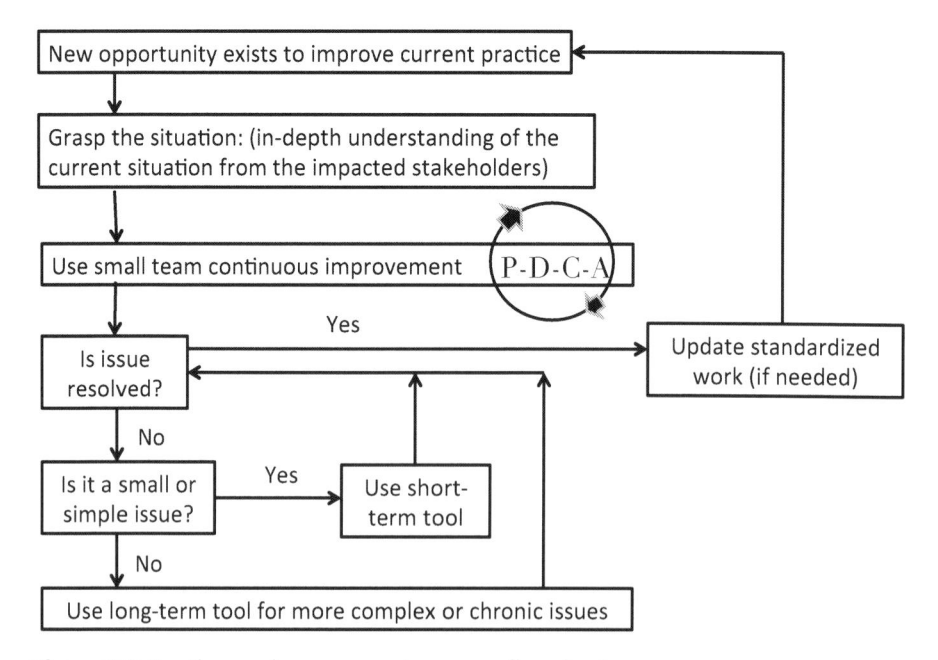

Figure 2.3: Continuous improvement process flowchart

2.3 Lewin's Model

Change, in its most basic form, is described by Kurt Lewin, a German psychologist and pioneer in his field who later came to the United States, as

$$B = f(PE)$$

In his formula, behavior (B) is a function (f) of the interaction between a person (P) and the environment (E). This interaction is constantly changing, with varying degrees of resistance to behavioral change. One of Lewin's many contributions was the force field analysis, which provides a process for looking at forces that influence change, both positive and negative, and provides an indication of readiness for change.

2.3.1 Force Field Analysis

A good tool to use to determine if you are ready for change is force field analysis. It provides a visual framework for showing forces that support or hinder a desired change or goal. It can be used to depict an individual's or group's state of mind at that point in time regarding a desired outcome.

Numerous ways have been developed to display a force field analysis. However, the methodologies all follow the same basic approach and key elements.

1. Write down/explain the proposed change.
2. In a driving forces column, list all forces supporting or pushing toward the change.
3. In a restraining forces column, list all forces opposing or pushing away from the change.
4. Each driving force does not require an opposing restraining force.
5. The length of the force arrow under each driving and restraining force should reflect the strength of the force.

According to Lewin's theories, human behavior is caused by an interaction of various positive and negative forces. The forces are a compilation of beliefs, habits, group norms, knowledge, expectations and more. These opposing forces hold an issue in balance or equilibrium. In order for change to occur, there must be sufficient driving forces to overcome the restraining forces and shift the equilibrium.

After doing the analysis, you can better decide if it's feasible to initiate implementing the change. It is a quick and good measure of your chances of success. An interim course of action is to work on solutions to reduce or eliminate the resisting forces or increase driving forces. Simply stated, force field analysis provides an indication of whether or not you are ready for the first or next step toward implementing a change. As resisting forces are reduced and/or driving forces increase, you can repeat the analysis as often as needed to see if you are getting closer to change readiness.

Chapter 2

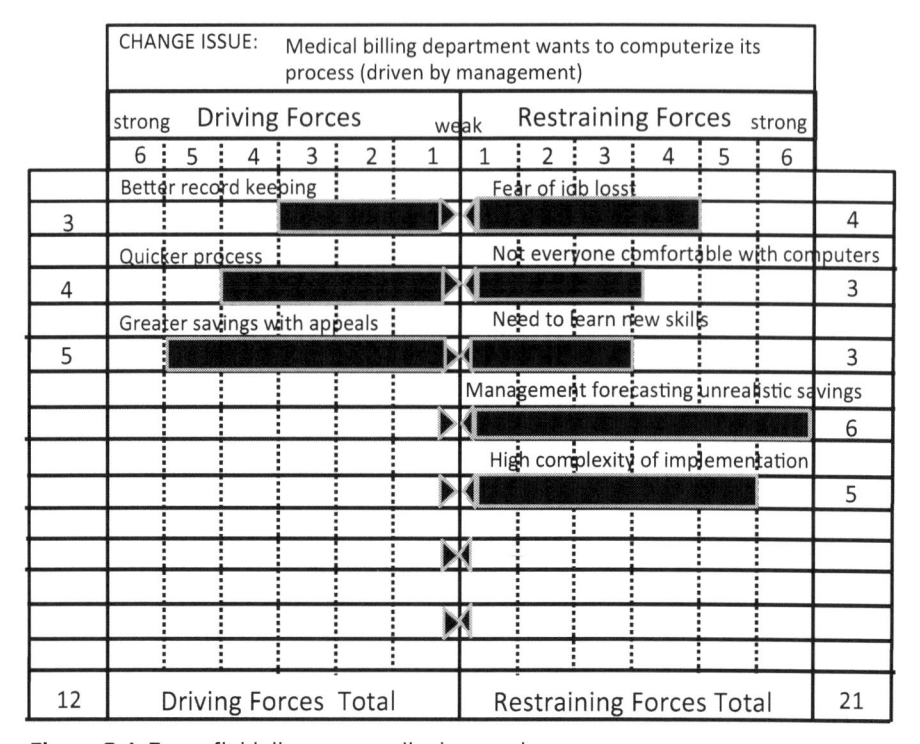

	CHANGE ISSUE:	Medical billing department wants to computerize its process (driven by management)											
	strong	Driving Forces			weak		Restraining Forces				strong		
	6	5	4	3	2	1	1	2	3	4	5	6	
	Better record keeping						Fear of job loss						
3				▰▰▰▰▰◁			▰▰▰▰▰▰▰▰						4
	Quicker process						Not everyone comfortable with computers						
4			▰▰▰▰▰▰◁				▰▰▰▰▰						3
	Greater savings with appeals						Need to learn new skills						
5		▰▰▰▰▰▰▰◁					▰▰▰▰▰						3
							Management forecasting unrealistic savings						
						◁	▰▰▰▰▰▰▰▰▰▰						6
							High complexity of implementation						
						◁	▰▰▰▰▰▰▰▰						5
						◁							
						◁							
12	Driving Forces Total						Restraining Forces Total						21

Figure 2.4: Force field diagram, medical example

Figure 2.4 is a medical example of a filled out force field diagram. There are many manual and computerized versions in use. At the top is a space to write down the change issue. On the left side are spaces to write down driving forces. Similarly, spaces on the right side are for listing restraining forces. Under each driving and restraining force issue are six spaces that can be shaded in or marked to indicate how weak (1=weakest) or strong (6=strongest) a force is. On the far left and right are spaces to write in the weak/strong score. By listing the driving and restraining forces and rating their magnitude with a one to six score, you can more easily decide if the group/department is ready for the change. Of course, you want the driving forces total score to be higher than the restraining forces total score. However, make sure the big restraining force issues are taken care of regardless of scores.

When scoping the change issue, be specific as to whom is driving the change and the group being assessed for change readiness. For each large restraining force, you should attempt to have a communicated countering action to lower the resistance. For example, if the largest restraining force is fear of job loss, then share with the team the reason for the change. It might be because the volume of billings is increasing, so the change will both enable the handling of the increased volume and allow better analysis for cost-saving decisions. Each significant restraining force needs to be remedied until the equilibrium score shifts enough to support the change. Take the time needed to get buy-in. Do not

Change Implementation Concepts and Models

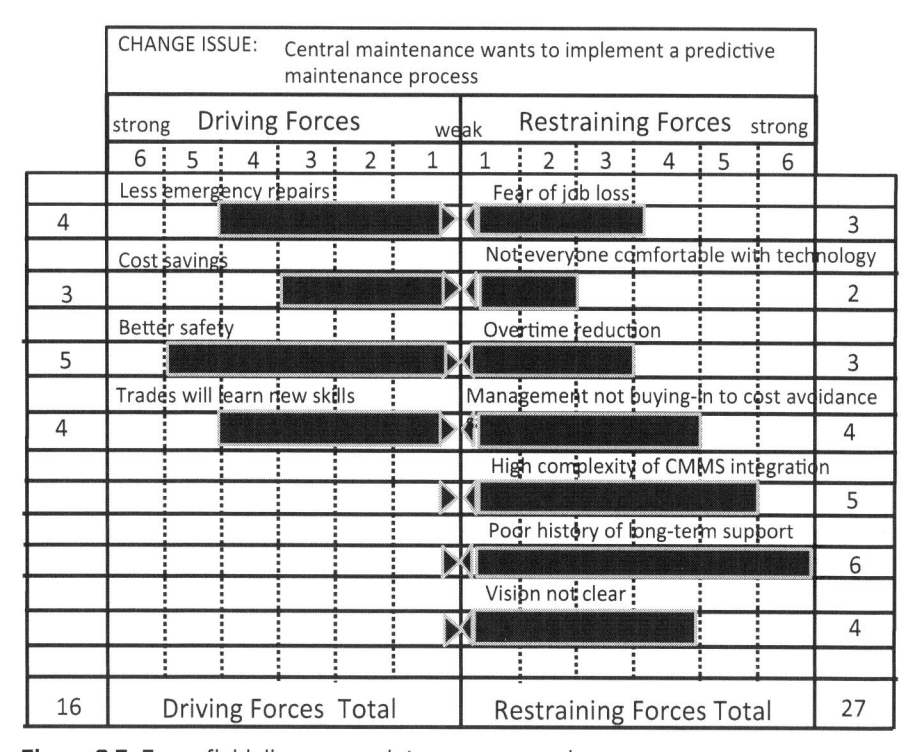

CHANGE ISSUE:	Central maintenance wants to implement a predictive maintenance process											
strong	Driving Forces				weak		Restraining Forces				strong	
	6	5	4	3	2	1	1	2	3	4	5	6
4	Less emergency repairs						Fear of job loss					3
3	Cost savings						Not everyone comfortable with technology					2
5	Better safety						Overtime reduction					3
4	Trades will learn new skills						Management not buying-in to cost avoidance					4
							High complexity of CMMS integration					5
							Poor history of long-term support					6
							Vision not clear					4
16	Driving Forces Total						Restraining Forces Total					27

Figure 2.5: Force field diagram, maintenance example

just make an announcement of what you are going to do to improve the restraining force. Communicate and implement the driving forces and assess the readiness for change as often as required. Implementing too early can further raise the restraining forces.

Another force field diagram using a predictive maintenance example is shown in Figure 2.5. A blank force field diagram is in Appendix A.

2.3.2 Current State – Unfreeze – Change – Refreeze – Future State

After the force field analysis is done and there is a perceived need for change, a good overall visualization of what needs to happen for change is an early model developed by Lewin. It is a three-stage process (Figure 2.6) that depicts the change management steps. Stage one is unfreezing the current state, which requires getting over the restraining forces. Before the future state can be instilled, the current state must be discarded. You must overcome the inertia of the status quo. Getting ready for stage two, the force field analysis, determines future state readiness. As the change is occurring and a future state is now being put into practice, it's important to carry out stage three, freezing/refreezing to get everyone on the new process and on the same page. This is an often overlooked step because once you've energized a group to change, some will want to go further. It is important that expectations are aligned

Chapter 2

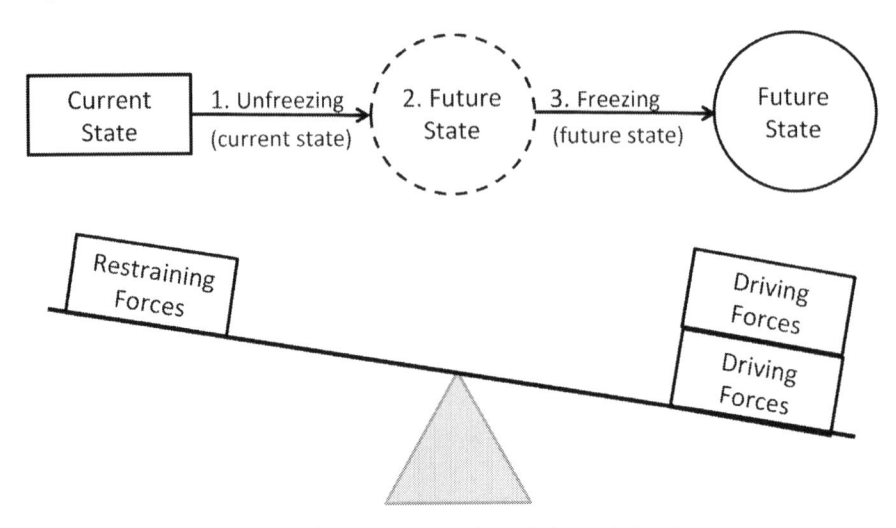

Figure 2.6: Schematic of Lewin's current state to future state steps

so team members with higher or slightly different expectations are not unhappy with the future state. So, refreezing at the proper place – one that has been well communicated with buy-in – requires a clear understanding of what the future state is.

2.4 Gleicher, Beckhard and Harris Change Equations

The change equation by David Gleicher, Richard Beckhard and Reuben Harris is both simple and effective. I have found it to be a great tool for grasping and clarifying readiness for change.

Change = Dissatisfaction x vision x first steps > resistance to change or written as the equation:

$$\Delta = D \times V \times F > R$$

Δ = symbol for change
D = dissatisfaction with the current state
V = vision of the future state
F = first steps toward the vision, both achievable and believable
R = resistance to change.

This shows that in order to get change (Δ), the three elements (D, V and F) must be present in sufficient quantity to overcome the resistance to change (R). Stated another way, if any of the three items are too small, then there is not enough momentum to enable the change. For example, you may work in a group of seasoned employees who like what they do and how they do it, and they may be producing a popular product, meaning their jobs are secure. So, why would they want to change, even if there are more efficient ways to perform the work? To start with, you would need to clearly communicate a highly desirable vision, with initial steps that are unquestionably achievable and believable. A well-defined vision with an attainable first step supports the change and takes away ambiguity, which causes resistance and fear. It is critical that leadership consistently demonstrates the vision.

When I helped to start up the Lansing Grand River (LGR) Cadillac facilities, each core value was discussed in individual meetings as previously mentioned. It's also important to point out that although our Union contract allowed specific competitive practices, they were not directly implemented. They were phased in to bring the employees along in understanding and buy-in. For example, teams of trades, operators and engineers reviewed all maintenance tasks to decide what could/should be done by plant floor operators in their machinery and equipment start-up checks. If you want to attain a future state, you need to act as if you are already there. Do it long enough and it becomes your reality. If getting a change is critical and other efforts aren't working, you may need to create dissatisfaction to initiate movement. It may simply mean showing the team how their performance compares to known competitors' best practices and explaining the two scenarios of continuing as is or using best practices with their likely outcomes. I have found that it is often a lack of knowledge, or ambiguity, and implementing too fast that increases resistance to change. Generally, people don't resist change as much as they resist how it impacts their lives. At the LGR plant, work practices were going to be different, with much more team member involvement. Hourly employees interested in working at LGR were invited to work one day in a simulated work environment, building basic wooden cars on a moving assembly line. The work intentionally started out unbalanced and was improved upon throughout the day, with team members' input on safety, quality, work practices and productivity. At the end of the day, the teams had a fairly balanced workload and highly improved workplace. They were then asked if they wanted to be part of that type of work environment. A large majority said something like, "If that's what you're going to do, I want to be part of it." It was the first step in acknowledging and stepping away from dissatisfaction with the current state of work practices where they presently worked.

It's also important that the first step is believable. That can be as simple as:

- Having operators and skilled trades review all maintenance tasks to decide what can be done by the operator in daily checks. This gives the trades more time for predictive and other proactive maintenance. Operators should have major involvement or lead the effort.
- Letting team members finalize the standardized operating practices, with input from all stakeholders.
- Implementing and adhering to a robust, small team continuous improvement plan, giving teams direct authority for changes up to a specific dollar amount.
- Asking why and how when resolving issues versus telling what should be done, and demonstrating the proper use of the problem-solving process.

A different situation I heard about during a sightseeing bus tour of Manhattan in New York City, New York, also fits this change equation. When the Brooklyn Bridge was

Chapter 2

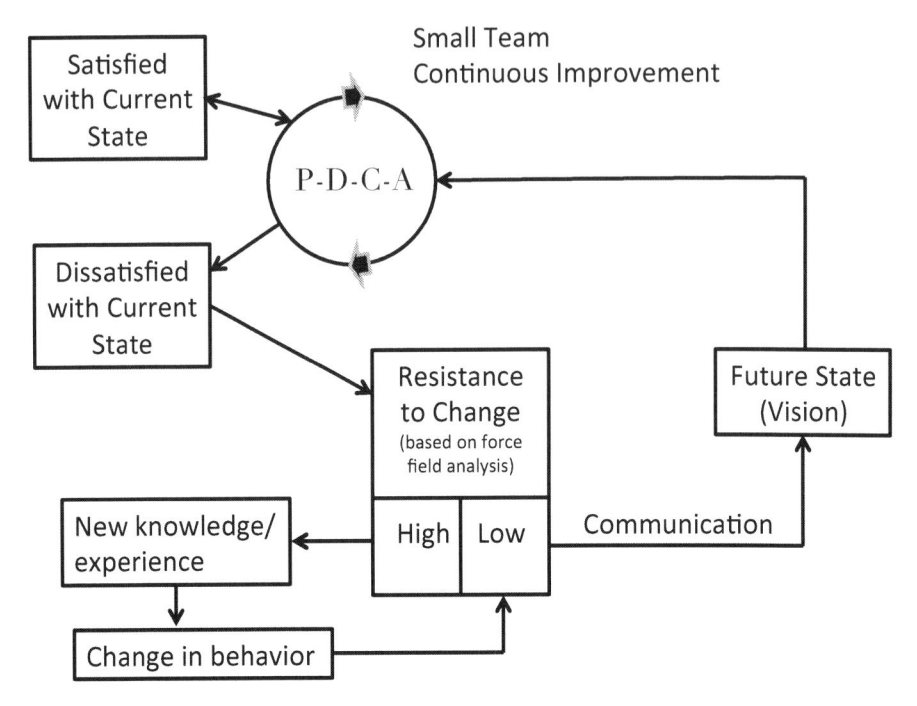

Figure 2.7: Schematic of integrated improvement models

finished after thirteen years of construction, people were afraid to cross it. It connects the boroughs of Brooklyn and Manhattan and goes over the East River. It was also the first steel wire suspension bridge. At first, people started to use it, but six days after its opening, rumors about the bridge collapsing caused a stampede, leading to concerns over its stability. On May 17, 1884, P.T. Barnum marched a troupe of 21 elephants and other animals over the bridge to squelch any fears about its stability.[11] It was the step needed to show the bridge's safety was achievable and believable.

Figure 2.7 integrates the general concepts of the Gleicher, Beckhard and Harris equation and Lewin's steps into a simplified model of continuous improvement. If the current state is working and periodic reviews using plan-do-check/study-act cycles confirm it, then no other action is necessary. If the check step shows issues or dissatisfaction with the current state, then move through the flowchart and next measure your readiness for change using a force field analysis. Once resistance is low enough, implement the new practice and check it over a specified time. The improvement steps should be small enough to be seen as doable. These steps should be repeated until the future state is realized. Once it has proven out, it becomes the new standardized work and the process starts all over again.

Change Implementation Concepts and Models

	Lewin	Gleicher, Beckhard, Harris	Kotter
From the Current State	Unfreeze	D = Dissatisfaction V = Vision	Establish a sense of urgency Form a strong coalition Create a vision for change Communicate the new vision and strategy
During Transition	Transition	F = First Concrete Step	Empower team members to act on the vision Create short-term wins to grow support Consolidate improvements and use the momentum to continue
Establish the Future State	Refreeze	$\Delta = D \times V \times F > R$ R = Resistance to Change	Institutionalize the change

Figure 2.8: Schematic of integrated improvement models

2.5 Kotter's Eight-Step Model

John Kotter's eight-step change process has been widely used in many organizations to instill change. According to Kotter, eight stages are required to ensure successful changes. Here is a summary list of Kotter's eight stages for creating change:[12]

1. Establish a sense of urgency if it doesn't already exist.
2. Form a strong coalition, a team capable of guiding the change.
3. Create a clear vision.
4. Communicate the new vision and strategy.
5. Empower team members to act on the vision.
6. Create short-term wins to grow support.
7. Consolidate improvements and use the momentum to continue on with more and/or larger changes.
8. Institutionalize the change.

Each stage can require significant effort and time to accomplish. However, it is critical to complete each stage. As often as needed to assess readiness, a force field analysis can be performed to decide what still needs to be resolved before moving to the next step.

Figure 2.8 summarizes the steps or stages of change from Lewin, Kotter, and Gleicher, Beckhard and Harris. It depicts all the models aligning, just with increasing levels of detail.

An often debated topic is the importance of a significant emotional event to motivate change. The generally accepted theory of change points toward unfreezing the existing

Chapter 2

state before progress can be made toward the desired state. Outcomes of historical cases have shown that emotional events can help produce change if they are interpreted as proving compelling reinforcement of the need to change. Change is still possible without a traumatic event, but requires a very clear vision of the direction for change, taking into account the underlying interests, and consistent leadership support. Based on my experience, leading change with a clearly defined future state or vision is attainable. Having change without a significant event, such as a potential plant closing, will take longer, but may result in a more sincere workforce buy-in. If leadership provides long-term, consistent support, this change path can work equally well.

2.6 Implementation and Expectations

Leaders are often expected to show short-term results, typically quarterly and annually. Fundamental change, however, typically does not occur in one major event. It is more often a series of steps, with several identifiable, pivotal events. This is further complicated by leadership turnover. Thus, viewed from a short-term perspective, the results may not be seen as impressive. But, from a long-term viewpoint, the results may be much more substantial. Making the change a daily practice is where most change process implementations slow down. In a typical change implementation scenario, it appears everything is working during the pilot setup. But when the new work methods are put on the plant floor on a larger scale, people quickly revert back to their old work habits. Why? The key reason is behavioral change. If it is not established, the transfer of the change to daily practice will be slow or nonexistent, as evidenced by resistance to

Stage 1	Stage 2	Stage 3	Stage 4	Stage 5
Raising Awareness	Commitment Readiness	Transfer to Daily Practice (standardized work)	Gaining Momentum	Continuous Improvement (after the change)
Willing	Wanting	What	Working	Why
to change	to change	to change	the change	change/ sustain

This will only happen with change of behavior

Increasing Benefits

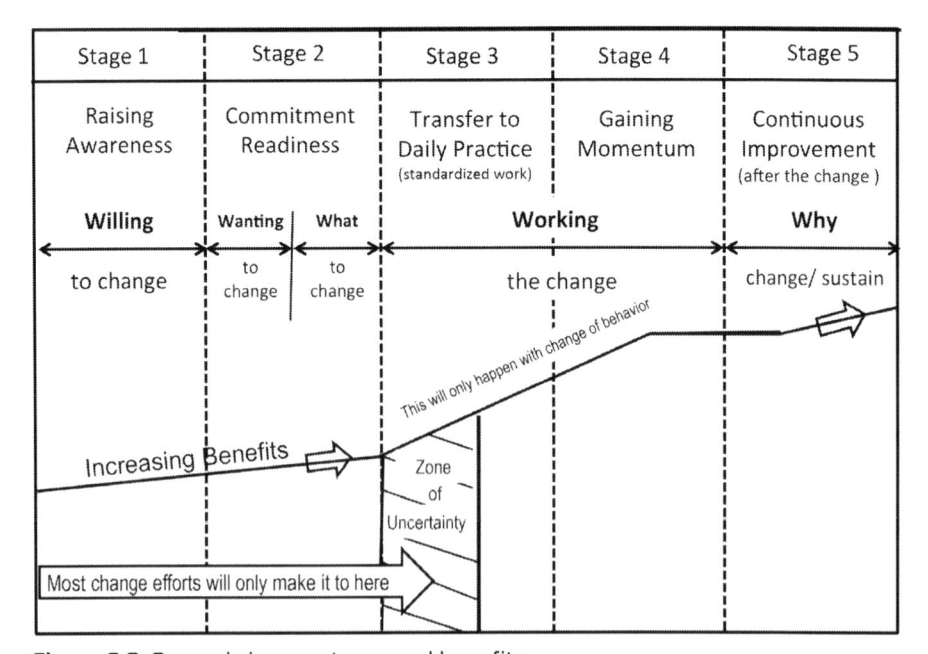

Zone of Uncertainty

Most change efforts will only make it to here

Figure 2.9: General change stages and benefits

Change Implementation Concepts and Models

change. Referring to CEO Roger Smith, "Smith rearranged North American operations to modernize GM's manufacturing, and paralyzed the company for 18 months because he destroyed the informal networks that actually got the work done in a highly bureaucratized company."[13] Being able to nurture the fundamental skills, informal processes and employee enthusiasm needed to instill readiness for such changes points to the heart of change management.

Figure 2.9 depicts five general stages of change and the associated magnitude of its benefits.

To decide on personal support for a change, you need to ask yourself three questions.

1. What do I know about the change?
2. What do I believe about the change?
3. What am I willing to do in terms of actions supporting or opposing the change?

From an individual perspective, a person needs to progress through the five Ws of engaging change.

Stage 1: **W**illing to change
Stage 2: **W**anting to change
  What to change (knowing how)
Stages 3 & 4: **W**ork the change (repetition, standardized work practices, gaining momentum)
Stage 5: **W**hy the change (improving on the institutionalized change)

The stages map well against the historical models as shown in Figure 2.10

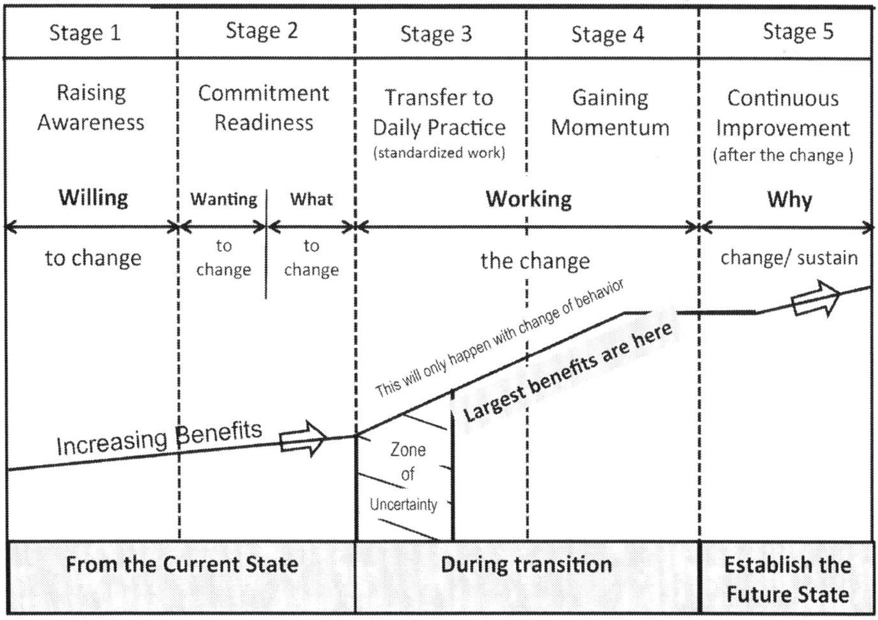

Stage 1	Stage 2	Stage 3	Stage 4	Stage 5
Raising Awareness	Commitment Readiness	Transfer to Daily Practice (standardized work)	Gaining Momentum	Continuous Improvement (after the change)
Willing	**Wanting**	**What**	**Working**	**Why**
to change	to change	to change	the change	change/ sustain
From the Current State		During transition		Establish the Future State

This will only happen with change of behavior
Largest benefits are here
Increasing Benefits
Zone of Uncertainty

Figure 2.10: Mapping the five general change stages with historical models

35

Chapter 2

Many change efforts stall out somewhere around Stage 3 (Figures 2.9 and 2.10) when it's time to transfer the desired change to daily practice. This is a critical time where you need to build enough support and momentum for the change to take hold. At Stage 5, the change has been institutionalized. With every new idea, you ask: Why change? Will it be an improvement or should you simply sustain the current best practice?

Figure 2.10 integrates Figures 2.8 and 2.9, mapping the five general change stages with the current, transition and future states used in the historical models. Although most failures occur when putting the change into daily practice, it's also when most of the change benefits will be experienced.

In implementing the basics of lean, a key guiding principle is support for the operator or the person closest to adding value to your product. This person may be a vehicle assembly operator, a nurse in a hospital, an aluminum remelt operator, an employee in an insurance office, a medicine packaging technician, a warehouse operator, or other team member. This concept is often illustrated as an upside-down pyramid as shown in Figure 2.11.

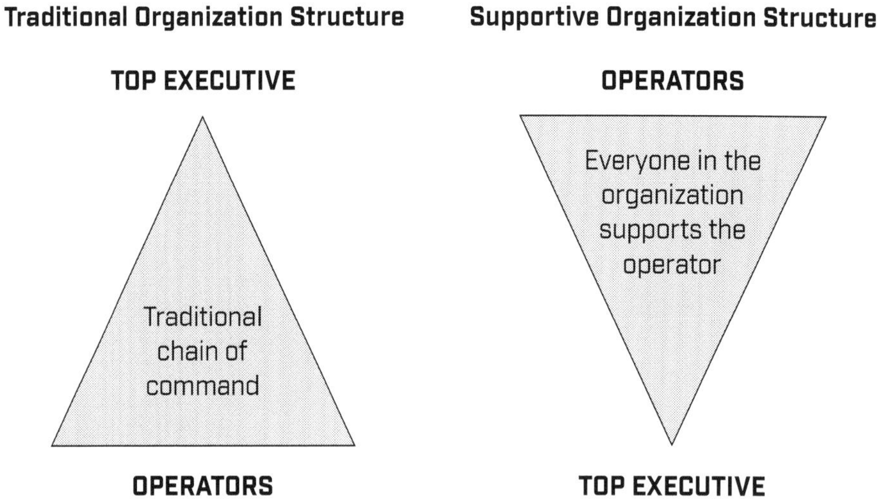

Traditional Organization Structure

TOP EXECUTIVE

Traditional chain of command

OPERATORS

Supportive Organization Structure

OPERATORS

Everyone in the organization supports the operator

TOP EXECUTIVE

Figure 2.11: Traditional and supportive organization structure

Using the same support the operator/team member thinking, Figure 2.12 shows how you want the change from current to future state to look, with everything staying in balance and a clear and agreed upon expectation of the future state.

Change Implementation Concepts and Models

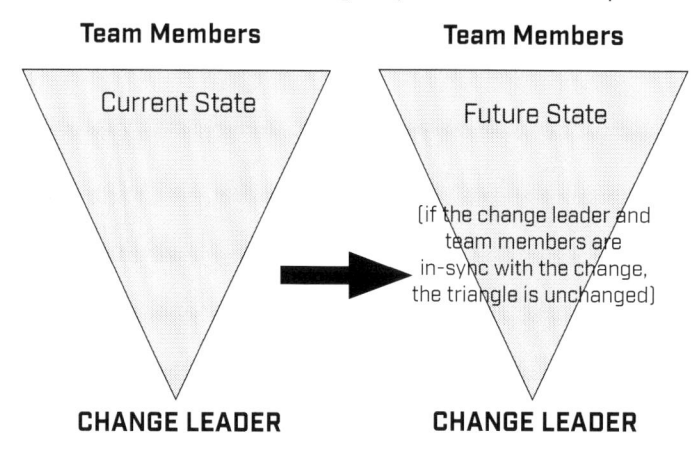

Figure 2.12: Current to future state while staying in balance

Figure 2.13 displays various possible outcomes or levels of alignment when moving from the current state to the future state. Note that what you want is an anchored future state, with the operators' and leader expectations of the future state aligned. The word change leader refers to any person taking a leadership role on a change. If the change leader's expectations regarding the change run somewhat ahead of team member expectations, then the team members will put up resistance. Using the visual example, the triangle (B_F) is out of balance. What you want is the triangle moving forward in the position shown in C_C, meaning the change leader and team members are moving toward the future state at the same pace. Think of the change leader point of triangle C_C (Figure 2.13) moving forward quickly and balance is lost. Resistance by team members is causing

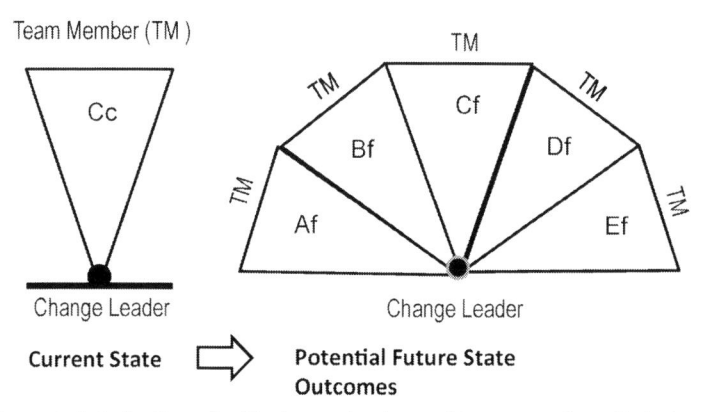

Cc = Current state is aligned with change leader and team members (in balance)
Af = Change leader's expectations are ahead of team members' expectations
Bf = Change leader's expectations are slightly ahead of team members' expectations
Cf = Change leader and team members are aligned on future state
Df = Team members' expectations are slightly ahead of the change leader's expectations
Ef = Team members' expectations are ahead of the change leader's expectations

Figure 2.13: Levels of alignment from current to future state

the triangle to fall to the left, indicating the effort is failing. If nothing is done, resistance most likely will get worse. This is depicted as the triangle falling completely to the left (A_F). Likewise, the reverse can happen, with team members' expectations going beyond the change leader's expectations. This results in resistance from the change leader, causing the triangle to topple to the right.

If everyone in the organization supports the change, then the triangle simply moves to a new position as an entire unit. However, that is rarely the case. More typical is that leadership wants the change ahead of organizational readiness.

Having alignment provides a stable situation. If some team members get beyond or behind the leader's expectations, it will not change the situation much, assuming there is a still a high percentage of team members supporting the change. However, if a few leaders get beyond or behind the operator's expectations, the new situation triangle will topple quickly and the change will fail.

Understand where resistance resides. Is the issue/roadblock person to person, person to team, team to team, team to department, department to department, department to plant, plant to plant, or plant to corporate headquarters?

Change comes from physical change, such as a new boss or having to move to a new location, and new knowledge that changes how you view your particular situation in terms of what you can do and have control of. How well an organization is capable or willing to manage or simply cope when implementing and sustaining change readiness is a key factor in long-term success and viability.

REFERENCES

1. Doolen, Toni L.; Van Aken, Eileen; Farris, Jennifer; and Worley, June. "Research Examines Kaizen Event Success and Sustainability." *Reliable Plant* Issue 8, 2007.
2. Laraia, Anthony C.; Moody, Patricia E.; and Hall, Robert W. *The Kaizen Blitz: Accelerating Breakthroughs in Productivity and Performance.* Hoboken: Wiley, 1999.
3. Aberdeen Group. *The Lean Strategies Benchmark Report.* Boston: Aberdeen Group, June 2004.
4. Change Management, www.bain.com.
5. *ERP Software Implementation Failure Analysis and Causes: Top ERP Implementation Failure Factors,* http://www.erp.asia/erp-failures.asp.
5. "Worldwide Productivity Movin' Right Along." *Quality Digest,* October 2005, p. 9.
6. Williamson, Robert M. *Lean Machines for World-Class Manufacturing and Maintenance.* Columbus: Strategic Work Systems, Inc., March 2006.
7. Blache, Klaus. *Reliability and Maintainability Modeling Applications and Benefits 2014 study.* Knoxville: The University of Tennessee, College of Engineering, Reliability and Maintainability Center.
8. Roth, William F. *Comprehensive Healthcare for the U.S.: An Idealized Model.* Boca Raton: CRC Press, 2010.
9. Hawkins, Lee, Jr. "As GM Battles Surging Costs, Workers' Health Becomes Issue." *The Wall Street Journal,* 7 April 2005.
10. Bildner, Phil. *Twenty-One Elephants.* New York: Simon and Schuster, 2004.
11. Kotter, John P. *Leading Change.* Boston: Harvard Business Press, 1996.
12. Taylor, Alex, III. "GM and Me." *Fortune,* 8, December 2008, p. 97.

Chapter 3

Using Lean Tools and Other Techniques for Continuous Improvement

> *"The fish only knows that it lives in water after it is already on the river bank."*
> — French Proverb

> *"We aren't where we want to be, we aren't where we ought to be, but thank goodness, we aren't where we used to be."*
> — Lou Holtz

3.1 Lean Thinking

There is an overwhelming number of tools and techniques available for achieving continuous improvement. Just a select, but partial list, in no particular order, includes, 5 Whys, 5S, A3 problem-solving, benchmarking, change readiness assessment, failure mode and effects analysis (FMEA), fishbone analysis, overall equipment effectiveness (OEE), reliability and maintainability assessment, reliability centered maintenance (RCM), root cause analysis (RCA), seven wastes, spare parts assessment, theory of constraints analysis, complexity reduction analysis, and value stream mapping (VSM) for current and future state. There are many textbooks available on each specific tool and technique. These tools and techniques are often used within the overall processes of lean production and total productive maintenance (TPM).

The plants of both New United Motor Manufacturing, Inc. (NUMMI) in California and General Motors' Grand River in Lansing, Michigan, shared four production systems characteristics. These are commonly known to persons familiar with lean implementation as:

- Focus on the operator;
- Standardized work;
- Reduce waste;
- Continuous improvement.

As you review the continuous improvement tools, note how they all intertwine with these four characteristics.

Chapter 3

Continuous improvement is an ongoing journey. So, if you have employees who say, "I'm done with continuous improvement in my area," – I have heard that from individuals in various companies – they don't understand because, in reality, you are never done. It's not uncommon for leading companies to use at least ten percent of their workforce on kaizen. This enables high levels of year-to-year improvements.

However, it shouldn't be surprising that many organizations are not fully utilizing and taking advantage of benefits from each of these tools and techniques. They all take time to learn and require resources to implement and sustain. Many of them overlap in application. Lean implementation promotes using most of the tools. Lean manufacturing is the systematic removal of all waste in an organization. It is focused on one-piece flow and a pull production process. Yet, in practice, organizations need to start somewhere and often need to decide on two or three things to focus on at a time. Based on their maturity in the lean journey, that focus should change. It has been proven that lean production and practices can be implemented in all types of industries and in all parts of the world. Lean systems, when properly implemented, are exemplified by greater decision-making at the plant floor level, and timely identification and resolution of problems, both product and process. At the heart of all lean systems are teams doing continuous improvement.

Eaton Corporation's Lincoln, Illinois, plant was selected for the 2010 Assembly Plant of the Year award because it "…stood out based on strong overall performance and its ability to continuously improve, even during the difficult market environment. The production system and lean thinking have become an embedded part of the culture, where employees constantly strive for competitive advantage in their operations."[1] In their journey, 5S, TPM, standard work and proactive ongoing improvements were key.

Lean implementation has much to offer, so why is it that most lean implementations fail? In the past six years, I've been in about one hundred facilities on various issues, such as inventory control, lean, reliability, maintainability, assessments, research studies and training. Companies visited include assembly (e.g., cars, planes, trains), process (e.g., aluminum, steel, food, chemical), energy (e.g., nuclear, gas, coal), consumer products (e.g., household goods), construction, entertainment (e.g., theme parks) and many more. I've seen many issues, opportunities for improvement, weaknesses and strengths in all these companies.

Most of them are not satisfied with their current level of implementation of lean, reliability and maintainability. Most have a computerized maintenance management system (CMMS), but only have some of the total system capabilities implemented. Many say they want to do more predictive technologies. At some of these places, I found boxed up technologies, which were newly purchased, several years old, or never opened. Companies want to be doing more scheduled maintenance, proactive checks, condition based monitoring, reliability trending and so on, but don't know how to get there. Some say they know what to do, but not with the current level of resources.

Let's discuss the big picture by looking at lean as an example. There have been successes. Yet, why are there so many implementation failures? Figure 3.1 outlines a brief history of lean milestones. In the early days (1920s), there was mainly mass production. Later, there was Deming, Juran and Ishikawa (1950s). In the United States, lean as a

Using Lean Tools and Other Techniques for Continuous Improvement

Early Days
- Mass production (Henry Ford, 1926)
- Just-in-time (Kiichiro Toyoda, 1937)
- Deming, Juran, Ishikawa (1950s)
- Deming Prize (1960s)

2010, 2011, 2012, 2013, 2014, 2015, ...

Books
- The Machine That Changed The World, 1990
- Lean Thinking, 1996

Learning & Implementation

Why are so many lean implementations failing?

The Toyota Way (respect for people), 2001
TPS published in English, 1988
NUMMI (Toyota & General Motors, 1984)
Toyota Production System (TPS)
- Described & distributed
(late 1970s – early 1980s)

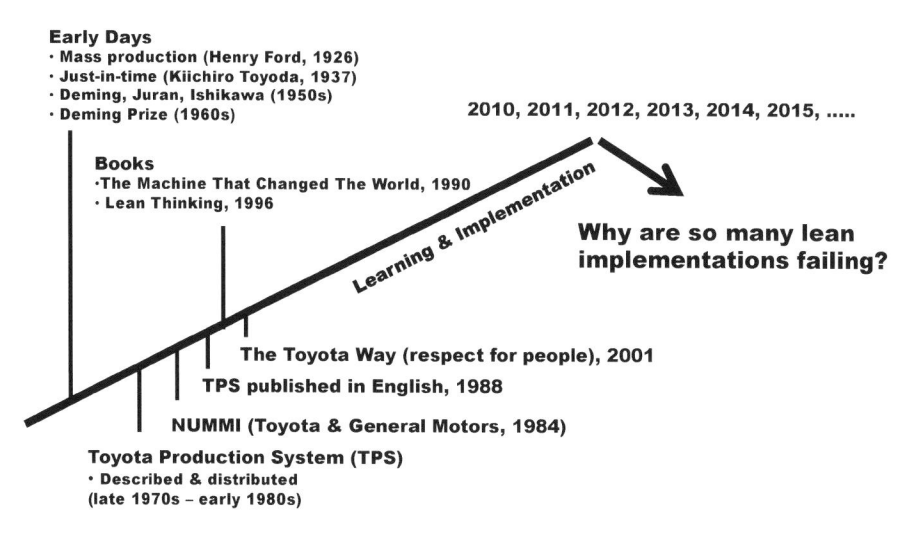

Figure 3.1: Lean milestones

popular movement started with the Toyota Production System (TPS) being described and distributed in the late 1970s to early 1980s. General Motors and Toyota started a joint venture (NUMMI 1984) and TPS was published in English (1988). But it was the publications of *The Machine That Changed the World* (Womack, Jones and Roos, 1990, revised 2007) and *Lean Thinking: Banish Waste and Create Wealth in Your Corporation* (Womack and Jones, 1996, second edition 2003) that made lean applications widespread across the U.S. and appear more doable.

Since the late 1980s until now, many companies have gone through lean learning, many with false starts mainly due to not understanding or willing to implement the full process. As described in Chapter 1, it's not surprising that seventy percent of lean implementations fail because they don't meet intended expectations, aren't sustainable, etc.

In an Aberdeen Group study, it was determined that:

- The top concern/challenge that potentially represents a barrier to adoption/expansion of lean strategies was "significant culture change required."
- The top lean-enabled business strategy is "implement continuous improvement culture and methods."
- Best in class companies had much higher "pervasive lean expertise through all organizations, kaizen events, launched top-down, bottom-up, corporate tracking of continuous improvement progress and results."[2]

Without a robust people process to support it, a lean process will be, at best, only somewhat successful. Organizations take on the tough journey toward lean implementation because they expect big results. Remember that Figure 1.7 in Chapter 1 showed that the

Chapter 3

high and very high impact of lean on continuous improvement is still low, even after five years of implementation.

You should be ready to support the people side of lean. For example, while observing several implementations of Andon systems – typically a display board in a highly visible location that notifies the team leader, maintenance, management and/or other workers about a quality problem, process problem, or needed action – there were numerous questions from the workforce about when to pull or not pull the Andon cord. This cord or button triggers an alert. From early implementations across several plants in Europe, the majority of plant floor questions pertained to the people process. The group leaders responsible for several teams knew most of the technical answers, but were not ready for the many people issues/questions. So, it's important to remember that lean is foremost a people process if it's going to be successful.

It took many years, from the 1950s to 1960s to today, to push TPS through Toyota. It didn't come easily and did not appear to be implemented with a people-friendly process when it first started. But, keep in mind that the management-worker relationship in the United States was not much better at that time. Taiichi Ohno, considered the father of TPS, was a great industrial thinker, but did not offer anything to engage the workforce in his teachings.

"Chihiro Makoa, one of Ohno's favorite pupils, worked with the master for more than twenty years but cannot remember ever receiving a compliment of any sort from Ohno for his efforts. He can, however, remember receiving tongue-lashings almost by the day."[3]

Eventually, the Toyota Production System evolved to a more people-oriented process. In Western cultures and many others, the lean process needs to be nurtured on a daily basis to sustain best practices. At the Lansing Grand River (LGR) plant in Michigan, we did a routine plant floor review of standard operating procedures being practiced. It happened every day and was a positive experience. It focused on improving the process and asking questions to develop knowledge, rather than blaming people.

Toyota, at the NUMMI joint venture plant with General Motors, maintained a high level of trust and respect from the viewpoint of the worker. For example, more attention was given to implementing suggestions, resulting in more than thirty per employee. This is significant since about eighty-five percent of the workforce hired by NUMMI were previous employees of the GM-Fremont plant, which probably averaged less than one suggestion per employee. Based on my benchmarking studies, low employee suggestions are not uncommon. However, it is fair to point out that NUMMI counted the many small team plant floor initiated and implemented improvements. Some other companies do this also, but don't count them.

""NUMMI's suggestion program has monetary rewards, but they're mainly small. We want to encourage quantity. The number of suggestions, rather than just focusing on suggestions with big payoffs. So I try to hold the line at least 95% acceptance. Even ideas that we reject are rarely just killed. The group leader or manager will go back to the team who made the suggestion and we work with them to find some better alternatives for achieving the same objective."[4]

It was unknown at that time how U.S. workers would react to the intense discipline of standardized work that Toyota required. I remember an early visit to talk to United Automobile Workers (UAW) union members, which included assembly line operators and trades. The UAW leaders visiting NUMMI with me were surprised to see employees working harder (i.e., more minutes per hour of assembly), but enjoying it more. Much has been learned since then about instilling lean practices. Also, keep in mind that not all practices can be similarly applied at your business, particularly if it's other than high volume, discrete manufacturing/assembly like automotive or similar parts. For example, high complexity and low volume processes need different considerations. Machine shops can use about half of the lean concepts as is, but need to revise strategies for the other half to make them efficient and effective. Remember that lean is only a process/tool to use. Your small team continuous improvement process will determine its long-term success.

3.2 Total Systems Thinking

A system can be defined as a group of interrelated and independent components that result in an outcome. It can be simple, yet most corporate systems are very complex. Total systems thinking is defined as being able to comprehend enough parts of the organization, project, or decision that you don't limit the desired outcome. Doing this often requires being able to see through or around the complexity to visualize a simplistic, yet realistic model of the issue.

It's been over twenty-five years since my first training session at the Avraham Y. Goldratt Institute in New Haven, Connecticut. I listened to Dr. Eli Goldratt discuss his principles of manufacturing and continuous improvement, concepts that can be applied to all types of businesses. More recently, at an October 26, 2010 lecture at the University of Tennessee Haslam College of Business, Dr. Goldratt made two key points:

- Reality has inherent simplicity.
- Common sense is when the logic is perfect.

By truly understanding with profound knowledge (i.e., grasping the situation), the problem becomes clearer and simpler, making the solution easier to find.

It brings to mind Achems razor, a well-known principle in the scientific community that is also known as Occam's razor, named after the 14th-century philosopher. In simplest terms, it states that all things being equal, the better solution is the simpler one.

I also include statistical thinking as part of total systems thinking.

"Statistical thinking helps us detect patterns or events that vary over time, such as shifts, drifts, and outliners, and avoid reacting to random variations or 'noise.' Systems thinking helps us to react appropriately to the patterns and events detected by statistical thinking because it helps us see how our actions and policies have no impact on the broader business landscape."[5]

Statistical thinking can help bring order to the vast amounts of information.

Chapter 3

3.3 Nominal Improvement Hierarchy

The schematic in Figure 3.2 was provided by Ron Moore, world-renowned expert in reliability and operational excellence. I think it's a very good representation of the order and sequence to using various tools. The Toyota Way/Production System schematic can represent any of a number of companies that understand proper lean implementation.

I believe over ninety percent of plant floor problems can be suitably addressed by the basic improvement tools of kaizen, 5S, standardization, 5 Whys and so on, and following the lean and TPM principles. Big, chronic and bottleneck issues can be handled by the more resource-consuming tools of Six Sigma and reliability centered maintenance (RCM). Root cause analysis (RCA) can be done somewhat quicker, so I am listing it separately. Viewing data from one hundred and fifty companies, the most frequent improvement tools used with high and very high impact on continuous improvement by companies attaining reliability and maintainability (R&M) savings are:

- 5 Whys/RCA,
- RCM,
- FMEA,
- Visual controls/P-D-C-A.

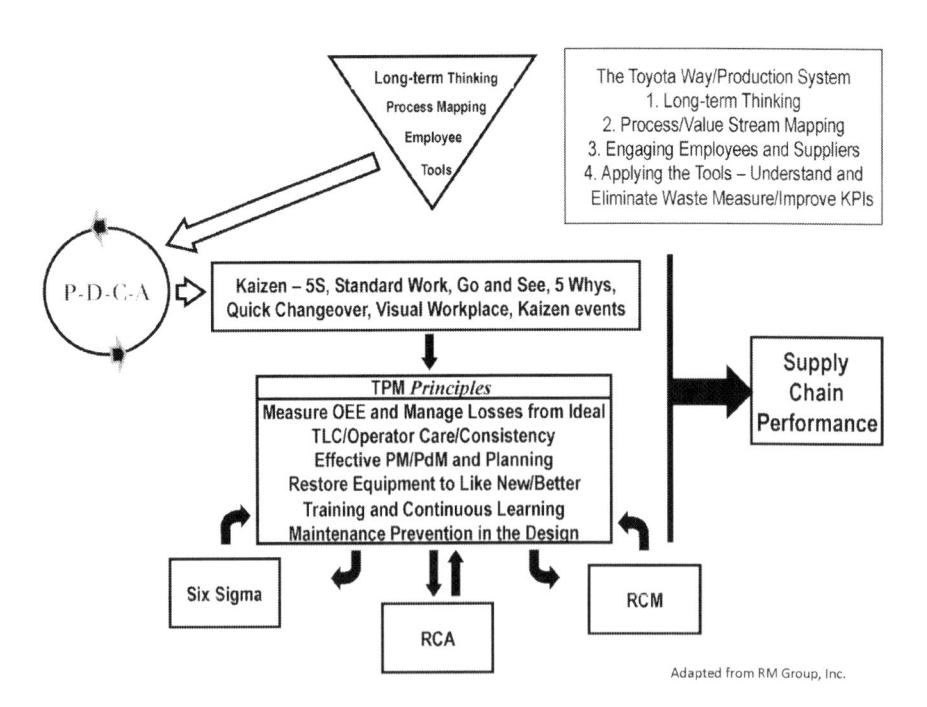

Figure 3.2: Nominal improvement hierarchy

Using Lean Tools and Other Techniques for Continuous Improvement

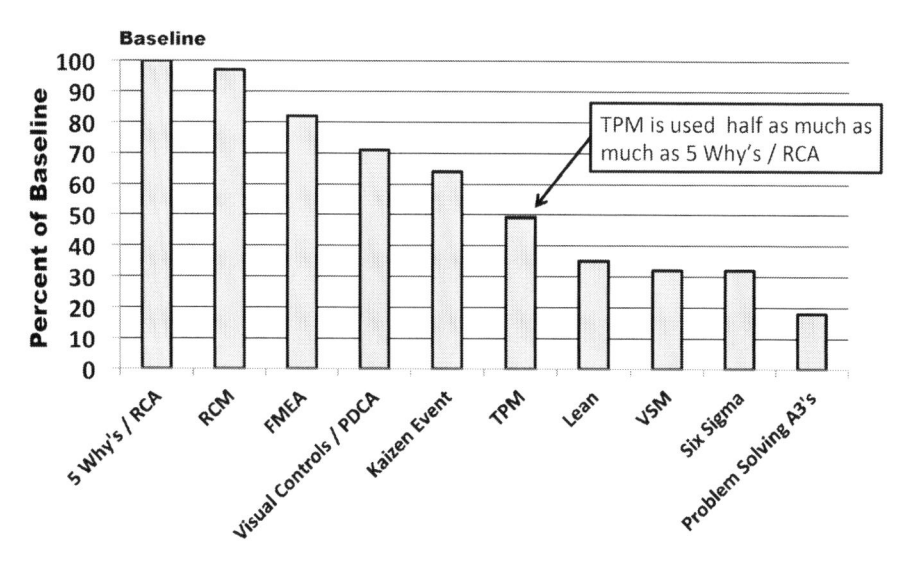

Figure 3.3: Improvement tools used with high and very high impact on continuous improvement by 150 companies attaining R&M savings

Although you do a FMEA as part of an RCM project, FMEA is also listed separately because it can be done alone, as many companies indicated. Likewise, some of these tools are also used in kaizen events, TPM and lean implementation. However, the recognized benefits are mostly being attributed to the first four tools listed in Figure 3.3.

3.4 Select Tools and Techniques as Related to Continuous Improvement

There are numerous tools available for solving problems and performing continuous improvement. I will include this sampling of tools and techniques mainly to discuss their importance and relevance towards contributing to the improvement effort. The intent is not to provide a detailed how-to for each tool and technique, but to discuss their contribution and importance in regards to making things better and sustaining change. So, a brief clarification of the selected tools/techniques is warranted. Figure 3.4 shows common continuous improvement tools and techniques and their typical use.

Many of the tools complement each other and are meant to be used together. However, it is critical to determine up front the scope and use of the improvement tools and techniques. This is important for knowing what tool to use at what time and to minimize wasting resources.

Having an effective process that gets the most continuous improvement from its people is the foundation for success. It's the people who need to be able and willing to use the tools and techniques.

Chapter 3

Figure 3.4: Continuous improvement tools and techniques

TOOL/TECHNIQUE	TYPICALLY USED FOR
5S	Many small changes to support standardized work when just starting a work process or ongoing improvement to reduce waste and improve efficiency and effectiveness in operations.
5 Whys	Small changes on a specific issue with iterative question asking to understand cause and effect. Can be used individually or as part of a fishbone diagram for more complex issues.
7 Wastes	Identifying and eliminating the seven fundamental forms of waste. Typically done with lean initiatives and kaizen events.
A3 Problem Solving	A standardized format/process that follows P-D-C-A type steps to solve moderate to tough problems. Versions of the form also can be used for proposals and status reports. An A3 size paper is about 11x17 inches. A good way to develop problem solvers.
Benchmarking	Process of comparing your organization or facility processes and practices to industry best practices, similar industry, or any industry with transferable processes. Comparing where you want to be to actual performance is referred to as a gap analysis.
Change Readiness Assessment	Evaluation of your organization or group's readiness for the next step in a change. It can be done with surveys or interactive tools, like a force field diagram, in a team setting.
Complexity Reduction Analysis	Analysis of an organization's value stream and how it is impacted by the proliferation of products, part numbers and complex processes.
Error or Mistake Proofing	Teaching and reminding the proper standardized work and identifying variation. Used when it's important to make a mistake immediately obvious.
Fishbone (Ishikawa) Diagram	Analyzing a broad or complex problem or restraining forces to identify possible causes of a problem.
Failure Mode and Effects Analysis	Identifying and ranking possible failures in a design, process, product, or service. A FMEA is done as part of an RCM effort or by itself to mitigate or eliminate potential failures
Force Field Analysis	Assessing the readiness for change and identifying what restrain forces need to be improved or removed.
Kaizen Event	Team-based improvement events, typically 3 to 5 days. Often a VSM is done first to select areas of focus. A 5S project can be done as a kaizen or numerous other initiatives.
Overall Equipment Effectiveness	To measure effectiveness of a production process or facility based on availability, performance and quality. Opportunities to improve are categorized into 6 losses, which can be targeted by teams.
Reliability Centered Maintenance	Developing a maintenance strategy. To identify components that can cause unwanted consequences upon functional failure to facility/assets. Then used to identify ways to prevent those failures by optimizing preventive maintenance (PM) tasks.

Using Lean Tools and Other Techniques for Continuous Improvement

Reliability and Maintainability Assessment	Evaluation of your organization's reliability and maintainability practices relative to industry best practices. It should provide enough details to result in identifying areas for improvement. An R&M assessment should focus on organizational knowledge, culture and skills, and determine the maturity of your processes and practices, such as identifying missing best practices.
Reliability and Maintainability Road Map	A detailed R&M plan, such as events, training, action items and timing, to get from where your organization is to where you want it to be.
Root Cause Analysis	Identify what and why it happened to correct the root cause of an event. Some basic RCA tools are fishbone diagrams, scatter diagrams and Pareto charts.
Spare Parts Analysis	Analysis to determine the proper level of replacement parts needed to sustain production. It also includes items, such as stocking strategies, holding costs and storage/delivery options.
Throughput Analysis	Any quantitative methodology used to analyze where bottlenecks exist for the purpose of production system design or continuous improvement. This is mostly done with computer models using simulation techniques. A popular technique is theory of constraints (TOC) by Eliyahu M. Goldratt.
Total Productive Maintenance	An overall maintenance process that works toward getting employees at all levels involved in improving reliability and maintaining machinery/equipment, while moving toward owner-operator practices. These efforts typically improve throughput, safety, quality and cost, while adding value to the customer. It works well together with efforts in improving OEE.
Value Stream Mapping	Identifying what problems to work on or where to improve throughout your value stream. Can do a gap analysis by doing a VSM of desired versus actual practices.

"We get brilliant results from average people managing brilliant systems. Our competitors get average results from brilliant people working around broken systems."
— Fujio Cho, Chairman, Toyota Motor Corporation

Other companies also understand the value of these concepts. For example, the Lansing Grand River plant opened in January 2002 and in mid-September 2013 produced its millionth Cadillac. It also was designed with people as the focus. A few key points are:

"LGR is designed around leading edge processes that provide the support and resources enabling individual operators, working in teams, to do their jobs as effectively and solely as possible.

47

Chapter 3

> *"Focus is on the operators as the most important person in the manufacturing system. Operators work in small teams, trained and empowered to run their areas. Continuous improvement is achieved in this way, and that is one of our most important goals."*[6]
> — Robert Anderson, LGR Plant Manager

3.4.1 5S

5S is often one of the first tools implemented in the introduction of lean concepts. It's simple to understand and the changes are typically not too extreme. Implementation provides an immediate visual impact to reducing waste and optimizing workplace organization in the office and factory. If implemented properly, it also provides the discipline to sustain the changes and builds the foundation for larger efforts, such as lean, reliability and maintainability, spare parts, tools and materials best practices.

Think about whether this scenario has happened at your facility: An employee goes to the supply cabinet and cannot find the item he or she is looking for or the bin is empty. This happens in hospitals, manufacturing and process operations, utility plants and assembly plants, and with many different situations that have a wide range of consequences and costs. For example, an electrician has an emergency repair that is affecting production. He can't find the part without looking in several places. No one is happy with the slow response, so the electrician gets extra parts and stores them. He does not want to go through that again. Over time, for various like situations, others hoard parts and inventory costs go up. A 5S process can help standardize such spare parts issues using numerous 5 Why activities to find the root cause of mediocre and bad practices. Without a good control process, parts also get obsolete or mishandled. At just one small production facility, with the help of its maintenance team, we removed $2.5 million of excess inventory after checking critical equipment and planned maintenance needs.

"As a nurse with many years in the trenches, one of the most frustrating realities in the hospital is the inconsistencies associated with relatively standard spaces and work tasks. Why can't highly repetitive spaces, such as a medication room, nourishment room, or even a med-surgery patient room, be truly standardized so that no matter where you are deployed to work, you are instantly familiar with the environment and standard work is accomplished without the waste of searching for supplies and equipment."[7]

There are numerous versions of English terms used to depict the original Japanese 5S methodology of seiri, seiton, seiso, seiketsu and shitsuke. Here is a brief summary of the original 5S English terms.

5S

Sort: The first S focuses on eliminating unnecessary items from the workplace that are not needed for current production operations. An effective visual method to identify these unneeded items is called red tagging, which involves evaluating the necessity of each item in a work area and dealing with it appropriately. A red tag is placed on all items that are not important for operations, are not in the proper location, or do not have the proper quantity. Once red tag items are identified, these items are then moved to a central holding area for subsequent disposal, recycling, or reassignment. Organizations often find that sorting enables them to reclaim valuable floor space and eliminates such things as broken tools, scrap and excess raw material.

Set In Order: Arrange parts so they are easy to find and use. This is an opportunity to utilize visual controls for improving storage areas.

Shine: Clean the work area. By doing the cleaning, you notice the little defects. For example, if you wash your own car versus going through a car wash, you observe the scratches, wear and minor damages. Then you know what to improve and what to watch for in the future.

Standardize: Implement the best practices and procedures so everyone knows what to do in a uniform manner.

Sustain: Establish the discipline for maintaining the improvements. Instill the habits, rules and procedures to prevent backsliding. This could include such things as posters to show results for learning; photos for before and after comparisons; pocket cards with checklists or reminders; plant or area layouts showing where improvements were implemented; standardized methodology sheets; and calibration walks to coach the ongoing use of best practices.

Some companies add one more S for safety.

5S is a simple concept, but implementation is not always easy. It requires making plant floor level decisions and changing habits, usually as a team. When implementing 5S, make sure all persons impacted have input and understand the reasons for the change. Figure 3.5 is a good matrix showing 5S levels of achievement.[8]

5S provides key ongoing benefits by engaging employees, requiring teamwork and promoting continuous improvement. In addition, everyone in the organization can participate in it. By sustaining the current process and continually improving it, best practices are achieved.

3.4.2 5 Whys

The 5 Whys is an investigative method used to find the underlying reason for a problem. By asking why often enough and working through the symptoms, the root cause of the problem can be determined. Obviously, 5 Whys is not the limit, but it's been found that most root causes of problems are determined by then. Simply ask why at least five times to get to the root cause of a situation. Often, a clear understanding of the issue can be quickly found when done with a participative team and goes a long way to finding the underlying why. A few examples follow.

Chapter 3

Figure 3.5 5S Levels of Achievement (Maturity Level)

Level V: Continuously Improve	Cleanliness problems are identified and mess prevention actions are in place.	Needed items can be retrieved within 30 seconds and require a minimum number of steps	Potential problems are identified and counter measures are documented	Reliable methods and standards for housekeeping, daily inspections and workspace arrangement are shared and are used throughout similar work areas.	Root causes are eliminated and improvement actions focus on developing preventive methods.
Level IV: Focus on Reliability	Work area has documented housekeeping responsibilities & schedules and assignments are consistently followed.	Needed items in work area are minimized in number and are properly arranged for retrieval and use.	Inspection occurs during daily cleaning of work areas and equipment and supplies.	Reliable methods and standards for housekeeping, daily inspections and workplace arrangement are documented and followed by all members of the work group.	Sources and frequency of problems are documented as part of routine work, root causes are identified, and corrective action plans are developed.
Level III: Make It Visual	Initial cleaning has been performed and sources of spills and messes are identified and corrected.	Needed items are outlined, dedicated locations are properly labeled and required quantities are determined.	Visual controls and identifiers are established and marked for the work area, equipment files and supplies.	Work group has documented agreements on visual controls, labeling of items, and required quantities of needed items.	Work group is routinely checking area to maintain 5S agreement.
Level II: Focus on Basics	Needed and not-needed items are identified. Those not needed are removed from work area.	Needed items are safely stored and organized according to frequency of use.	Key work area items to be checked are identified and acceptable performance levels documented.	Work group has documented agreements for needed items, organizations and work area controls.	Initial 5S level has been determined, and performance is documented and posted in work area.
Level I: Just Beginning	Needed and not needed items are mixed throughout the work area.	Items are placed randomly throughout the workplace.	Key work area items checked are not identified and are unmarked.	Work area methods are not consistently followed and are undocumented.	Work area checks are randomly performed and there is no visual measurement 5S.
	Sorting	**Simplifying**	**Systematic Cleaning**	**Standardizing**	**Sustaining**

Used with permission and adopted from: http://reliabilityweb.com/index.php/articles/the_5s_method_of_improvement__enhancing_safety_productivity_and_culture/

5 Whys - Everyday Example

Issue: Many restrooms in restaurants have piles of paper on the floor from improper disposal of hand towels.

1. Why: Is there paper on the floor?
   Because: People don't like to grab the bathroom door in public restrooms after washing their hands, so they toss the paper toward the trash can.

2. Why: Doesn't the paper get into the trash can?
   Because: It has a lid on it, is under a counter and is difficult to open.

3. Why: Is it under a counter?
   Because: It's too far away to reach the trash can foot pedal and hold the door open at the same time. However, at the current spot, a pipe prevents the trash can from opening completely.

4. Why: Not just put it next to the exit door?
   Because: The manager doesn't want a trash can next to the exit because it would not look good.

SOLUTION: Since people are going to toss the paper towels at the trash can anyway because they aren't going to touch the door, it's better to put the trash can by the door. It looks better there than all the paper on the floor.

It's a simple solution for a common issue, yet how many places do you see that have not corrected a similar restroom situation? On my recent cross-country driving trip, it was about half the places.

5 Whys – Reliability/Maintainability Example

Issue: PM data is not getting into the computer system.

1. Why: Do skilled trades refuse to enter data into the system?
   Because: They say it's not part of their job or it's too much data entry.

2. Why: Don't trades like to enter the data?
   Because: It takes too long since they don't type.

3. Why: Does it really take so long?
   Because: They can't read the small screen that well.

4. Why: Can't they read the screen well?
   Because: The screen print is small to fit the formatting and the older workforce can't read it well.

Chapter 3

5. Why: Can't the software be reformatted to larger print?
   Because: Someone needs to fund the change.

SOLUTION: Fund the software change.

5 Whys - Medical Insurance Example

Issue: Betty does not want to change to the mostly paperless system.

1. Why: Does she not want to change?
   Because: She thinks it will slow her down.

2. Why: Does she think it will slow her down?
   Because: She is not familiar with the new system.

3. Why: Is she not familiar with the new computer system?
   Because: She is not really interested in learning it because there will be higher production expectations.

4. Why: Is she concerned about higher targets if the system is faster?
   Because: She thinks the expected benefits were oversold to justify the purchase of the new computer system, now putting a higher burden on her.

5. Why: Does she think that way?
   Because: She has been through this twice before with similar negative outcomes.

6. Why: Has she been through this twice before with similar negative outcomes?
   Because: Most of the production (i.e., billing volume) issues cannot be fixed by software. They are process issues. (Note that this is the true root cause.) Management doesn't understand the roadblocks in attaining production numbers.

SOLUTION: Do a value stream map of existing and future processes to better assess the new software decision.

Once you've identified the root cause, a good check is to go through the 5 Whys logic backwards. To illustrate, start with the final why in the reliability/maintainability example:

1. Someone needs to fund the change so the software can change to larger print.
2. When we go to larger print, the tradespeople will be able to read the screen better.
3. When being able to read the screen better, they can now enter responses, etc.

Using the 5 Whys avoids assumptions and jumping to conclusions, and traces back to the root cause of the problem. It's important to get subject matter experts involved so correct and in-depth questions are asked and answered. The major criticisms of the 5 Whys are it may not be repeatable and it's too simplistic of a tool.

3.4.3 Cause and Effect (Fishbone) Diagram

The fishbone (Ishikawa) diagram (Figure 3.6) is also called the cause and effect diagram. It is a visual, problem-solving tool created in 1943 by Kaoru Ishikawa while a professor at Tokyo University. The fishbone diagram states the problem on the right and all potential causes, sub-causes, or causes of the causes. These inputs are typically collected in a brainstorming meeting if a problem or resistance to change is more complex than the 5 Whys alone can resolve. The tool has an easy to use format and goes after root causes in an organized way. The fishbone diagram is a good visual tool to promote participation. A typical practice is to do the 5 Whys at each leg of the fishbone diagram as needed. The categories, such as people, machine and methods, can be changed as needed. Generally, the fishbone diagram is not a tool to use for very complex problems. A blank fishbone diagram is in Appendix B.

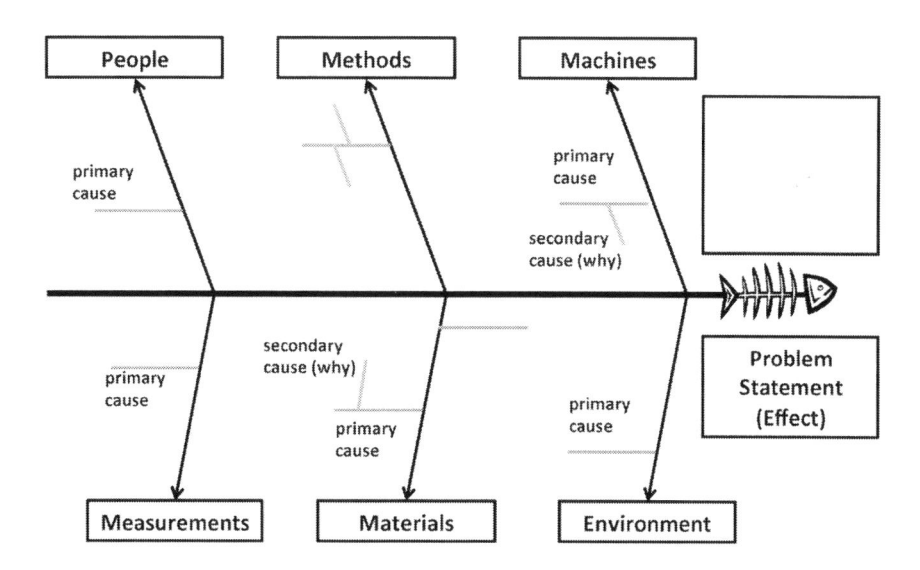

Figure 3.6: Cause and effect (fishbone) diagram

3.4.4 Root Cause Analysis

Root cause analysis (RCA) encompasses various problem-solving methodologies that systemically help identify the root cause of a problem. Analysis is typically done after an event has occurred. The focus is to find the cause or causes of an event and solve the underlying problem, issue, or question. RCAs can be done for safety, engineering, maintenance, reliability, production and more. Just a few examples of events that can be investigated by root cause analysis are:

- Reason for an accident and how best to prevent it from happening again.
- Reason for a data center outage and how to maximize computer uptime.
- Reason for a quality defect on a product and how to detect it earlier in the value chain.

The Office of Safety and Mission Assurance of the National Aeronautics and Space Administration (NASA) defines and describes root cause analysis as:

"A structured evolution method that identifies the root causes for an undesired outcome and the actions adequate to prevent recurrence. Root cause analysis should continue until organizational factors have been identified or until data are exhausted.

"RCA is a method that helps determine:

- What happened?
- How it happened?
- Why it happened?

"It allows learning from past problems, failures, and accidents.
"An overview of the steps used in RCA are:

- Clearly define the undesired outcome.
- Gather data, including a list of all potential causes.
- Create an event and causal factor tree.
- Continue asking "why" to identify root causes.
- Check your logic and eliminate items that are not causes.
- Generate solutions that address both proximate causes and root causes."[9]

Root cause analysis includes such tools as, 5Whys, Pareto charts, scatter plots, fault tree analysis, fishbone diagrams, brainstorming, force field analysis and failure mode and effects analysis. RCA is an overall process that describes all the tools and techniques mentioned. All these methodologies are well-known and described in detail in various books and Internet sites. What's good is these tools are visual and require no or minimal statistics. It enables easier understanding for decision agreement. Figure 3.7 lists typical questions, per NASA's Air University, to ask when doing an RCA with a fishbone diagram.

Figure 3.7: Typical Questions to ask when performing RCA - fishbone

PEOPLE
Was the document properly interpreted?
Was the information properly disseminated?
Did the recipient understand the information?
Was the proper training to perform the task administered to the person?
Were guidelines for judgment available?
Did the environment influence the actions of the individual?
Are there distractions in the workplace?
Is fatigue a mitigating factor?
How much experience does the individual have in performing this task?

MACHINES
Was the correct tool used?
Is the equipment affected by the environment?
Is the equipment being properly maintained (e.g., daily/weekly/monthly preventative maintenance schedule)?
Was the machine properly programmed?
Is the tooling/fixture setup adequate for the job?
Does the machine have an adequate guard?
Was the tooling used within its capabilities and limitations?
Are all controls, including emergency stop button, clearly labeled, color-coded and/or differentiated by size?
Is the machine the right application for the given job?

MEASUREMENT
Does the gauge have a valid calibration date?
Was the proper gauge used to measure the part, process, chemical, compound, etc.?
Was a gauge capability study ever performed?
Do measurements vary significantly from operator to operator?
Do operators have a tough time using the prescribed gauge?
Is the gauge fixture setup adequate?
Does the gauge have proper measurement resolution?
Did the environment influence the measurements taken?

MATERIAL
Is a material safety data sheet (MSDS) readily available?
Was the material properly tested?
Was the material substituted?
Is the supplier's process defined and controlled?
Were quality requirements adequate for part function?
Was the material contaminated?
Was the material handled properly (e.g., stored, dispensed, used and disposed)?

ENVIRONMENT
Is the process affected by temperature changes over the course of the day?
Is the process affected by humidity, vibration, noise, lighting, etc.?
Does the process run in a controlled environment?

METHODS
Was the canister, barrel, etc. labeled properly?
Were the workers trained properly in the procedure?
Was the testing performed statistically significant?
Have you tested for true root cause data?
How many "if necessary" and "approximately" phrases are found in this process?
Was this a process generated by an integrated plant floor engineering team?
Was the integrated plant floor engineering team properly represented?
Did the integrated plant floor engineering team employ design for environmental (DFE) principles?
Has a capability study ever been performed for this process?
Is the process under statistical process control (SPC)?
Are the work instructions clearly written?
Are mistake proofing devices/techniques employed?
Are the work instructions complete?
Is the tooling adequately designed and controlled?
Is handling/packaging adequately specified?
Was the process changed?
Was the design changed?
Was a process failure mode and effects analysis (FMEA) ever performed?
Was adequate sampling done?
Are features of the process critical to safety clearly spelled out to the operator?

Adapted from NASA RCA Overview

Chapter 3

Figure 3.8: The Seven Wastes

WASTE	DEFINITION	MANUFACTURING/ PRODUCTION	OFFICE/ ADMINISTRATION
Correction	Work that results in repairs, rework defects, or scrap in a previous step	Repairing a quality defect; having to repeat an operation to make it to specification	Misplaced records or information; data entry error; invoice error; engineering change orders
Overproduction	Making more than required faster or sooner	Producing extra product just in case there are production problems; working ahead in a production line to get more rest between jobs	Extra copies; unnecessary e-mails; compiling reports that nobody reads; providing too much information; buying items before they are needed
Motion	Walking or wasted motions to pick up/ store parts; any kind of travel	Walking to a parts crib to get a part for a planned maintenance work order; poorly organized workplace layout requiring extra movements	Excessive handling of paperwork or reports; walking to the copy machine; repeated searching for files
Material movement	Unnecessary transfer, conveyance, or transport	Product is loaded and unloaded without value being added; parts are moved long distances because there is not enough line side storage systems	Going to a central copy room to get work done; having to get unnecessary signatures; e-mail attachments that aren't needed
Waiting	Operator or machine idle time; people waiting for machinery, information, or people	Operator waiting for a machine to cycle before being able to load the next part; machine can produce twice as fast as the operator can load parts	Waiting for fax confirmation or copies at copy machine; system is down due to repair or is just slow
Inventory	Having extra raw materials, work in process, or finished goods	Stockpiling between operation; keeping extra product just in case to ensure making production goals	Excess office supplies, like unnecessary files and items in desks; old e-mails, vendor information letters, etc.
Process	Overprocessing more than the customer is willing to pay	Using elaborate and expensive equipment when it's not required; doing more work, mental or physical, then is necessary	Repetitive, manual data entry; using inadequate software; compiling reports that nobody needs

With experience, it's easy to decide which tool to use and when. For example, a Pareto chart is good for analysis or displaying the frequency of problems in a process, such as a list of maintenance bad actors based on total downtime over the past six month. A scatter plot is a good tool when you have paired numerical data and are trying to check if two variables are related (i.e., cause and effect), such as the percent of reactive maintenance and production throughput. There are also many programs available that do a good job of taking you through a comprehensive RCA, such as Kepner-Tregoe®, PROACT®, RealityCharting®, TapRoot®, NASA's root cause analysis tool (RCAT) and Reliasoft's XFRACAS. Also, many enterprise management systems now have good built-in RCA capability.

3.4.5 Seven Wastes

Waste in the value chain of your business is anything that does not add value to your end product. There are several acronyms that have been used to remember them. The one I was taught at General Motors Institute (now Kettering Institute) many years ago was COMMWIP (Correction, Overproduction, Motion, Material movement, Waiting, Inventory and Process. Figure 3.8 is an overview of the seven wastes and their definitions, along with manufacturing/production and office/administration examples. Note that the worst kind of waste is overproduction because it generates and/or hides all other wastes.

Two additional key concepts that are often hidden costs because they impact so many areas are flow that is not level and being unreasonable. If the flow of a product or information is not constant, it can cause many other types of waste, such as lack of consistency in schedules, high inventory, lack of information, etc. Being unreasonable refers to both machines and people overburdened beyond reasonable capabilities. Is your production equipment running faster than designed or longer than recommended between maintenance checks? How well is ergonomics used to set up your workplaces and do you understand the impacts of an aging workforce? Going through the seven wastes to identify what can be improved in your work area is a good start to improving and leveling flow of your work process.

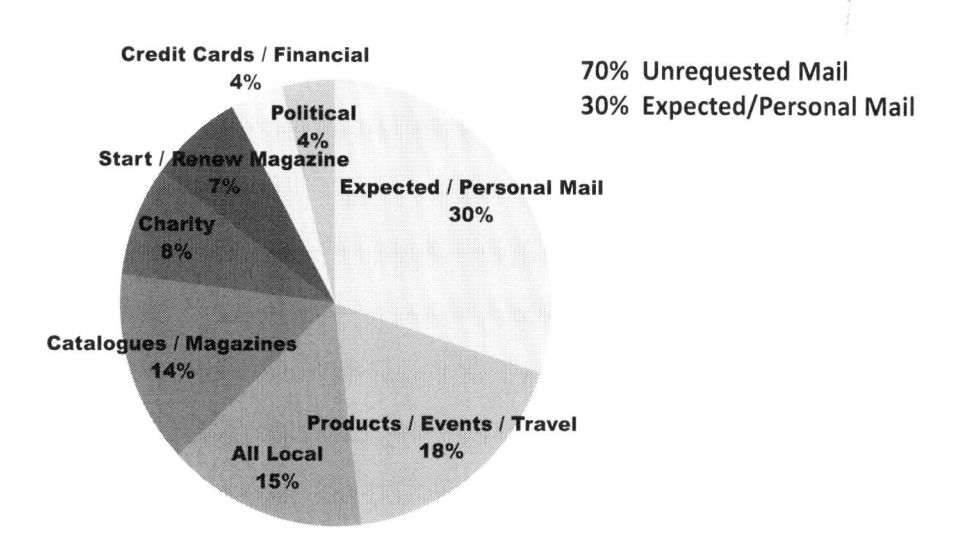

Figure 3.9: One year of mail history

Chapter 3

At our local post office, I had a business mailbox that I had to clean out on a regular basis because of all the local ads, newsletters, newspapers and other junk mail. I asked if I could stop the non-business mail, especially since I already get the same junk mail at my home address. The answer was no. The garbage container next to the locked boxes was full and had about one foot of junk mail on top of it that patrons were directly throwing away. Who is responsible for controlling this waste? During this time, I also tracked my mail for exactly one year (Figure 3.9). Seventy percent of the mail was junk mail or overproduction waste.

All cards, letters, bills, magazines, etc., that I expected, ordered and wanted made up only thirty percent of my total mail deliveries. Seventy percent of my mail goes directly into the weekly garbage pickup or recycling. "Over fifty percent of this unsolicited junk mail ends up in landfills annually."[10] In 2014, the United States Postal Service published[11] that 523 million pieces of mail are processed and delivered every day. The letter carriers and truck drivers drive four million miles daily. If you did a value stream map of what happens and what the customer (i.e., the mail recipient) really wants, it would also show wasted gasoline, energy, material movement and more. Of course, if you are the postal service, you get paid to deliver, so that's what you do. It gets back to who is looking at the big picture and doing the systems thinking to unravel these kinds of issues.

3.4.6 Overall Equipment Effectiveness

Overall equipment effectiveness (OEE) is a popular measure of production uptime and is typically measured against scheduled time. The formula is:
OEE = Availability x Performance x Quality.

OEE is often used as a key performance indicator. When used properly, it's also an effective tool for continuous improvement. To better drill down into what is causing losses, the three categories used to calculate OEE are further broken down into six big losses. The wording in the current OEE categories (shown in parentheses) is a little different than that in the 1989 book by Seiichi Nakajima, who first described OEE as a main component of TPM.

"Downtime (Availability)
1. Breakdowns due to equipment failure
2. Setup and adjustment, such as exchange of die in injection molding machines, et

Speed Losses (Performance)
3. Idling and minor stoppages, such as abnormal operations of sensors, blockage of work on chutes, etc.
4. Reduced speed, such as discrepancies between designed and actual speed of equipment

Defects (Quality)
5. Defects in process and rework, or what production rejects.
6. Reduced yield between machine start-up and stable production, for example, start-up rejects until acceptable quality parts at rate"[12]

Typically, an OEE of around eighty-five percent is in the best in class range. Availability (90%) x Performance (95%) x Quality (99.5%) = 85%. I have seen OEEs between forty percent and ninety-five percent in companies, with wide ranges among those in the same industry and plants within the same company.

OEE and the six losses can be used as a tool to remove waste. In practice, you may not be willing to trade a higher OEE number for lower quality, even if it means more performance and an overall higher OEE. Too often, OEE is used mainly by upper management to compare performance between factories. That's when all the gamesmanship begins, with a long list of rules, exceptions, adjustments for types of processes, age of equipment, and so on. It doesn't mean that some of the reasons for wanting adjustments aren't valid, but comparisons quickly go into a gray area.

OEE should be calculated based on three hundred and sixty-five days a year and twenty-four hours per day. This metric is called total effective equipment performance (TEEP). After calculating a baseline TEEP, all continuous improvements should be measured against it. Many plants measure OEE based on scheduled hours. As soon as it becomes a comparison between plants, the concern for where your plant will fall on the list overpowers some of the potential opportunities for real plant floor team improvement. To deal with this, some companies calculate factory OEE or TEEP for only throughput roadblocks, then analyze where losses are coming from to target improvements, such as the production line or specific machinery or equipment. OEE or TEEP is then calculated for the problem area and focused on until the roadblocks are removed and OEE or TEEP is acceptable. These successes are then reported as improvements in OEE or TEEP for that specific area. The impact on overall plant OEE or TEEP still can be reported, while keeping the focus on continual improvement.

3.4.7 Visual Aids/Controls

Visual control is a technique used to signal abnormal conditions quickly and easily to see if a machine is running to standard. It can be used to guide everyday decision-making at the plant floor level where it's needed. At a glance, anyone walking by should be able to know if standardized work is being followed and if the production process is working to plan.

A visual workplace is one where work tasks are easily understood by all (i.e., self-explaining) and where visual displays are sufficient to enable employees to maintain standardized work and operational requirements, and perform continuous improvement. It also can be used to provide information, instruction and instant feedback to minimize variation.

Visual aids are used with many of the other lean tools, such as PDCA, 5S, mistake-proofing and more, and have resulted in these improvements:

"15% increase in throughput;
70% cut in materials handling;
60% decrease in floor space;
80% decrease in flow distance;

68% reduction in rack storage;
45% decrease in number of forklifts;
12% increase in engineering cycle time;
50% decrease in annual physical inventory time;
96% decrease in defects."[13]

Some examples of visual aids are:
- Shadow boards to display outlines of tools to easily see what is missing.
- Standardized labels for storerooms to reduce time to repair.
- Floor markings to put items in proper place and reduce congestion.
- Troubleshooting aids to speed up repairs.
- Indicators showing proper ranges on gauges for machine performance to minimize damage.
- Lubrication, inspection and predictive maintenance points identification to collect better data for decisions.

3.4.7.1 Mistake Proofing

Mistake proofing, also called error proofing and poka-yoke, refers to devices on machinery and equipment to ensure production without defects. This can be used to detect such things as a bad weld from a robot error. Other examples are:

- Correct part selection indicator;
- Bar code reader;
- Part racks with light curtains;
- Torque tools with indicators.

An early 1990s study done in conjunction with Stanford University discovered that "system defect rates were consistently correlated only with product and process complexity, pointing to the key role of mistakes in product quality. The link between complexity and defects points to the two most effective methods for improving quality as: a) mistake proofing and b) simplifying products and processes."[14]

Mistake proofing typically provides a much less expensive alternative than other processes. For example, at intersections inside a factory, you want storage to be low enough so forklift truck drivers can see around the corners for any traffic. One facility I toured had tennis balls hung from a string to the allowable height at each intersection.

People make mistakes due to errors in perception, lack of training or skill, poor judgment, intentional acts, distractions, forgetting, lack of a standard and many more reasons. Mistake proofing minimizes or removes the chance of making an error, especially with things that cannot be easily reversed. Another good example of mistake proofing is the small notch in the memory card of most cameras. The memory card only can be inserted in the correct position. Mistake proofing also can be used to check for counterfeit parts, which is a growing issue. An organization that is mature in continuous improvement and plant floor involvement typically has a high number of mistake proofing ideas implemented.

3.4.8 Reliability Centered Maintenance

Reliability centered maintenance (RCM) is "a process used to determine what must be done to ensure that any physical asset continues to perform its intended functions in its preset operating context."[15]

The Military Handbook (MIL-HDBK-470A) defines RCM as: "A disciplined logic or methodology used to identify preventive and corrective maintenance tasks to realize the inherent reliability of equipment at a minimum expenditure of resources."

The NASA Reliability Centered Maintenance Guide explains: "The goal of RCM is to determine the most applicable and cost effective maintenance strategy, while minimizing the risk of impact failure in a safe environment and while protecting/preserving assets and their capability." It's a logical methodology to identify both preventive and predictive maintenance tasks to assure the reliability of your assets at the best cost.

The results of a FMEA and additional information are used to determine the best maintenance actions in typically four areas:

1. Reactive – for small and redundant items, non-critical, low consequence;
2. Preventive – items that wear out with an identifiable failure pattern;
3. Predictive technologies – items with random failures and to minimize human error;
4. Proactive – FMEAs, root cause analysis, trending/analysis of bad actors.

The RCM process involves asking seven questions of the assets to be analyzed and is defined by the technical standard SAE JA1011 Evaluation Criteria for RCM Processes. The SAE standard provides the minimum criteria that any process should meet before it can be called reliability centered maintenance. It begins by working through, in order, these seven questions.

1. What is the item supposed to do and its associated performance standards?
2. In what ways can it fail to provide the required functions?
3. What are the events that cause each failure?
4. What happens when each failure occurs?
5. In what way does each failure matter?
6. What systematic task can be performed proactively to prevent or diminish to a satisfactory degree, the consequences of the failure?
7. What must be done if a suitable preventive task cannot be found?

Similar questions and detailed information can be viewed in the late John Moubray's *Reliability Centered Maintenance* book[16] and other RCM process explanations.[17]

3.4.8.1 Failure Mode and Effects Analysis

A failure mode and effects analysis (FMEA) is a failure analysis tool that is best used in the design phase, but can be used for continuous improvement on existing products,

Chapter 3

components, or machinery/equipment. Typically, team members identify potential failure modes based on their collective experiences. Failures can come from things like, lack of maintenance, substandard material, poor design, improper part substitution, running conditions and environment, accidents and more. These possible issues are then designed out or minimized to improve the product, raise uptime, reduce mean time to repair, and so on. There are many types of FMEAs that can be used throughout the total product/process lifecycle.

FMEAs can support many objectives, such as:

- "Identify and prevent safety hazards.
- Minimize loss of product performance or performance degradation.
- Improve test and verification, as in the case of systems or design FMEAs.
- Improve process control plans, as in the case of process FMEAs.
- Consider changes in the product design or manufacturing process.
- Identify significant product or process characteristics.
- Develop preventive maintenance plans for in-service.
- Develop online diagnostic machinery and equipment techniques."[18]

Failure mode, effects and criticality analysis (FMECA) is similar to a FMEA, but has some minor differences. The main difference is a criticality analysis to analyze risks. The probability of each failure mode is analyzed with the severity of the consequences. Rating scales are different, as well as the guiding standards, such as MIL-STD-1629A. FMECA tends to be used more for military and high risk applications.

Stepwise, there are many logic flowcharts that can be followed through an RCM analysis, which includes a FMEA or FMECA. Most strive to be in compliance with SAE JA1011 (standard for Reliability Centered Maintenance), SAE J-1739 (FMEA – Automotive Systems) and SAE ARP-5580 (Non-Automotive Applications). A very detailed flowchart can be found at the NAVAIR Reliability Centered Maintenance Flowchart link.[19]

An ongoing debate is whether or not to do a full or short form of an RCM/FMEA. A full-blown FMEA takes more resources and is more comprehensive. Shortened versions, like Backfit RCM, RCM Blitz™ and Streamlined RCM, are faster and leverage commonality of assets. John Moubray gave me a copy of his *Reliability Centered Maintenance* book many years ago in Scotland. Those who have had the opportunity to meet John know that he only supported doing a full RCM/FMEA analysis to avoid risk. Keeping the scope specific and maintaining good facilitation can keep the time much shorter. I am not going to debate the advantages/disadvantages of short versus full RCM/FMEA because it really depends on the severity of risk or potential consequences. If risk is minimal, I see no reason why a group of assets, like pumps, cannot be done with a shorter RCM/FMEA. Equally important is getting the plant floor experts to the meeting and doing lots of pre-work with data to get ready. By understanding the process, risks and benefits of a full RCM/FMEA, you can make a decision if a long or short version is appropriate.

3.4.9 Learning Curve

The learning curve in any industry is a pattern of improvements as you make more products or perform a task. The concept started in the 19th century with German psychologist Hermann Ebbinghaus. The premise is that people learn in a predictable pattern. Some examples of where learning curves can be applied are:

- Maintenance replacement of parts;
- Number of automobiles;
- Barrels of oil;
- Tons of aluminum or steel;
- Gallons of chemicals.

The learning curve theorem states that: "Every time the production or experience doubles, the new cumulative average cost declines by a fixed percent."[20]

Simply, the more times you do the same task, the faster you can perform a subsequent task. The learning curve typically plots cost or time per repetition for producing a product versus the cumulative number of repetitions for production volume. The plots are often done on log-log scales so they result in straight lines defining the learning curve. Examples of studies[21, 22] are:

- Direct labor hours per unit to assemble an aircraft versus units produced.
- Average time to replace specific equipment parts versus number of maintenance replacements.
- One-year death rates from heart transplants versus the number of transplants done.

Many learning curve slopes are between seventy-five and eighty percent. That means with an eighty percent learning curve, the eighth item produced only took eighty percent of the time of the fourth item produced. Likewise, the two hundredth item only took eighty percent of the time of the one hundredth item to produce, and so on. In one of my plant assignments, learning curves were used to keep training and acceleration of new engine builds on target. Similar results were obtained.

Figure 3.10 is an example of an actual plot that can be used for such things as planning, budgeting and providing feedback to production teams, especially for focusing timely production start-ups. Follow these steps:

1. Based on the below recommendations, plot the expected learning curve for production:[23, 24]
    a. 40% for all manual
    b. 80% (25% automated, 75% manual)
    c. 85% (50% automated, 50% manual)
    d. 90% (75% automated, 25% manual).

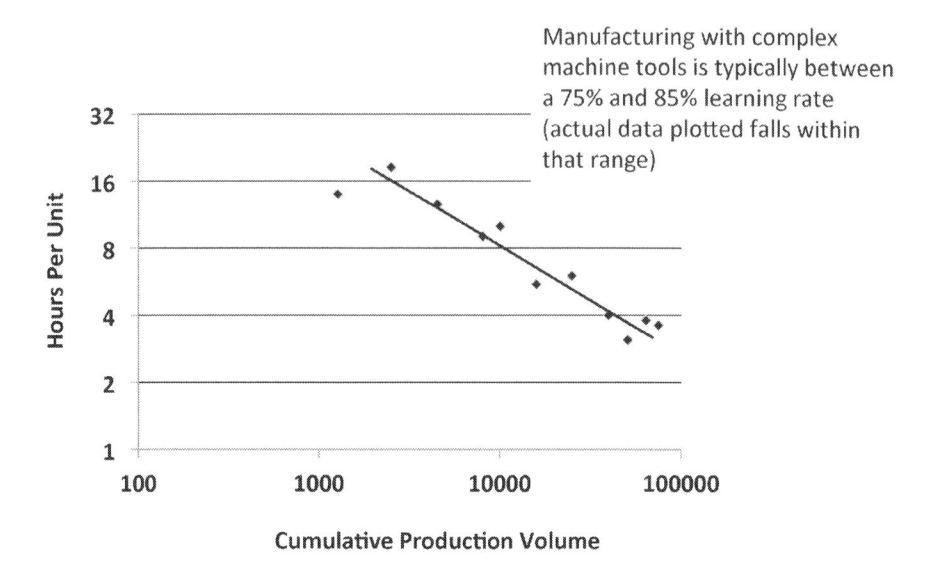

Figure 3.10: Learning curve log-log plot from manufacturing plant

2. Calculate the + 95 percent confidence limits for the learning curve.

3. Plot actual data, adjust the learning curve if needed and communicate results.

After collecting enough data, you will have better information to understand learning in your type of facility, culture and equipment. Many things can affect learning, like a new policy, training, layout change, process improvement, line rate change, etc. A significant change should be evident in the learning curve plot. Learning curve applications have almost no limitations. They can be used for calculating expected factory costs, training progress, purchasing, the supply chain, make/buy decisions, strategy, product reliability, scrap reduction, quality, maintenance shutdown/start-up, visual controls to provide feedback and motivation, and much more.

3.4.10 Total Productive Maintenance

"Total productive maintenance (TPM) is a plant improvement methodology that enables continuous and rapid improvement of the manufacturing process through the use of employee involvement, employee empowerment and closed-loop measurements of results."[25]

Organizations that understand that TPM is first and foremost a continuous improvement process for teams versus just a maintenance process are more successful. It's about the entire plant being involved in improving operations (e.g., OEE, six big losses), reliability, and utilization of assets. Another big part of TPM is the owner–operator concept, where operators have an active role in asset care, with inspection at a minimum. TPM falls short in many organizations for the same reasons as lean. The main cause is a lack of cultural readiness and active problem-solving capabilities. Companies attempt to implement, or partially implement, TPM, expecting great results without building up the underlying foundation of continuous improvement teams and management's understanding of how to coach it on a daily basis. Without informal and formal processes at work, including things you can't see, just copying the physical observations of a successful TPM program never works. After twenty-five years of TPM being in existence, how many organizations or factories can say, "We have fully implemented TPM and are doing ongoing improvement?" TPM touches almost every process in an organization, so if it's not strategically and tactically planned, other groups start to visibly or quietly resist as it touches their part of the organization. However, when implemented properly, there are numerous well-documented benefits.

Almost all the hundreds of early articles on total productive maintenance reported huge opportunities, like the Japan Institute of Plant Maintenance's (JIPM's) results on plants that receive the preventive maintenance prize for TPM.[26]

- Fifty percent greater productivity
- Unexpected equipment failures fell ninety-eight percent
- Process detects down ninety percent
- Maintenance cost down thirty percent
- Zero injuries and zero pollution are prerequisites for winning the prize

"….time it takes to implement TPM into an existing facility without these labor divisions is five to seven years. If the facility has a labor structure, it could take five

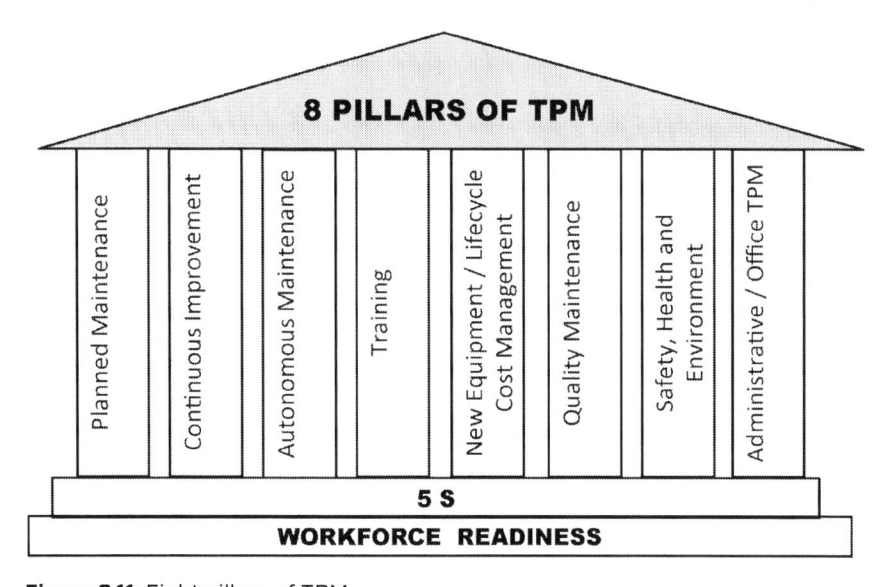

Figure 3.11: Eight pillars of TPM

to ten years. However, if the facility is new, the pros predict that TPM could be fully implemented within three years. The labor division being referred to is a strong separation between operations and maintenance. If we are even close to having a solid TPM program here by the end of five years, we will be very lucky."[27]

There are many similar versions, like Figure 3.11, depicting the pillars of TPM, but the general objectives are always to maximize uptime and throughput, improve safety, eliminate quality defects, reduce costs and support teams (e.g., operations, maintenance, and others) at all levels to enable continuous improvements. It starts with confirming workforce readiness and establishing engaged teams. Then, 5S is typically implemented to instill the discipline of standardized work. If that is successful, efforts can continue through the eight pillars of total productive maintenance.

3.4.11 Six Sigma

Six Sigma is a tool that can be applied as a continuous improvement strategy. It identifies and removes defects while reducing variation in the process. Six Sigma is typically done as projects with a specific goal (e.g., reduce quality defects, reduce cost and improve machine throughput). By statistical definition, a Six Sigma process operates at 3.4 defects per million or 99.997 percent process capability. It requires statistical knowledge for the analysis of data. More importantly, it requires a significant change in culture to be most beneficial. Six Sigma flows through five phases, more commonly known as the acronym, DMAIC.

1. "Define the projects, the goals and the deliverables to customers.
2. Measure the current performance of the process.
3. Analyze and determine the root cause(s) of the defects.
4. Improve the process to eliminate defects.
5. Control the performance of the process."[28]

It can make use of FMEA and many statistical tools, like hypothesis testing, design of experiments, control plans and so on. For example, Six Sigma can be used with FMEA to determine the anticipated DMAIC levels of quality. My experience is that Six Sigma is a good tool for mainly complex or difficult problems. When it comes to the majority of issues, it's more productive to utilize simpler tools and techniques that most team members can apply (e.g., 5S, 5 Whys, kaizen events) and further develop problem-solving skills.

3.4.12 Simplify and Reduce Complexity

Increasing complexity usually brings with it more errors and costs. Complexity also drives such things as:

- Higher inventory,
- Increased floor space,

- Increased tooling,
- Rising engineering costs,
- Higher labor and material costs,
- Shrinking benefits from economic scale.

"The complexity our organization will have to master over the next five years is off the charts – a 100 on a scale from 1 to 5."[29]

"In 2010, the Harvard Business Review estimated that a typical car contains approximately 2,000 functional components, 30,000 parts and 10 million lines of software code."[30]

Things around us and in organizations continue to get more complex. Service gets slower and more mistakes are made, with too many interchangeable or similar parts in manufacturing and assembly. Also, proliferation of electronics, substitution of parts, reused parts and software risks from supporting systems leaves room for much higher failure potential.

I often travel by car over lengthy distances, leading to many opportunities to stop for coffee. At one fast food stop, three people had ordered and were waiting in line for their orders to be filled. After using the restroom, I walked up and ordered only a coffee to go. While waiting for a single cup of coffee, the same attendant tried to take my order again and just stood there and watched while drive-through orders were being filled. I noted the next car driving towards the back to order and watched the occupant get his order completed before I was served one cup of coffee inside. It was obvious the priority was on keeping the drive-through moving, without paying any attention to efficiency and effectiveness with the inside customers. Drive-through focus and increasing order complexity has resulted in a broken process. Relative to assembly line operators, one study showed that, "operators with ten parts made forty-six percent more errors and needed thirteen percent more decision time that operators with four parts." Furthermore, the relief and untrained job operators made three times more errors than the trained operators."[31]

When it comes to buying products, like groceries, insurance, retirement investment and cars, if it becomes too difficult, people tend to walk away or make a simpler decision.

- "When Procter and Gamble went from twenty different kinds of Head and Shoulders™ shampoo to fifteen, they saw an increase in sales of ten percent.
- The more funds that were offered in a plan, the fewer participated.
- Go from lower to higher complexity when making choices. For cars, if you have consumers, choose the color before the gears and engine; they will be more likely to disengage in the choice.
- Choice overload reduces engagement, decision quality, and satisfaction."[32]

Manage your complexity for competitive advantage.

3.4.13 Ergonomics

Ergonomics is a methodology used to help people work productively in a safe manner. It organizes job tasks and tools to fit the person, instead of having the person fit into the

Chapter 3

work situation. Detailed definitions can be found at the Human Factors and Ergonomics Society (www.hfes.org) and the U.S. Department of Labor's Occupational Safety & Health Administration (OSHA) (https://www.osha.gov/SLTC/ergonomics/). In simplest terms, ergonomics is the scientific study of people at work. The word comes from two Greek words, *ergon* meaning work and *nomos* meaning laws. OSHA states that it helps lessen muscle fatigue, increase productivity and reduce the number and severity of work-related musculoskeletal disorders (MSDs). These MSDs affect muscles, nerves and tendons, and are the main cause of injury and illness in the workplace. In 2011, the U.S. Bureau of Labor Statistics identified maintenance and production workers in the top ten occupations for MSD issues. Many of those issues are muscle strains and back injuries. The 387,820 MSD cases accounted for thirty-three percent of all worker injury and illness cases in 2011. From various studies done in ergonomics, I have found:

- A statistical relationship between lack of ergonomic implementation and absenteeism, with the absenteeism resulting in lower quality.
- That overall plant operations improve. For example, implementation at one manufacturing facility resulted in a two percent increase in production, ten percent improvement in quality and twenty percent reduction in absenteeism.

There are many ergonomic publications on repetitive type tasks, such as part assembly, at work, but not much on maintenance work. Technicians and trades are equally at risk.

- The static loads from holding tools/parts for a long time are more prevalent.
- Because of the unpredictable nature of repair, awkward postures and hand-wrist positions are more likely.
- The tools, harnesses and sometimes tight work spaces lead to awkward body postures, such as more twisting and unbalanced lifting.
- Safety helmets and glasses, hearing protection, arc flash suits and gloves, and other protective wear.
- Technology is changing quickly, making clear information and cognitive skills more important.
- The emergency nature of some work may not promulgate the best ergonomic practices, even though all safety practices are followed.
- Climbing and working at heights usually leads to awkward postures.
- Ergonomic data and visual displays/error proofing needs are different for skilled trades who need to maintain focus while checking diagnostics and repairing.
- The impact is greater with more shift work and long hours.
- The workforce is aging.
- Extreme environments, such as working in heat or cold, near noisy equipment, etc., have a greater impact.

The winning plants of the future will win at the plant floor level. Ergonomics can support various initiatives, such as design for maintainability, minimizing physical stress, improving decision-making to reduce defects, and more.

3.4.14 Safety

Most continuous improvement tools and techniques, like 5S, 5 Whys, FMEA, RCM and RCA, all have ongoing roles in improving safety. For example, when you perform a kaizen event, the identified safety issues are usually tagged with a special safety color so they can be quickly found again and corrected. Use the tools to analyze where your safety improvement areas are. By analyzing historical data of trades versus entire facility from twenty-one companies, including manufacturing, mining, paper, aluminum, steel, chemical, automotive and energy covering over one hundred facilities, it was found that eighty-five percent of the time maintenance department employees were, on average, about three times more at risk. In order for the workplace to be truly supportive, employees need to be convinced that you/organization care about their well-being. Safety should be at the top of your priority list regardless, but without it, getting team involvement will be extremely difficult.

Safety, health and environment is one of the eight pillars of total productive maintenance. The Japan Institute of Plant Maintenance requires zero accidents as a prerequisite for entry to their award process. As stated earlier, a reliable plant is also a safe and cost-effective plant. Ergonomics and safety are closely tied together as higher job stress (e.g., mental, physical, etc.) on the human body results in more safety-related issues. It should be no surprise that it's all related. Figure 3.12 shows the strong relationship between injury rate and overall equipment effectiveness.

When plants are running with high OEE or asset utilization, then injuries are less likely. Best in class operations have outstanding safety results.

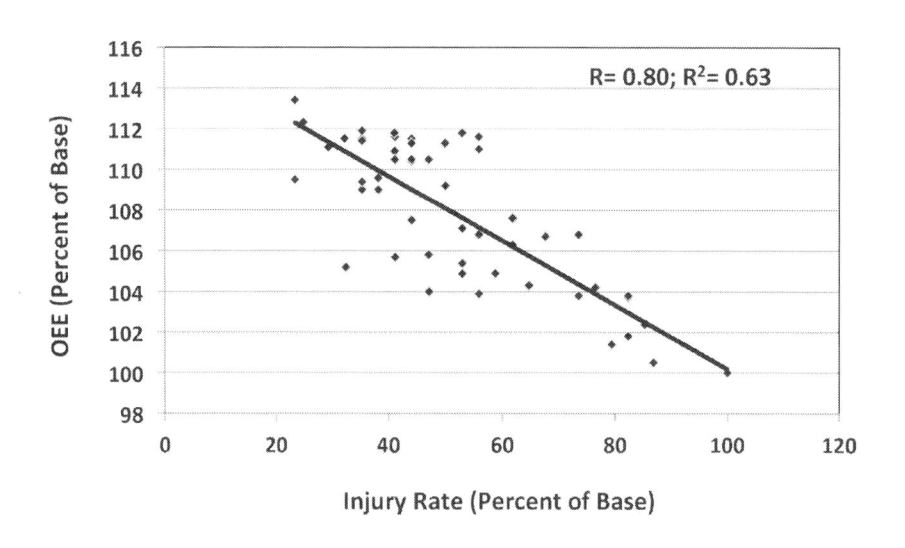

Used with permission from RM Group, Inc., Knoxville, TN

Figure 3.12: Safety and OEE

3.4.14.1 Safety Process (Contextual Risk Assessment Tool)

Operational excellence requires a high level of maturity in your safety process. It's not a coincidence that the best companies in throughput, quality and cost also do well in safety. The glue that holds it all together is the underlying culture that demonstrates your support for people and it's all linked with a cause and effect. The safety risk assessment tool went through a history of development from the early 1990s to 2008. Thanks to General Motors and Mike Douglas, its Senior Manager of New Technology and Standards, the University of Tennessee's Reliability and Maintainability Center shares the process in training courses. The contextual risk assessment (CRA) is simple, flexible and has a great range of applications. As an overview, it:

- Allows you to identify the **issues** as they relate to what you're **observing**.
- Provides an analysis area to **evaluate** the observations and issues based on the required discipline and the level of expertise needed according to the circumstances.
- Provides the ability to show the **impact** on the company, project, equipment, quality, responsiveness, etc.
- Enables looking at a glance at all the possible **safety category** combinations where actions can be performed based on the hierarchy of controls.
- Facilitates the convergence to the **optimal solution**, with **responsibility** and **estimated completion date**.

The CRA tool, using the risk assessment worksheet (RAW), provides you with the flexibility to perform due diligence based on the defined scope. It can be used at any step in the manufacturing lifecycle (MLE) and with machinery and equipment design elements. There are eight design elements throughout the three MLE stages: MLE-Design, which includes preliminary design, pre-award quote and award purchase order; MLE-Pipeline, which includes the detailed design, the supplier building the equipment or buying off-the-shelf and accepting the finished asset; and MLE-Plant Floor, which includes install/debug and run production.

The risk assessment worksheet:

- Focuses on what to capture and analyze.
- Provides the framework for how to ensure that due diligence was performed in the analysis.
- Provides the details to verify that action items were completed.
- Creates the ultimate format to enable a fluid and effortless spontaneous dialogue for risk assessments at any stage of a system's lifecycle.

Figure 3.13 is a high-level look at and explanation of the risk assessment worksheet.

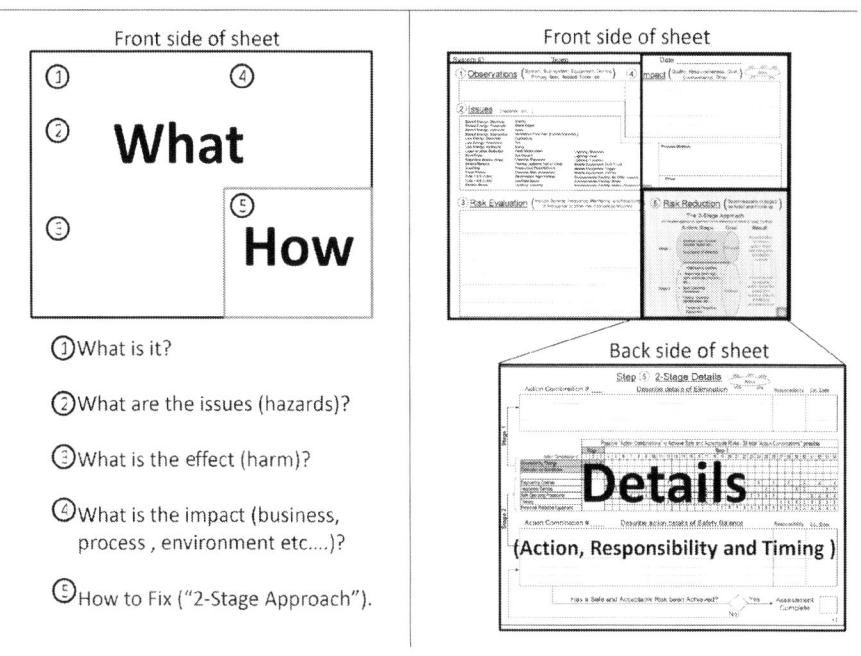

Using Lean Tools and Other Techniques for Continuous Improvement

①What is it?

②What are the issues (hazards)?

③What is the effect (harm)?

④What is the impact (business, process, environment etc....)?

⑤How to Fix ("2-Stage Approach").

Figure 3.13: General Motors' risk assessment worksheet

Figure 3.14 provides more details behind the hierarchy of health and safety controls or protective measures. General Motors implemented a two-stage approach (Figure 3.13) to capture the multiple actions required for safety applications. Stage one eliminates hazards with a combination of actions within its two categories. Stage two reduces risks to a safe and acceptable level, with combinations. To design or improve on an initially used hierarchy of controls (e.g., eliminate or substitute engineering controls, warnings, training and personal protective equipment), examples of health and safety hierarchy of controls are listed in Figure 3.14.

After filling out steps one through four in Figure 3.15, next follow the two-stage approach (step five) illustrated on page one under risk reduction (Figure 3.15) and detailed on page two of the RAW (Figure 3.16).

The two-stage approach is an iterative application of the hierarchy of health and safety controls. If elimination is not possible, then the actions in the remaining hierarchical categories (stage two) are considered until a safe operational level has been achieved. With further development, the two-stage approach matures into an action choice matrix (see the due diligence matrix in Figure 3.16). It also has been termed a contextual risk assessment. This process:

- Is a five-step, problem-solving tool you can start at any step, with no sequence required, and proceed to the other four in any order. The five parts are observation, issues, evaluation, impact and risk elimination/reduction.

Figure 3.14: Hierarchy of Health & Safety Controls (Protective Measures)

	Protective Measure	Examples	Influence on Risk Factors	Classification
Most Preferred ↓	Elimination or Substitute	• Eliminate pinch points (increase clearance) • Intrinsically safe (energy containment) • Automated material handling (robots, conveyors, etc.) • Redesign the process to eliminate or reduce human interaction • Reduced energy • Substitute less hazardous chemicals	• Impact on overall risk (elimination) by affecting severity and probability of harm • May affect severity of harm, frequency of exposure to the hazard under consideration and/or the possibility of avoiding or limiting harm depending on which method of substitution is applied.	Elimination
	Guards and Safeguarding Devices	• Barriers • Interlocks • Presence sensing devices (light curtains, safety mats, area scanners, etc.) • Two hand controls and two hand trip devices	• Greatest impact on the probability of harm (Occurrence of hazardous events under certain circumstance) • Minimal if any impact on severity of harm	Engineering Controls
	Awareness Devices	• Lights, beacons, and strobes • Computer warnings • Signs and labels • Beepers, horns and sirens	• Potential impact on the probability of harm (avoidance) • No impact on severity of harm	Administrative Controls
	Training and Procedures	• Safe work procedures • Safety equipment inspections • Training • Lockout/Tag out/Tryout	• Potential impact on the probability of harm (avoidance and/or exposure) • No impact on severity of harm	Administrative Controls
Least Preferred	Personal Protective Equipment (PPE)	• Safety glasses and face shields • Ear plugs • Gloves • Protective footwear • Respirations	• Potential impact on the probability of harm (avoidance) • No impact on severity of harm	Administrative Controls

Using Lean Tools and Other Techniques for Continuous Improvement

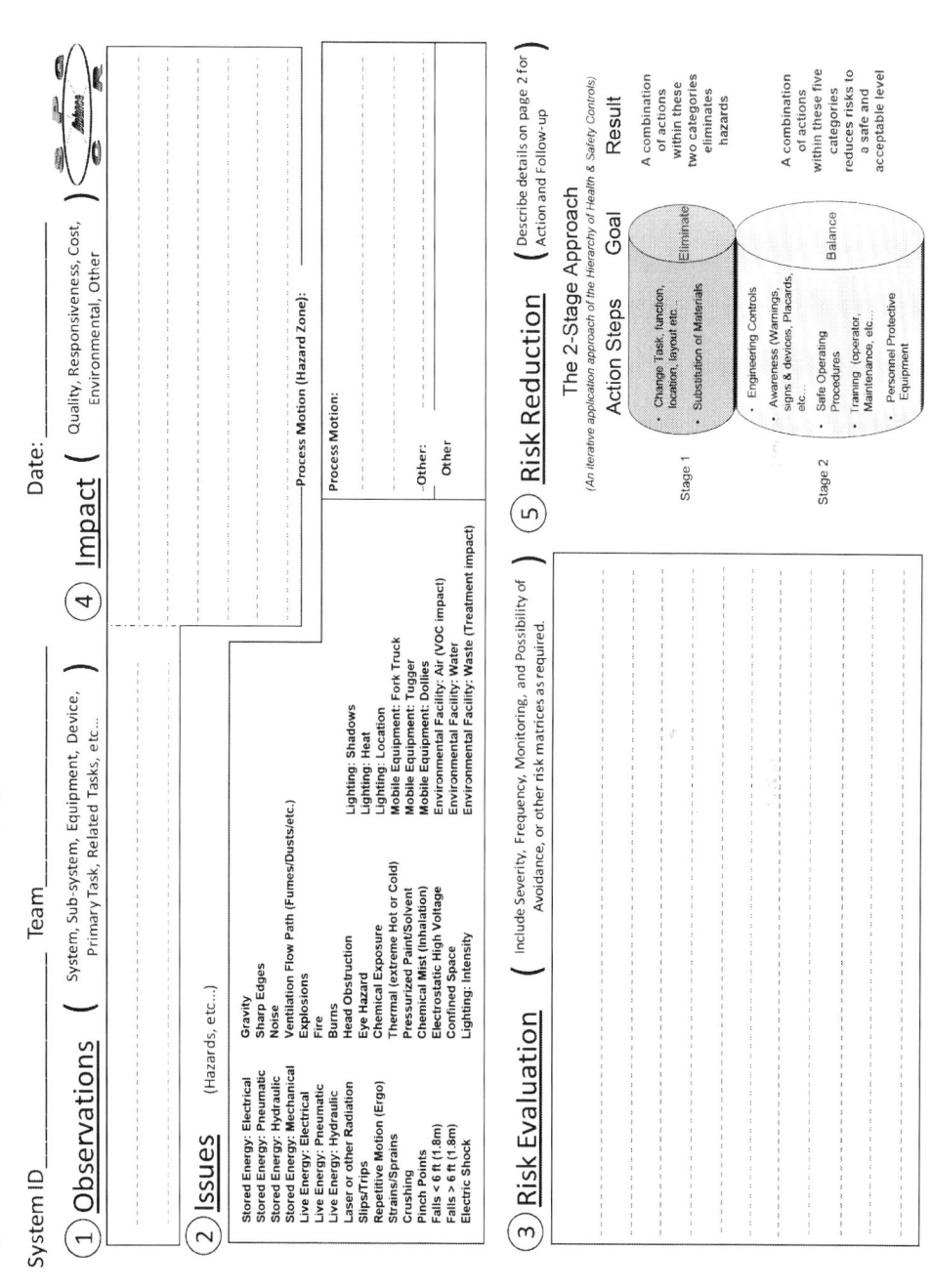

Figure 3.15: Risk assessment worksheet, page one

System ID _____ Team _____ Date: _____

① Observations (System, Sub-system, Equipment, Device, Primary Task, Related Tasks, etc....)

② Issues (Hazards, etc...)

- Stored Energy: Electrical
- Stored Energy: Pneumatic
- Stored Energy: Hydraulic
- Stored Energy: Mechanical
- Live Energy: Electrical
- Live Energy: Pneumatic
- Live Energy: Hydraulic
- Laser or other Radiation
- Repetitive Motion (Ergo)
- Slips/Trips
- Strains/Sprains
- Crushing
- Pinch Points
- Falls < 6 ft (1.8m)
- Falls > 6 ft (1.8m)
- Electric Shock

- Gravity
- Sharp Edges
- Noise
- Ventilation Flow Path (Fumes/Dusts/etc.)
- Explosions
- Fire
- Burns
- Head Obstruction
- Eye Hazard
- Chemical Exposure
- Thermal (extreme Hot or Cold)
- Pressurized Paint/Solvent
- Chemical Mist (Inhalation)
- Confined Space
- Lighting: Intensity

- Lighting: Shadows
- Lighting: Heat
- Lighting: Location
- Mobile Equipment: Fork Truck
- Mobile Equipment: Tugger
- Mobile Equipment: Dollies
- Environmental Facility: Air (VOC impact)
- Environmental Facility: Water
- Environmental Facility: Waste (Treatment impact)

④ Impact (Quality, Responsiveness, Cost, Environmental, Other)

Process Motion (Hazard Zone):

Process Motion:

Other:

Other

③ Risk Evaluation (Include Severity, Frequency, Monitoring, and Possibility of Avoidance, or other risk matrices as required.)

⑤ Risk Reduction (Describe details on page 2 for Action and Follow-up)

(An iterative application approach of the Hierarchy of Health & Safety Controls)

The 2-Stage Approach

Action Steps   **Goal**   **Result**

Stage 1
- Change: Task, function, location, layout etc.
- Substitution of Materials

Eliminate

A combination of actions within these two categories eliminates hazards

Stage 2
- Engineering Controls
- Awareness (Warnings, signs & devices, Placards, etc.
- Safe Operating Procedures
- Training (operator, Maintenance, etc.
- Personnel Protective Equipment

Balance

A combination of actions within these five categories reduces risks to a safe and acceptable level

73

Chapter 3

Figure 3.16: Risk assessment worksheet, page two

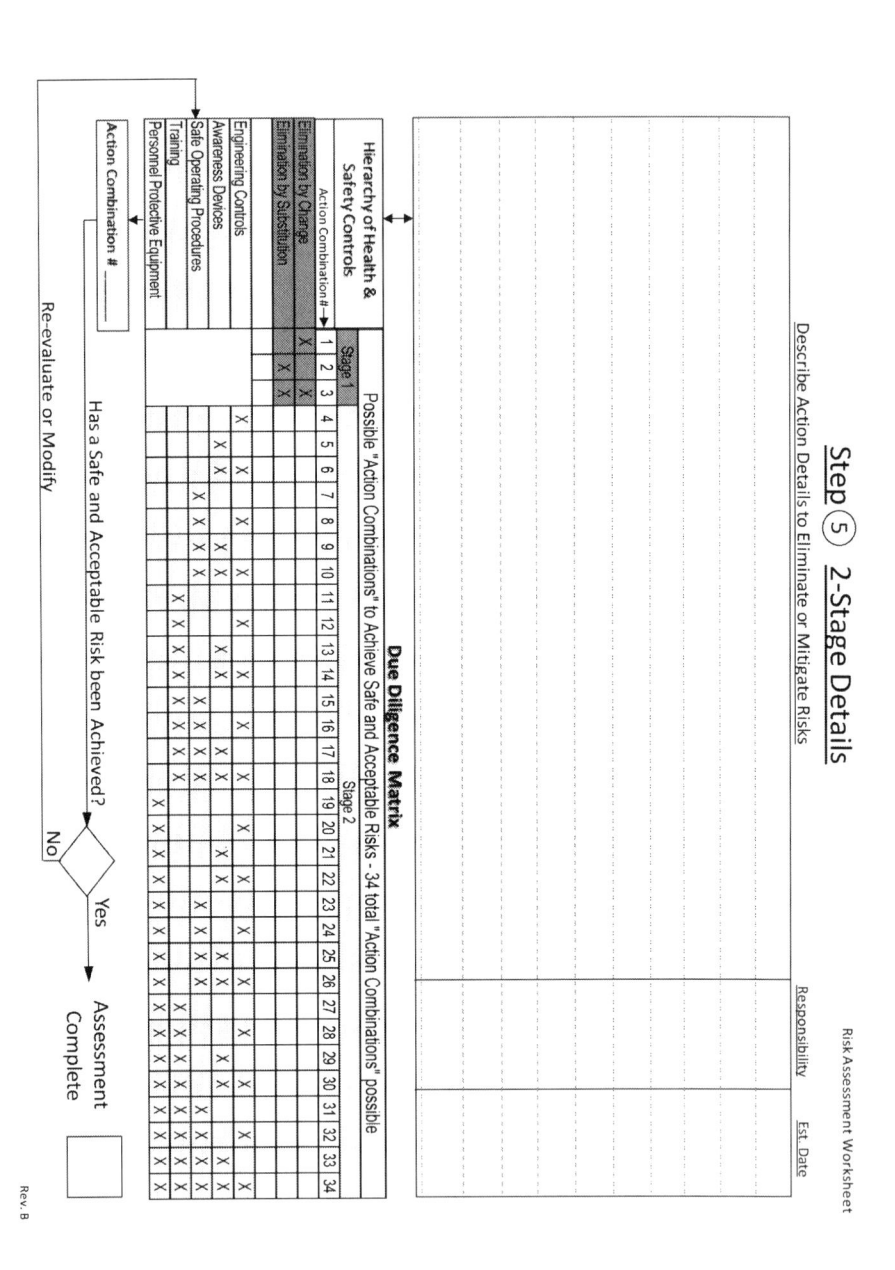

74

Using Lean Tools and Other Techniques for Continuous Improvement

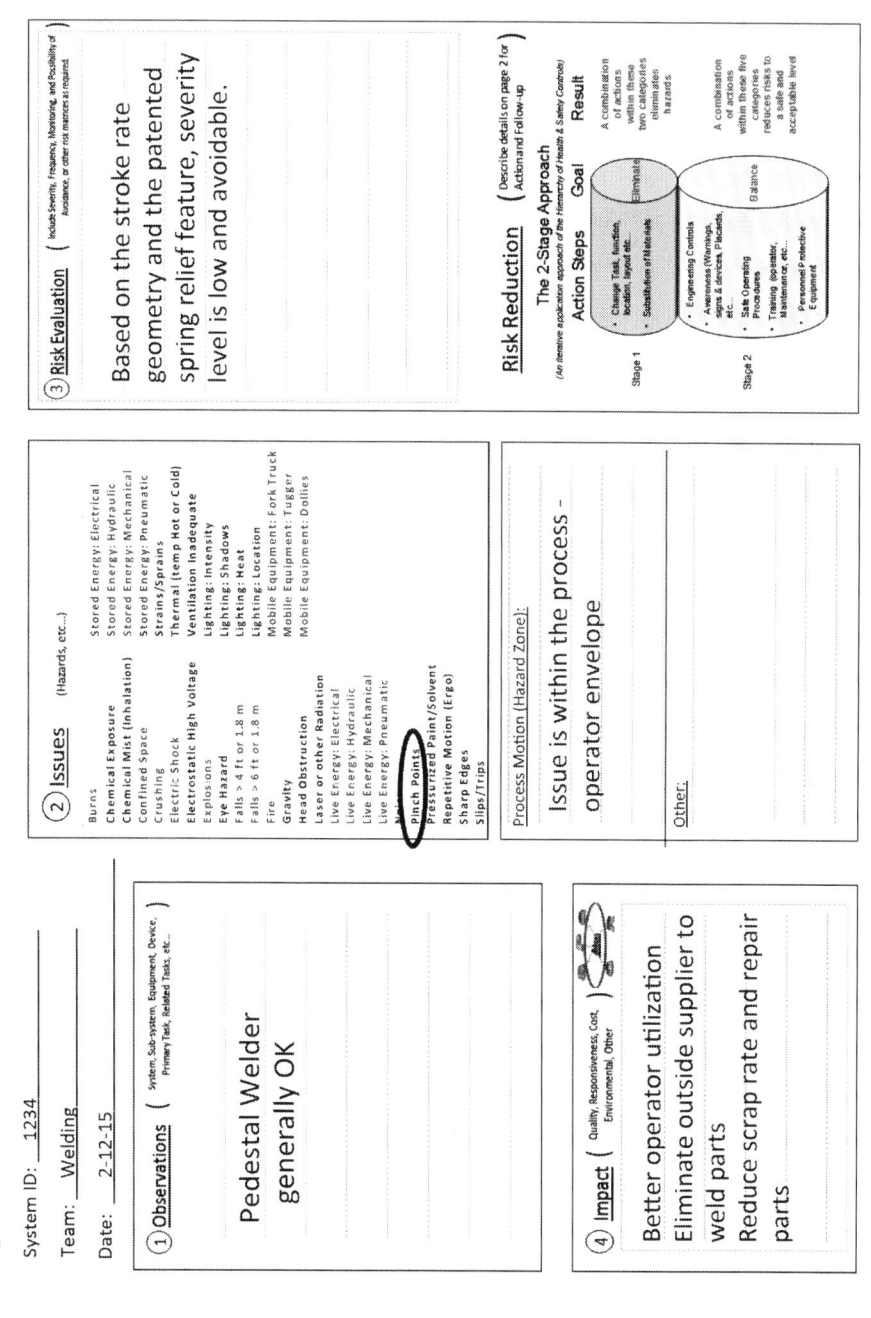

Figure 3.17: Risk assessment worksheet example, page one

System ID: __1234__

Team: __Welding__

Date: __2-12-15__

① Observations (System, Sub-system, Equipment, Device, Primary Task, Related Tasks, etc.)

Pedestal Welder generally OK

② Issues (Hazards, etc....)

Burns	Stored Energy: Electrical
Chemical Exposure	Stored Energy: Hydraulic
Chemical Mist (Inhalation)	Stored Energy: Mechanical
Confined Space	Stored Energy: Pneumatic
Crushing	Strains/Sprains
Electric Shock	Thermal (temp Hot or Cold)
Electrostatic High Voltage	Ventilation Inadequate
Explosions	Lighting: Intensity
Eye Hazard	Lighting: Shadows
Falls > 4 ft or 1.8 m	Lighting: Heat
Falls > 6 ft or 1.8 m	Lighting: Location
Fire	Mobile Equipment: Fork Truck
Gravity	Mobile Equipment: Tugger
Head Obstruction	Mobile Equipment: Dollies
Laser or other Radiation	
Live Energy: Electrical	
Live Energy: Hydraulic	
Live Energy: Mechanical	
Live Energy: Pneumatic	
Pinch Points	
Pressurized Paint/Solvent	
Repetitive Motion (Ergo)	
Sharp Edges	
Slips/Trips	

Process Motion (Hazard Zone):

Issue is within the process – operator envelope

Other:

③ Risk Evaluation (Include Severity, Frequency, Monitoring and Possibility of Avoidance, or other risk manners as required)

Based on the stroke rate geometry and the patented spring relief feature, severity level is low and avoidable.

Risk Reduction (Describe details on page 2 for Action and Follow-up)

The 2-Stage Approach
(An iterative application approach of the Hierarchy of Health & Safety Controls)

Action Steps	Goal	Result
Stage 1: • Change Test, function, location, layout etc. • Substitution of Materials	Eliminate	A combination of actions within these two categories eliminates hazards
Stage 2: • Engineering Controls • Awareness (Warnings, signs & devices, Placards, etc. • Safe Operating Procedures • Training (operator, Maintenance, etc... • Personnel Protective Equipment	Balance	A combination of actions within these five categories reduces risks to a safe and acceptable level

④ Impact (Quality, Responsiveness, Cost, Environmental, Other)

Better operator utilization

Eliminate outside supplier to weld parts

Reduce scrap rate and repair parts

75

Chapter 3

Figure 3.18: Risk assessment worksheet example, page two

Step ⑤ 2-Stage Details

List of Actions Required to Eliminate or Mitigate Risks	Reponsibility	Est. Date
1. - One or both Pilz safety relays could be removed in future designs if the encoder speed can be limited and calibration, procedures, ~~awareness and operating procedures are defined~~ and followed.	John Smith	Future Designs
14. - Limit the speed of the encoder.	John Smith	3-15-15
- Create an awareness label to notify operators of the minimum part size.	Jim Lewis	3-15-15
~~- Discuss with Central Engineering and UAW~~ leadership	Bob Holt	3-15-15
- Create operator training manual.	Bob Holt	3-15-15

Due Diligence Matrix - To assure that all possible "Hierarchy of Control" combinations have been considered

Hierarchy of Health & Safety Control	Possible "Action Combinations" to Achieve Safe and Acceptable Risks - 34 total "Action Combinations" possible																																		
	Stage 1													Stage 2																					
Action Combination #	①1	2	3	4	5	6	7	8	9	10	11	12	13	⑭	15	16	17	18	19	20	21	22	23	24	25	26	27	28	29	30	31	32	33	34
☐ Elimination by Change	✓	✓																																
☐ Elimination by Substitution		✓	✓																															
☐ Engineering Controls				✓	✓	✓	✓	✓	✓	✓		✓	✓	✓	✓	✓		✓	✓		✓		✓	✓		✓	✓		✓		✓	✓	✓	✓
☐ Awareness Devices					✓	✓			✓	✓			✓	✓			✓	✓			✓	✓			✓	✓							✓	✓
☐ Safe Operating Procedures						✓	✓	✓	✓						✓	✓	✓	✓					✓	✓	✓	✓					✓	✓	✓	✓
☐ Training							✓	✓	✓	✓	✓	✓	✓	✓													✓	✓	✓	✓	✓	✓	✓	✓
☐ Personnel Protective Equipment																✓	✓	✓	✓	✓	✓	✓	✓	✓	✓	✓	✓	✓	✓	✓	✓	✓	✓	✓

Action Combination # _____

Has a Safe and Acceptable Risk been Achieved? → Yes → Assessment Complete ☐
Revise Action List Requirements ← No

- Can be used in any conversation, meeting, dialogue, etc.
- Helps you deal with the dynamics inherent in all types of situations.
- Satisfies the due diligence requirement referenced by regulations, directives, local codes and standards.
- Provides an excellent platform for continuous improvement.

The matrix (Figure 3.16) consists of three parts:

1. Stage One
   Two categories, with three possible action combinations within the two categories
2. Stage Two
   Five categories, with thirty-one possible action combinations within the five stage two categories.
3. A communication line for quick reference

Showing the thirty-four possible action combinations or choices, it identifies what needs to be worked on to achieve elimination (stage one) or reduce the remaining risks to a safe level (stage two).

The risk assessment worksheet can be easily brought to a meeting and used to record comments, issues and potential solutions. Figures 3.17 and 3.18 show a completed example in an interactive, meeting friendly format. In Appendix C at the end of this book is a blank safety risk assessment worksheet.

"Safety in General Motors has been a continuous improvement journey over the past twenty plus years. However, the growing maturity and capabilities of the resulting processes and tools have resulted in significant benefits."[33] In 1993, the General Motors North American facilities incident rate, although already one of the best in automotive,

Figure 3.19: The Meaning of kaizen

Kai = Change   **Zen = Good or for the better**

Kaizen means continuous improvement and change for the better.   **(Japanese)**
Small incremental changes; break apart and put back together better

Blitz means flash or lightning   **(German)**

Kaizen Blitz = Quick kaizen event

Chapter 3

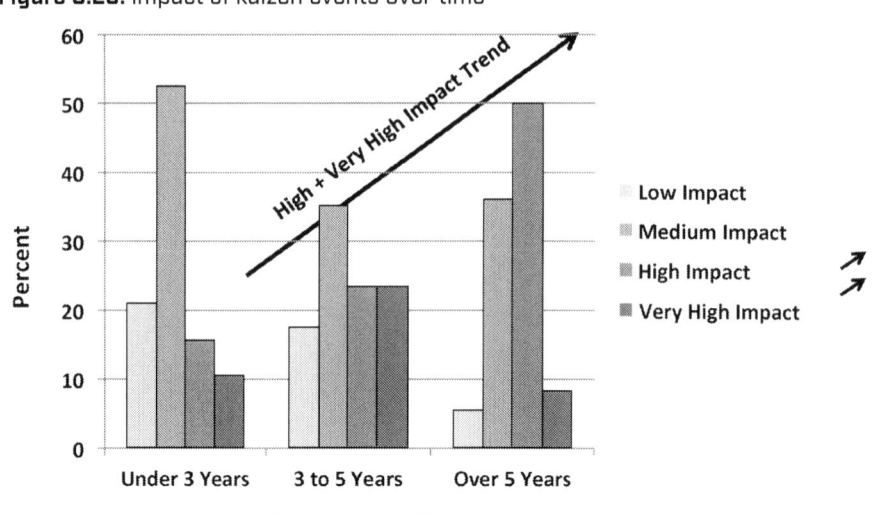

Figure 3.20: Impact of kaizen events over time

was twenty-nine per one hundred employees, with a lost workday case rate of 4.5 per one hundred employees. By 2008, the injury rate dropped to 1.69 and lost workday rate to 0.14.

GM's Mike Douglas likes to start his safety talks with this quote. I will use it to close this section and appropriately place emphasis on plant floor readiness.

> "Readiness is the mother of luck. The most consistently lucky people happen to be those that are the best prepared." Seventeenth century manual of success,
> *The Art of Worldly Wisdom* by Baltasar Gracian

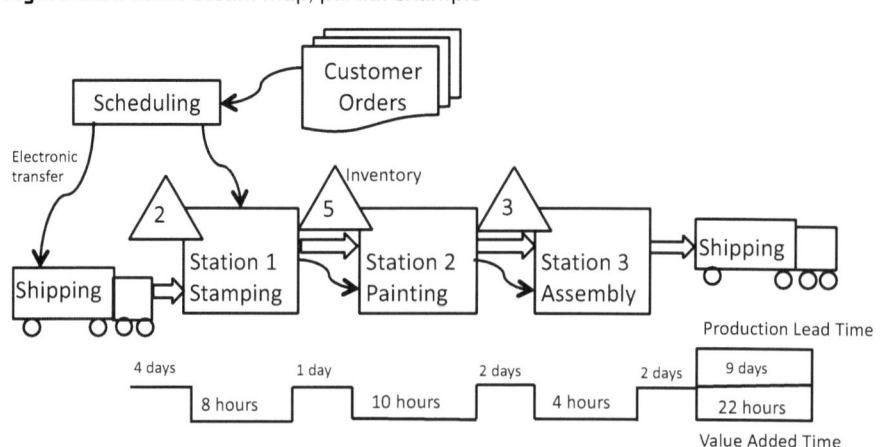

Figure 3.21: Value steam map, partial example

Figure 3.22: Practical problem-solving A3, basic template

Owner: PPS#:	Team:	Signatures Dates
Problem definition (Grasp the Situation):		Countermeasures (Based on RCA Findings):
Target/Goal (Specific Issue to Resolve):		Implementation (Who/What/When/Actual):
Analysis (Using 5 Why, Fishbone, Pareto, etc. as needed):		
^		Follow-up(Planned vs. Actual):

3.5 Kaizen

In Japanese, *kai* means change or the action to correct. In Chinese, *gai* means change for the better and *shan* means good or benefit. Benefit here also infers that one should not benefit at the expense of another person. This is systems thinking or viewing the bigger picture in decision-making. Putting it together, *kaizen* means change for the better and improvement. By its very definition, the act of improvement requires change. A frequently used process is a kaizen event. In Assembly Magazine's State of the Profession 2009 Survey,[34] continuous improvement/kaizen was selected by seventy-one percent of the respondents as the highest factor contributing to competitive advantage. Kaizen is the Japanese word for continuous improvement. A fast kaizen event has been given several names, one being kaizen blitz (Figure 3.19).

In a business environment, kaizen focuses on improving standard activities/work and processes. It's a continual process of eliminating waste and difficult work. The process is based on numerous small improvements within the job scope of those involved that cumulatively result in large improvements and minimal risk. Based on issue difficulty and organizations/task complexity, kaizen events come in many different formats, team sizes and duration of time. Kaizen events are good because:

- They provide opportunity for implementing workforce suggestions from many employees at different levels, learning new skills and building enthusiasm.
- The results are implemented quickly, showing immediate support for the team's input.
- The subtle significance of a kaizen event shows that change is doable.

Chapter 3

Kaizen events can be done on just about anything, including waste reduction, plan for every part, safety, machine improvement, maintenance tasks optimization, productivity improvements, and more. One team focused on one part number, with these results:

"…the required equipment space was cut twenty-two percent, inventory decreased forty percent, walking distance shrank eighty-seven percent, parts travel distance dropped sixty-seven percent, and cycle time decreased twenty-six percent. The team concluded that with minimal investment, similar percentage improvements could become a reality for almost all six hundred and fifty part numbers processed in the area."[35]

In a coil making operation between 1984 and 1992 during Japan's Showa period, "every activity was rethought and improved at least once. And eventually, in pursuit of perfection, every activity was kaizened at least ten times. Productivity soared, inventories were slashed to a quarter of their former value, and the amount of space needed to make a given amount of output was cut by seventy-five percent."[36]

Kaizen events don't simply promote change; they also stimulate the thinking process, which results in increased learning and problem-solving skills. Figure 3.20 shows that kaizen events continue to make a difference even after five years of continuous improvement. Kaizen is a key pillar in reducing waste within the larger umbrella of lean production methods. Lean concepts are applicable to all types of businesses, both in the factory and office. Typically, value stream mapping and/or 5 Whys on simple issues are used to target improvement areas and projects. Common attributes of all types of kaizen events are short-term, typically one to five days, done by teams and results oriented. Kaizen teams may follow selected methodologies in performing an event, such as standardized work, seven wastes, single-minute exchange of die (SMED), etc. Kaizen events can focus on problem resolution, small and large impacts, training and implementations.

Kaizen can align with gradual improvements by teams, or it can focus on more quickly implemented changes, as with kaizen blitz. Most companies have some version of this called rapid improvement teams, go-fast workshops, 3P and so on. For example, "3P (production, preparation, process) is a method originated by Chihiro Nakao in which employee teams conceptualize, develop, validate, and deploy radical improvement in product and process design. It's a systematized way to achieve kaikaku-sporadic, step-level change."[37] If a successful kaizen is to become the new standardized work, make sure the key persons are sufficiently trained in the updated standard and check the results on a regular basis.

"If enough people do a thing wrong often enough, it becomes right. Quantity is protection from criticism."[38]

To properly discuss kaizen and ongoing improvement, the concept of *kata* must be discussed. A kata is a standard form of movement or a routine.

"Toyota's way is characterized less by its tools or principles than by sets of procedural sequences – thinking and behavior patterns – that when repeated over and over in daily work lead to the desired outcome. If there is one thing to look at in trying to understand and perhaps emulate Toyota's success, then these behavior patterns and how they are taught may well be it."[39]

Using Lean Tools and Other Techniques for Continuous Improvement

James Womack, keynote speaker at the 2011 IndustryWeek Conference, defined kata as a practice that becomes a way of doing things. He stressed becoming a gemba walker (gemba is the Japanese word for workplace). He stated:

"….go see, ask why, and show respect and that Gemba is the place where value is created.

- Value flows horizontally, yet organizations are organized vertically.
- The gemba walk is the best way to truly grasp the situation so that good lean things can happen."[40]

In the summer of 2014, I took a group of University of Tennessee College of Engineering students to Munich, Germany, to teach a course on "Global Perspectives in Lean, Reliability and Maintainability." We also visited several industries to view and assess plant floor operations, including the Technical University of Munich's Lean Learning Center. For a textbook, we used the *Toyota Kata* book. Although the class was based on lean, reliability and maintainability, with materials provided by me, the key focus was around understanding how to continuously improve in a factory setting.

3.5.1 Grasp the Situation

By truly taking time to understand an issue and look at the big picture, many facts can be gathered to better resolve the situation. This refers both to problem-solving and really understanding what you have been asked to do. Look around and grasp the situation.

Here are a few examples that we can all relate to:

- My wife and I were paying for food at a popular grocery store. In the aisle next to us, we noticed an employee getting up on the food belt that transports food to the cashier. She was very vocal and proud that she was up there cleaning off every spot on the light covers that display the checkout line number. But, she wore her shoes while standing on the food belt and never cleaned the belt after getting off it. Did she really grasp the bigger situation and what customers were seeing?
- I had an international flight with a 10:15 a.m. departure and instructions were to be there three hours early (7:15 a.m.) to get through slow lines. The staff to check passports finally showed up about 8:15 a.m. Later, we were told that final security check doesn't open until 8:30 a.m. Who at this major European airport really understands the big picture?
- I get my medical checkup at a major, highly-rated hospital. In most areas, I see a bottle of disinfectant for people to use. Within the building, there is a pharmacy for convenient service. As I'm waiting in line, I notice some people coughing and several others with various congestive issues. At checkout, everyone has to use the same pen for a required electronic signature, with no disinfectant in sight. All it takes is for someone to walk typical patient paths from entering to leaving the hospital to notice

Chapter 3

the improvement opportunities. This is similar to the day in the life walks that are done with maintenance to understand and improve current practices.

- At a large conference, I noticed the way the tablecloths were intentionally ruffled on the coffee table. It looked nice, but the problem was with the way it was ruffled. You could not put down a single cup of coffee to add sugar and cream. I pointed it out to the nearby waiter who agreed with me and said he had previously mentioned this to his boss. He was told to ruffle the tablecloths "because they look nice and that's the way we do it."
- I take my coffee with sugar, no cream. No matter how clearly and carefully I try to order it that way, about eighty percent of the wait staff bring cream. If you observe carefully throughout the day, you will find many examples where people ask a question to fit the situation, but don't really listen to the answer. Just like I noticed every time I get cream, so do others in the workforce on other similar verbal exchanges. Listen attentively and grasp the situation.

It's important to observe, ask and listen to fully grasp the relevant situation, whether it's everyday examples like these, a machine uptime issue, reasons for a dissatisfied work group, why trades won't enter computer data, why shortcuts are taken during maintenance routes, or why engineers aren't getting the needed input from technicians and trades teams.

3.5.2 Value Stream Mapping

Value stream mapping (VSM) is a process that provides a visual representation, such as a flowchart that uses symbols, of a value stream. The mapping process, typically done with a team of key stakeholders close to the process, results in a combination of value-added and non-value-added steps/activities in a process. It is applicable to production, non-production and office/administrative processes. By laying everything out in an organized manner that all can understand, VSM provides a road map for improvement. Often done in a team setting utilizing a large wall, it's a visual way to identify waste and eliminate it. Often, other improvement techniques, like 5 Whys and seven wastes, are utilized in conjunction with VSM. Common symbols are used to help provide the same meaning to all participants. The exact symbols will vary, with some based on the ones you make common or the templates/software you utilize. They can display things like safety stock, shipments, inventory, production control, processes, etc., as needed. Figure 3.21 is a basic, partial example of a VSM flowchart. At the bottom is a summary of production lead time and value-added time. It shows both material and information flow throughout your entire process, from order to delivery. VSM identifies waste and problems that disrupt flow. Ideally, you should draft your future vision with value stream mapping. When your value stream maps are done, you would have created both a schematic for the current state and a desired future state, and enough clarity to engage in improvements.

The gaps between this and actual practices are your challenges. Various computer programs are available to do the mapping and calculations, but I recommend doing them manually, especially initially, for developing better understanding and enhanced involvement by all persons involved. Once a future state VSM has been completed, a computerized model could be used to clean it up. Then, additional improvements on the mapped process should again be done manually.

3.6 Practical Problem Solving and A3s

A3 reporting forms, which measure about 11 inches by 13 inches, can be used for project management, project status, small or large project coordination, meeting minutes and follow-ups, make-buy decisions, proposals of new ideas or changes in practical problem solving (PPS), or just about any type of communication audience. I have used PPS forms for all these purposes in the planning, construction and running of the Lansing Grand River Assembly Plant. The same format was used, with commonality between forms, but some differentiated slightly for safety, quality and maintenance/manufacturing reliability purposes. There are many available templates to do PPS forms. Some are formatted to do the eight disciplines of problem solving (8D), which can handle more complex problems. Most A3s have informational areas, such as:

- Problem description area;
- Focus area clarification/deliverables;
- 5 Whys, root cause and/or tools;
- Countermeasures;
- Implementation steps;
- Timing and progress tracking;
- Sketch or other clarification;
- Follow-up;
- Place for signatures for buy-in;
- Sharing learning.

Basically, the A3 is a single page communication tool, with everything you need to convey a message or make a decision. It's much easier to throw lots of information and data in front of people instead of consolidating your message clearly and concisely on one page.

> "If you can't explain it simply, you don't understand it well enough."
> Albert Einstein

Some A3s have a signature box for individuals to approve specific actions. Another use of the signature box is to get some buy-in for controversial or difficult decisions in advance of your presentation. Others would see up-front that you have support for your proposal, which quickens decision-making time. The use of a practical problem-solving A3:

- Supports PDCA/PDSA;
- Helps identify problem root causes;

- Facilitates kaizen;
- Promotes team member involvement at all levels;
- Guides problem-solving thinking.

Figure 3.22 is a PPS A3 basic template that shows, at a very general level, areas that are typically included. The amount of detail in each area depends on the intended use. The best PPS forms are those that you design to fit your organization and its tools and techniques, processes, flow of information, etc. So, the forms can be very simple, with not much more than what's shown in Figure 3.22, or they can have much more detail. Just remember, keep it to one page. If you are starting with no background in the use of A3s, there are some good overview books available now. More importantly, keep in mind that although A3s stimulate continuous improvement, the implementation of A3s is a cultural change in itself that requires understanding and support.

The key thing about a PPS form or any A3 is the ability to adjust or change it to what you need to best convey your message or perform problem-solving actions. Key sections of each form should be standardized and required, with some flexibility for specific needs. A3 forms can be computerized, but I recommend filling out the form by hand to keep it plant floor focused. The A3 also can be used as a visual control to monitor progress, provide feedback and transfer lessons learned from one area or plant to another.

REFERENCES

1. Weber, Austin. "Lean Thinking Helps Eaton Stay Healthy." *Assembly Magazine*, October 2010: pp. 30-37.
2. Aberdeen Group. *The Lean Strategies Benchmark Report: Manufacturing Excellence Moves to the Value Chain*. Boston: Aberdeen Group Inc., June, 2004.
3. Womack, James P. and Jones, Daniel T. *Lean Thinking: Banish Waste and Create Wealth in Your Corporation*. New York City: Simon and Schuster, 1996.
4. Adler, Paul S. *The 'Learning Bureaucracy': New United Motor Manufacturing, Inc*. Los Angeles: School of Business Administration, University of Southern California, 1992.
5. El-Homsi, Anwar and Slutsky, Jeff L. *Corporate Sigma: Optimizing the Health of Your Company with Systems Thinking*. Boca Raton: CRC Press, 2009.
6. Lansing Grand River Assembly Plant opening and related public presentations in 2001 and 2002.
7. Carpenter, Teresa. "Widespread Workplace Organization – Taking 5S Strategies to the Next Level." *Lean Healthcare Exchange*. June 2, 2010, http://www.leanhealthcareexchange.com/?p=777.
8. Bresko, Mike. "The 5S Method of Improvement – Enhancing Safety, Productivity and Culture. *Uptime Magazine* Aug/Sept 2009: pp. 32-35.
9. NASA. *Root Cause Analysis Overview*. Office of Safety & Mission Assurance, Chief Engineers Office, 2003; http://www.hq.nasa.gov/office/codeq/rca/rootcauseppt.pdf.
10. Younes, Lina. "Put an End to Junk Mail." *It's Our Environment*. EPA Blog About Our World, February 26, 2009.
11. United States Postal Service. Postal Facts 2014.
12. Nakajima, Seiichi. *TPM Development Program: Implementing Total Productive Maintenance*. New York City: Productivity Press, 1989.
13. Galsworth, Gwendolyn. *Visual Workplace, Visual Thinking*. Portland: Visual-Lean Enterprise Press, 2005.

14. Hinckley, Martin. "Controlling Pharmaceutical Manufacturing Mistakes." *Pharmaceutical Manufacturing*, June 23, 2008; http://www.pharmamanufacturing.com/articles/2008/078/.
15. Moubray, John. *Reliability-Centered Maintenance*. New York City: Industrial Press, Inc., 1997.
16. Ibid.
17. The Aladon Network. *7 Basic Questions*; http://www.thealadonnetwork.com/about-rcm/about-rcm2-2/7-basic-questions-of-rcm/.
18. Carlson, Carl S. *Effective FMEAs: Achieving Safe, Reliable and Economical Products and Processes Using Failure Mode and Effects Analysis*. Hoboken: John Wiley and Sons, Inc., 2012.
19. Naval Air Systems Command. "Acquisition & In-Service Reliability Centered Maintenance (RCM) Flowchart." *NAVAIR 6.0 Logistics and Industrial Operations*, www.navair.navy.mil/logistics/rcm/.
20. Wright, T.P. *Factors Affecting the Cost of Airplanes, Section II*. Copies of original publication provided in a training class at General Motors Institute, 1970s: p.2.
21. Hirschmann, Winfred. "Profit from The Learning Curve." *Harvard Business Review* No. 64107, January 1964: pp. 105-119.
22. Smith, D.B. and Larsson, J.L. "The Impact of Learning on Cost: The Case of Heart Transplantation." *Hospital & Health Services Administration*. Spring 1989: pp. 85-97.
23. Hirsch, W.Z. "Firm Progress Ratios." *Econometrica*, Vol. 24, No. 2, 1956: pp. 136-143.
24. Ibid, Section II.
25. Nakajima, Seiichi. *TPM Development Program: Implementing Total Productive Maintenance*. New York City: Productivity Press, 1989.
26. Plant Engineering Technical Staff. *Total Productive Maintenance*. Tokyo: Japan Institute of Plant Maintenance (JIPM), March13, 1986: pp. 119-123.
27. Feature Focus. "TPM Raises Equipment Efficiency and Cuts Plant Maintenance Costs." *Industrial Maintenance & Plant Operation Magazine*, September 1990: pp. 46-48.
28. Brue, Greg. *Six SIGMA for Managers*. New York City: McGraw-Hill, 2002.
29. Lonergan, Edward. Quoted in *Capitalizing on Complexity: Insights from the Global Chief Executive Officer Study*. Somers: IBM, 2010.
30. SAE International White Paper. *Systems Engineering/Complexity Reduction Through Industry Collaboration: Mobility Industry Works to Simplify Today's Electronics-Intensive Integrated Vehicles*. June 2014: p. 1.
31. Gatchell, S. *The Effect of Part Proliferation on Assembly Line Operators' Decision Making Capabilities*. SAE Technical Paper 790498, 1979.
32. Iyengar, Sheena. "How to Make Choosing Easier." *TED Talk*, November, 2011.
33. Katzel, Jeanine. "Safe Journey: GM Program Strives to Make Safety Everyone's Job." *Control Engineering Magazine*, 7 July 2010.
34. Weber, Austin. "State of the Profession 2009: Ready for the Recovery." *Assembly Magazine* 29 June 2009; http://www.assemblymag.com/articles/86601-state-of-the-profession-2009-ready-for-the-recovery.
35. Galsworth, Gwendolyn D. and Tonkin, Lea A.P. "Invasion of the Kaizen Blitzers." *Target Marketing Magazine*, Volume II, Number 2: p. 34.
36. Ibid, Womack, J.P., et al, pp. 223-224.
37. Meyerhofer, Andy. *Kaikaku: Moving Beyond Kaizen: One Organization's Story of Radical Process Change Using 3P*. Shelton: Productivity, Inc.: 2012; http://www.productivityinc.com/resources/case-studiesarticles/kaikaku-moving-beyond-kaizen/.
38. Livingston, William L. *The New Plague: Organizations in Complexity*. Stewart: F.E.S. Limited Publishing, 1985.
39. Rother, Mike. *Toyota Kata*. New York City: McGraw-Hill, 2010.
40. Womack, James. Keynote talk on Gemba Walks, IndustryWeek Conference, April 5, 2011.

Chapter 4
Enablers for Successful Change and Sustainable Continuous Improvement

> *"It is no use saying, 'We are doing our best.' You have got to succeed in doing what is necessary."*
> — Winston Churchill

> *"Not everything that counts can be counted, and not everything that can be counted counts."*
> — Sign hanging in Albert Einstein's office at Princeton University

4.1 Core Enablers

"Only a third of excellent companies remain excellent over the long term. An even smaller percentage of organizational change programs succeed."[1]

The question continually being asked is, "What are the enablers for successfully implementing my change?" Of course, there are common things that can and should be done as depicted by the various change models. However, some things are very situational and need to be handled for change to take place. So, predictions of success are often difficult with the numerous potential influences that can drastically and, sometimes, almost instantaneously change the anticipated outcome. As Yogi Berra stated, "It's tough to make predictions, especially about the future."

People change because they are inspired by a clear, believable vision, or there is a desperate situation, like your plant is the poorest performing in your company or when compared to your competitor's plants. Having said that, there are still many things that can be done to greatly improve your chances of success. To achieve or maintain competitive advantage in any industry, you must recognize the need for and be skilled in implementing change. How well your organization accepts change is critical to the continuous improvement of your operations in any field (e.g., medical, manufacturing, process, assembly, energy, logistics, etc.). At the core of successful applications are four major categories[2] that are regularly evidenced.

I. People as the center
II. Quality as the driving force
III. Engaging management style
IV. Small team continuous improvement

Chapter 4

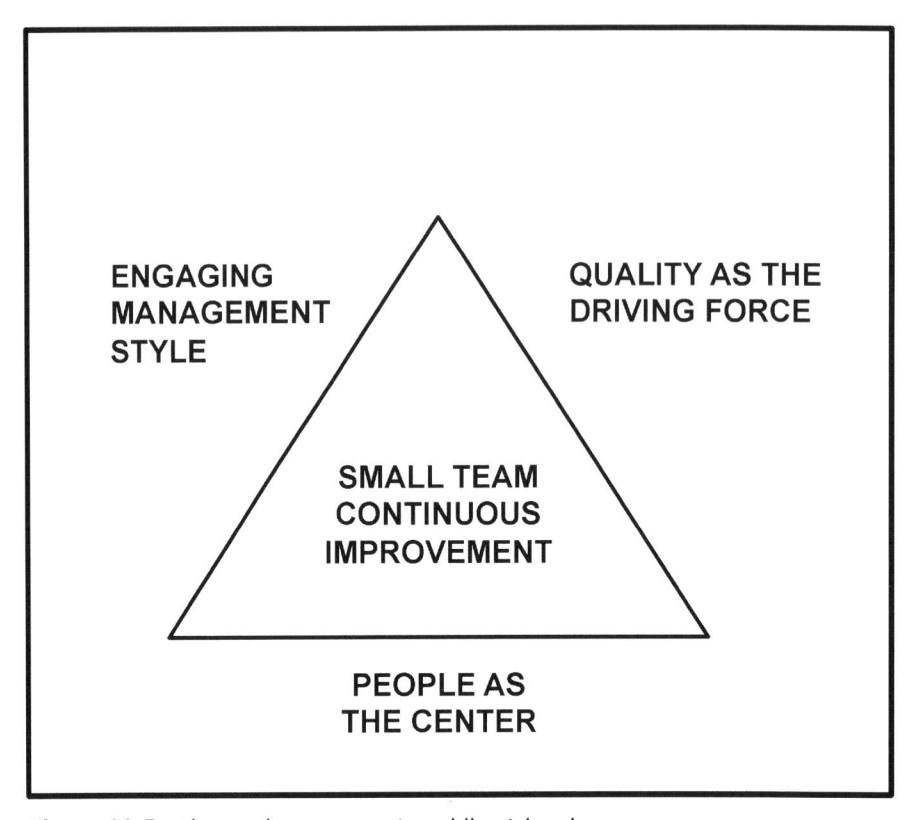

Figure 4.1: Continuous improvement enabling triangle

Each of the three categories (Figure 4.1) must be congruent with the other two, with the fourth category, continuous improvement, persisting in all of them. Most companies will agree with these items, but critical is the detail to which they are understood and applied. Presented for each category are several opportunities and the corresponding actions/understandings needed to improve the chances for successful application. The more enablers you have in place, the greater your likelihood of success.

4.1.1 People As the Center

Opportunity #1. Recognize that people still run the place.
Actions/Understandings

1. Use early employee involvement to enable successful continuous improvement.
2. Introducing successful change requires an understanding of the impact on both the work system and social system.
3. Assure everyone that people will always be the most essential part of any production system.
4. Bring decision-making to the lowest level.

5. Make certain everyone understands the big picture in running the business/production system.
6. If change is required, make sure the change is wanted. The new state must be more rewarding/desirable than the present state for the change to take hold.
7. Have flexibility with the final form based on the workforce.
8. Involve the first level of supervision in the planning and implementation of change programs. This can minimize the related risks. Change the foreperson/supervisor role and title to team leader or coach.

Opportunity #2. Manage stress in the workplace.
Actions/Understandings

1. Managers need to better understand and be sensitive to stress related to various activities, such as:
   a. stress of an operator working with a robot/automated device.
   b. when the supervisor no longer understands the technical language of those above him/her.
   c. when the supervisor no longer understands the intricacies of the technology below him/her.
   d. stress of change.
   e. stress from increasing organizational and competitive complexity.
2. Properly pace the rate of change.
3. Ensure the change is manageable.

Opportunity #3. Apply ergonomics.
Actions/Understandings

1. Provide working conditions (e.g., workplace, environment, job tasks) that consider human limitations and capabilities to make the workers in the process most effective, while optimizing the working conditions.
2. Consider and plan for ergonomics at the design stage of projects and programs. Then, utilize a follow-up program to evaluate and improve.
3. Ergonomists interested in implementation must develop an acute sensitivity to the relationship between human performance and business needs. Measures should be developed to show how human performance contributes to the needs of the business.

Opportunity #4. Develop a highly trained workforce.
Actions/Understandings

1. Enhance transfer of technology, but keep in mind that the best solution is the simplest one that works.
2. Recognize and promote the critical nature of education and training.
3. Support and adhere to the training schedule.
4. Develop and maintain skills in the core technologies needed for the business.

4.1.2 Quality As the Driving Force

Opportunity #1. Manage quality into the business.
Actions/Understandings

1. Develop a sense of customer. Measure what the customer values as quality.
2. Make decisions based on long-term customer satisfaction.
3. Evaluate the quality impact of any change.
4. Use profound knowledge/decisions based on data.

Opportunity #2. Implement statistical process control.
Actions/Understandings

1. Minimize variation.
2. Constantly improve quality.
3. Focus on the process.

Opportunity #3. Implement a robust reliability and maintainability (R&M) process.
Actions/Understandings

1. Implement people R&M to minimize human error.
2. Implement process R&M to minimize variability and maximize operations.
3. Implement product R&M to maximize quality and customer satisfaction.

4.1.3 Engaging Management Style

Opportunity #1. Manage workplace attitudes.
Actions/Understandings

1. Use positive leadership.
2. Make sure everyone understands the importance of their job.
3. Emphasize involvement, accountability and ownership of job tasks; empower the workforce.
4. Project vision with realistic expectations;
5. Work with a sense of urgency.

Opportunity #2. Use a management style that supports implementation of new ideas and change.
Actions/Understandings

1. Support teamwork.
2. Use consensus decision-making, but clearly define the scope up front.
3. Communicate what decision will be made by leadership, taking input and providing clarification.

4. Allow for organization learning.
5. Match the organizational and systems/procedural architecture.
6. Job descriptions should be minimal/flexible, but standardized work must be clearly defined.
7. Formal reviews and appraisals should be eliminated and replaced with continuous discussions to guide and remove barriers.
8. Promote information sharing.
9. Practice participative management.
10. Listen more to customers and employees.
11. Establish a reward system to reward those making the change.
12. Reward those who support the operators.
13. Desired state or change should support the strategic business objectives.
14. Your actions, in terms of what you spend time on and how you handle situations, will send a message to your organization. Management style will determine the organizational structure and how it actually functions, regardless of any organizational chart.
15. Reward balance to those who apply the proper level of people, technology and other resources.

Opportunity #3. Apply a common focus and actions toward objectives.
Actions/Understandings

1. The vision must be clear, focused and consistent, especially when leadership changes.
2. Build organization systems to support the vision.
3. Concentrate on a few things and do them well:
    a. Make the key items highly visible and simple to understand.
    b. Goals must be realistic and appear attainable.
4. Use the philosophy that everyone has a customer.
5. Discipline the organization to act in the agreed upon manner. Reward those who follow the discipline plan and do what they said they would.

4.1.4 Small Team Continuous Improvement

Opportunity #1. Plan extensively.
Actions/Understandings

1. Plan extensively, but execute in a timely manner.
2. Follow a plan to get from the current state to the desired state.
3. Stay with the plan and change direction only at predetermined evaluation checkpoints.
4. Implement incrementally.
5. Define tasks at different stages of development.
6. Management must set the vision, but decentralize execution.
7. Design for what will work in your organization.
8. Have the fundamentals in place before implementing the change or new technology.

Chapter 4

Opportunity #2. Manage complexity.
Actions/Understandings

1. Simplify.
2. Use the proper level of automation, with the proper balance between people and technology.
3. First make it work manually, then automate if necessary.
4. Commonize and standardize where feasible.
5. Emphasize practical application.

Opportunity #3. Make continuous improvements forever.
Actions/Understandings

1. Persist in solving problems.
2. Use root cause analysis.
3. Ask why until the real reason for the problem surfaces.
4. Use value-added justifications.
5. Use a practical problem-solving tool/process in all parts of the organization.

The four categories and accompanying issues and actions/understandings present key enablers to successful change implementation. Like most destinations, there are several paths that will lead to the same end point. Some paths are long, some short, some rough, some smooth, some slow, some fast. Several of the actions/understandings can be recognized in other strategies and programs. For example, Dr. W. Edwards Deming's 14 Points for management present a long-range quality control program. It may be more accurate to say that he outlines a combination of management styles and guidelines.

Dr. Deming's 14 Points[3] are:
1. Create constancy of purpose toward improvement of product and service, with the aim to become competitive, to stay in business, and to provide jobs.
2. Adopt the new philosophy.
3. Cease dependence on mass inspection to achieve quality. Build quality into the product in the first place.
4. End the practice of awarding business on the basis of price tag alone. Instead, minimize total cost. Move toward a single supplier for any one item on a long-term relationship of loyalty and trust.
5. Improve constantly and forever every activity in the company, to improve quality and productivity, and thus constantly decrease costs.
6. Institute modern methods of training and education on the job, including management.
7. Institute positive leadership. The aim of leaders should be to help people, machines, and gadgets to do a better job.
8. Drive out fear, so that everyone may work effectively for the company.

Enablers for Successful Change and Sustainable Continuous Improvement

9. Break down barriers between individuals, groups and departments.
10. Eliminate slogans, exhortations, and targets for the workforce asking for zero defects and new levels of productivity. Such exhortations only create adversarial relationships, as the bulk of the causes of low quality and low productivity belong to the system and thus lie beyond the power of the workforce.
11. Eliminate works standards (quotas). Substitute leadership.
12. Remove barriers that rob the worker (hourly and salary) of his/her rights to pride of workmanship. Emphasize quality above everything else.
13. Institute a vigorous program of education and retraining.
14. Take action to accomplish the transformation. Involve the entire workforce.

In Dr. Deming's 14 Points, quality is the driving force on which all is focused. Figure 4.2 groups Deming's 14 Points, which can be aligned with the three other success factor categories. Although several of the points could go into more than one category, note that seven of the fourteen points are mainly management style.

Figure 4.2: Deming's 14 Points grouped by success factor categories

	Success Factor Categories	Dr. Deming's 14 Points
I.	People as the center	6, 12, 13
II.	Quality as the driving force	Focus of all points
III.	Engaging management style	1, 2, 7, 8, 9, 10, 11
IV.	Small team continuous improvement	3, 4, 5, 14

Of the four success factor categories, quality as the driving force has the best foothold in industry. Employees in most industries are better in understanding the importance of minimizing variation, targeted and stable processes, and statistical process control at the plant floor level. Of greater concern is current industrial growth in the other three categories. Being people-centered and following an engaging management style both relate to the work social system, while small team continuous improvement must spread to all parts of the business. We must get better at getting better.

> *"Practice does not make perfect. Perfect practice makes perfect."*
> — Vince Lombardi

Continuous improvement is a journey. Having an engaged workforce continually striving for a better way of doing their jobs is also at the core of achieving business excellence. Ultimately, it's how well people accept and apply their current standardized work and how willing they are to change and improve that will decide the success of anything you do.

Chapter 4

On the journey of continuous improvement, companies typically will benchmark other companies that are doing it well. This eventually results in the identification of new tools and perceived concepts. Without living in the observed system on a daily basis, the tools, techniques and technology benefits are often misunderstood relative to the practices that enable the positive results.

As mentioned earlier, I had the opportunity to periodically work on the production floor of NUMMI, the Toyota and General Motors joint venture in Fremont, California. I did the same in Eisenach, Germany for the General Motors plant that was managed with similar concepts. I then had the privilege to be part of the leadership team that did the design, build and operation of the world-class Lansing Grand River assembly plant, where all leaders were required to teach and mentor these continuous improvement concepts with employees throughout the entire operation. It was these kinds of experiences that clarify what was often cited, but not initially completely understood:

> " – you have to see that the rigid specification is the very thing that makes the flexibility and creativity possible."[4]

Toyota uses four rules to guide the design, operation and improvement of everything. The rules are:

"**Rule 1:** All work shall be highly specified as to content, sequence, timing and outcome.

Rule 2: Every customer-supplier connection must be direct and there must be an unambiguous yes or no way to send requests and receive responses.

Rule 3: The pathway for every product and service must be simple and direct.

Rule 4: Any improvement must be made in accordance with the scientific method, under the guidance of a teacher at the lowest possible level of the organization."[5]

These rules provide an organized and rigorous, yet flexible, approach to continuous improvement.

4.2 Individuals and Teams

In order to have successful teams, you need to have engaged employees.

> "Coming together is a beginning; keeping together is progress; working together is success."
> — Henry Ford

If you have a high number of employees that are not engaged, things will most likely get worse. Good employees will start to make comments or ask questions, like:

Enablers for Successful Change and Sustainable Continuous Improvement

- Why am I going home late every day when others who don't accomplish as much go home on time?
- I work hard all day long while others take long lunches and perform non-work tasks during working hours and nothing is done about it.
- Goals change almost monthly. Is it volume or quality that we strive for?
- I make suggestions, but nobody pays any attention to them. Sometimes, these same ideas get implemented later by a management mandate and they ask why we haven't done it that way earlier.
- My boss doesn't step up to poor performers, so it can't be that important.
- There doesn't seem to be any standardized operating procedures, so best methods or any standardized practices are not followed by anyone. This makes continuous improvement difficult because everyone wants to do it their way, with no baseline for improvement.
- Regardless of how hard and long I work, it's never enough. The goal is just raised with no discussion on process or quality of work impact.

In this kind of work environment, your employees will function enough to keep their jobs, but you will not experience the benefits of an engaged workforce. When a team sees slackers or stars getting away with bad behavior or getting preferential treatment on a regular basis, it's just a matter of time before performance suffers. This may not be verbalized by team members, but more people start doing a little less here and there and the downward spiral has begun.

Furthermore, today's gadgets, phones and other electronic capabilities are making younger employees more impersonal. More and more people would rather send texts, e-mails and other social media rather than deal with individuals directly. At the Lansing Grand River plant, we had an informal rule that if you were going to see someone in the next 24 hours, handle the communication in person. It was a lesson observed at the Eisenach, Germany assembly plant. The more you share and discuss the daily issues and develop a relationship, the easier it will be to discuss the tough issues as they arise.

Compare that to when Carol Bartz, former CEO of Yahoo, broke the news of her firing in a memo from her iPad® to Yahoo employees. In the message, she wrote, "I am very sad to tell you that I've just been fired over the phone by Yahoo's chairman of the board."[6] It sent an immediate message to an entire organization. It's important to remember the need to build relationships with people who run the factories and organizations.

"According to a recent Watson Wyatt survey, highly engaged employees miss twenty percent fewer days of work and are almost eighty percent more likely to be top performers. About seventy-five percent of them exceed or far exceed expectations in their most recent performance review. These workers also tend to be more resilient to and supportive of organizational change initiatives."[7]

The Gallup Management Journal surveyed U.S. employees in 2005 to gain insight on how happiness and well-being affect their job performance. Respondents were categorized into three types of employees (Figure 4.3).

Chapter 4

(adapted from Gallup survey, Krueger and Killham, 2005)

Of engaged employees, 77% felt the supervisor focused on their strengths / positive characteristics

Of engaged employees, 45% of happiness experienced comes from work

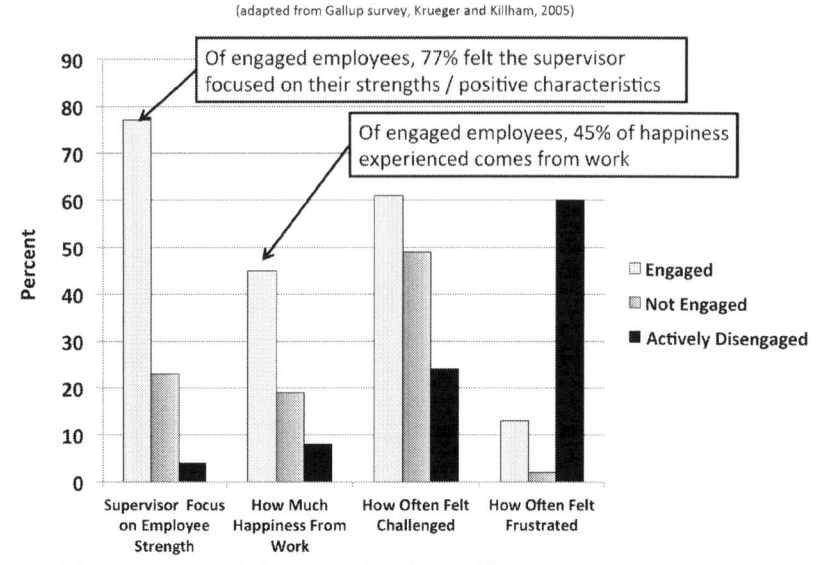

Figure 4.3: Importance of the supervisor in workforce engagement

"1. Engaged employees work with passion and feel a profound connection to their company. They drive innovation and move the organization forward.
2. Not Engaged employees are essentially 'checked out.' They're sleepwalking through their workday, putting time, but not energy or passion, into their work.
3. Actively Disengaged employees aren't just unhappy at work, they're busy acting out their unhappiness. Every day, these workers undermine what their engaged coworkers accomplish."[8]

Twenty-seven percent of the respondents were engaged employees, fifty-nine percent were not engaged employees and fourteen percent were actively disengaged employees. For me, the most important fact here is that you still have an opportunity with eighty-six percent (combined total of engaged and not engaged employees) of the workforce if you can motivate the not engaged group. If you are successful, you have more than six times (86/14 = 6.1) the likelihood of success in changes, based on their level of engagement at work. For engaged employees, forty-five percent of their happiness experiences came from work, compared to only eight percent for the actively disengaged.

The Gallup survey results,[9] based on about one thousand employees, show the importance of good supervision (i.e., direct boss) on engagement. Engaged employees who are happy are more likely to be able to handle change and be willing to solve problems in the workplace.

> *"People don't come to Toyota to work. They come to think."*
> — Taiichi Ohno

The four key items that NUMMI used to focus on team members were mutual trust and respect, fairness and equity, teamwork, and involvement. This built the foundation for all work processes. Also, highly engaged employees are more trusting of their leadership. What is it that gets people to want to work together? "Truth is the most resilient and lasting tie for connecting people and organizations."[10]

"We all have a deep need for a sense of:
1. *Uniqueness* as individuals.
2. *Union* with something greater than thyself.
3. *Usefulness* to others.
4. *Understanding* about our lives and work.

When these needs are respected and met, we're capable of experiencing deep fulfillment and personal satisfaction in our lives and in our work."[11]

"What used to be called the 'soft issues' of business will increasingly be the differentiators of sustainable excellence in every industry in the world."[12]

4.3 Leaders

The tools and techniques in Chapter 3 are all good for continuous improvement and to attack specific issues. But, it takes leadership to get there. "What drives the healthcare improvement engine? Most important is a leadership mind-set that expects everyone in the healthcare organization, including executives, to actively apply scientific thinking (PDCA/PDSA) to remove waste and variation."[13]

Leadership is the ability to motivate and influence the behaviors of other people. The performance of the organization is an extension of the demonstrated attitude of its leaders. This is a trait that can be found at any occupation and work level. Trust is at the foundation of every leader's ability to gain and sustain fellowship. Stephen Covey[14] categorizes trust into four components. They are integrity and intent, which define your character, and capability and result, which define your competence. Measuring where trust is lacking in any of these four categories provides direction on where to build trust. The speed at which you can assess and extend trust determines how fast a business can benefit from improved employee involvement.

Figure 4.4 shows the most important enablers to sustain change. From one hundred and fifty companies, the three highest are leadership support, communications (clear vision/feedback) and trust/buy-in. When asking the same group how future improvements can be obtained, leadership and engaged workforce (buy-in) were the two highest responses (Figure 4.5). I don't see anything unique about these responses since the same list of enablers have been talked about for as long as I can remember. The opportunity is still there for companies to use them as a competitive advantage.

"Companies with the highest levels of effective communication experienced a twenty-six percent total return to shareholders from 1996 to 2002, compared to a fifteen percent return experienced by firms that communicate least effectively."[15]

Chapter 4

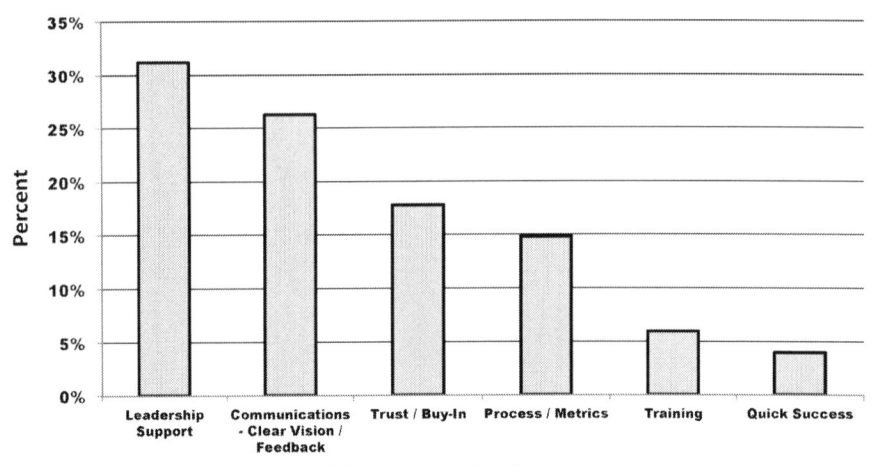

Figure 4.4: Most important enablers to sustain change

When touring a RockTenn Company mill and discussing teams, they shared a pocket card titled, "Making decisions with trust and integrity" that stated their culture. On the back, it had several reminders, questions such as:

- As a result of this decision or action, will people trust me more or less?
- Am I making this decision or action with integrity?
- Am I being honest?
- Am I withholding facts or information that might help others better understand the situation at hand?
- How would I want to be treated if roles were reversed?

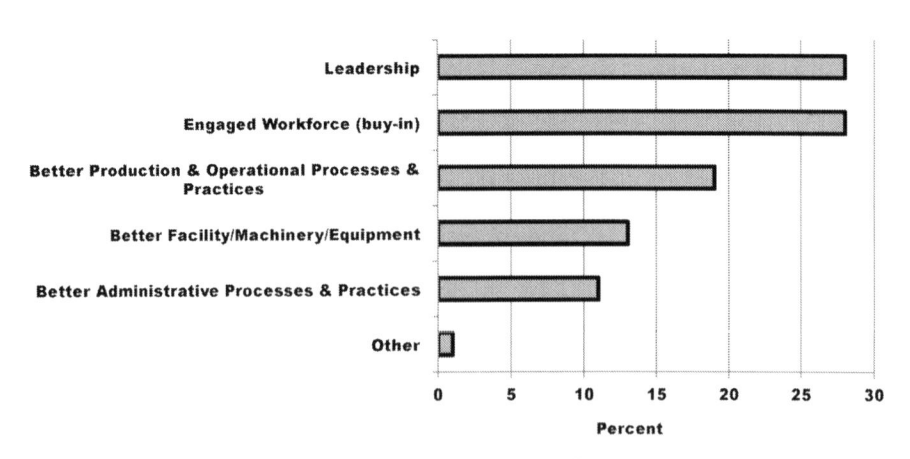

Figure 4.5: How future improvements can be obtained

It's important that leaders understand change management because being flexible and adaptable to future needs will be paramount to company survival. Operating along the lines of the old saying, "If you do what you always did, you will get what you always got," is risky in a quickly changing business environment. "A 2009 Swedish study tracking 3,122 men for ten years found that those with bad bosses suffered twenty to forty percent more heart attacks than those with good bosses."[16]

"Allied Signal used Six Sigma (1990s) to get thirty-one quarters of thirteen percent or more of growth (earnings per share). In 2000, there was new leadership and just eighteen month later, the Six Sigma culture was gone."[17] To instill a culture that will survive a top leadership change is very, very difficult. "At Toyota, the process and the principles are the star, not the CEO."[18] This works because when leaderships changes, it's still the same philosophy being practiced.

"By getting the leadership of Chrysler, Daimler gutted the culture that Chrysler was proudly building, a culture that made companies like Toyota nervous. Instead of building on this proud culture and protecting it, Daimler tore it down through radical cost cutting, eviscerating Chrysler's strengths. From Toyota's perspective, the appropriate response might be, 'Thank you, Daimler, for doing what we could not and would not do to a competitor. You destroyed its culture."[19]

The same one hundred and fifty companies in Figures 4.4 and 4.5 were also asked, "What is the best metric to measure involvement?" Figure 4.6 shows that thirty-nine percent replied "results." The problem is that good results can be attained in a negative way, at least for some time. Tracking the number of suggestions, kaizen events and FMEAs

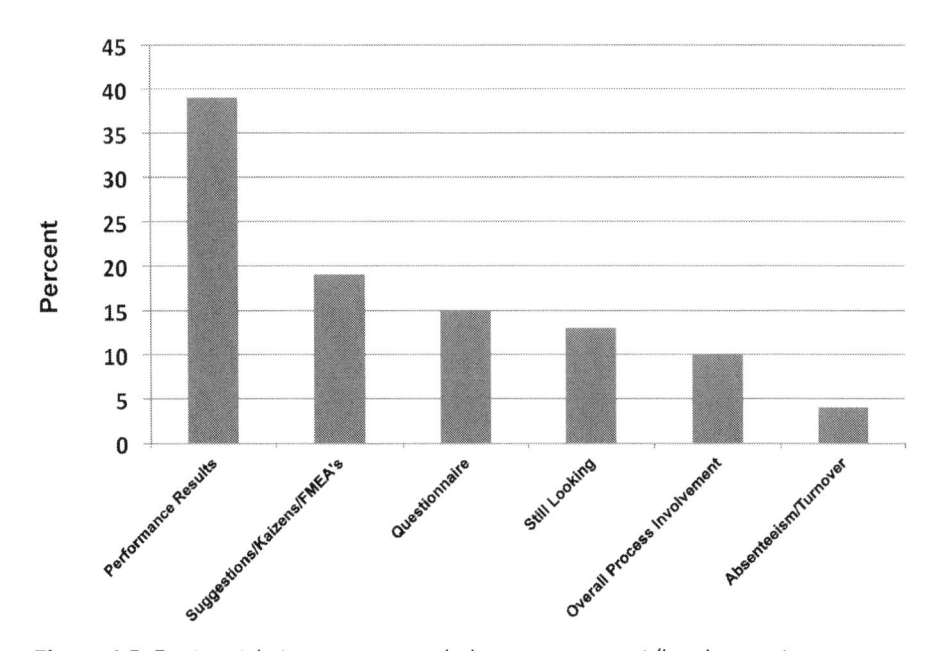

Figure 4.6: Best metric to measure workplace engagement/involvement

Chapter 4

are all good indicators if these are voluntary events versus a corporate mandate, such as everyone must do a specified number of kaizen events. Thirteen percent said they don't have a good measure. Fifteen percent use an outside party to collect information on employee satisfaction and engagement. Interesting was that just about every company that uses a questionnaire volunteered that, "They don't believe the responses." They feel employees just put down answers they think the company wants to hear. There is a lack of trust and good metrics (i.e., leading indicators) to monitor employee engagement.

Good leadership allows employees to grow and take risks. The focus should be on continuous improvement of the system. Poor leadership seeks to find blame and amplifies the issues, resulting in discouraged employees and lower performance. Early in my career, I was told that, "If you are leading and turn around and don't see any followers, you are just a visionary. If you are leading and turn around and see many followers, then you are a leader." It's important that all levels of the organization understand the vision. Top leaders sponsor most initiatives that are implemented at the grassroots level. Middle management or first-line supervisors are frequently left in the void. Sometimes, plant floor employees get more training on technology and processes than their direct supervisors because of the time available to get training. "Middle managers are not the problem. They're often accused of dragging their feet and causing bureaucracy, but this is more often a failure of top management to clearly articulate objectives related to operational excellence."[20]

"For the next twenty years, you are promoted once every thirty to fifty months. During this time, the culture becomes more and more an instinctive part of you. Indeed, one of the reasons you've gotten promoted is because you fit and get along with the people who decide on promotions. After a while, although you may not be aware of it, you are teaching the new hires the culture. Indeed, at age fifty, as a senior level manager, you may be almost oblivious to the culture."[21]

In *Good to Great*, Jim Collins states, "to be clear, the main point of this chapter is not just about assembling the right team – that's nothing new. The main point is to first get the right people on the bus and the wrong people off the bus before you figure out where to drive it."[22] I agree with this concept, in general, but if the same top leadership picks the people for the bus, what has really changed?

Five keys to effective leadership and empowerment were noted by William Byham, author of Zapp! and keynote speaker at the 2013 International Maintenance Conference (IMC).

1. Maintain or enhance self-esteem.
2. Listen and respond with empathy.
3. Ask for help and encourage involvement.
4. Share thoughts, feelings and rationale to build trust.
5. Provide support without removing responsibility to build ownership.

In commenting on Alan Mulally, CEO of Ford, Bill Vlasic, stated, "Admitting a shortcoming in Mulally-speak was a 'gem.' Coming back after a failure was a sign of 'emotional resilience.' Owning up to problems was 'liberating.' He had a knack for making people feel wanted and respected, whether in the employee cafeteria or in a dealer's showroom, around the boardroom or on the factory floor."[23]

The core competencies of a leader are:

<u>**Strong interpersonal skills**</u>, including the ability to assess other's behavior, organize ideas, communicate effectively and motivate.

<u>**Personal qualities**</u>, the right personal qualities help build confidence and make everything a leader attempts more effective. Although there are numerous qualities that could be listed, a strong and balanced work ethic and good personal efficiency skills are an excellent foundation on which leaders can build.

<u>**Technical knowledge**</u>, includes those skills related to the organization's products, services, or processes used to create them. Every leader, even those who are not in direct supervisory positions, should have this knowledge.[24]

On September 15, 2009, Colonel Henry "Hank" Hartsfield Jr., University of Tennessee (UT) alumnus and NASA astronaut, made a keynote address at UT on leadership and teams. As part of his presentation, he shared NASA's Foundations of Mission Control, which are:

➢ To instill within ourselves these qualities essential for professional excellence:

- Discipline – Being able to follow as well as lead, knowing we must master ourselves before we can master our work.
- Competence – There being no substitute for total preparations and complete dedication for space will not tolerate the careless or indifferent.
- Confidence – Believing in ourselves as well as others, knowing we must master fear and hesitation before we can succeed.
- Responsibility – Realizing that it cannot be shifted to others, for it belongs to each of us; we must answer for what we do, or fail to do.
- Toughness – Taking a stand when we must; to try again, and again, even if it means following a more difficult path.
- Teamwork – Respecting and utilizing the ability of others, realizing that we work toward a common goal, for success depends on the efforts of all.

➢ To always be aware that suddenly and unexpectedly we may find ourselves in a role where our performance has ultimate consequences.

➢ To recognize that the greatest error is not to have tried and failed, but that in trying, we did not give it our best effort.

4.4 Followers

By now, it should be evident that teams, groups, and corporations succeed or fail based on not just how well they are led, but how well followers follow. Leadership is still important. What the top bosses do is highly magnified in the eyes of most employees. If the CEO makes an emotional and factual presentation supported by walking the talk or leading by example, then the organization has a chance. If the CEO rides down the elevator with golf shoes in hand midday on a Friday and does not acknowledge others in the elevator, no future words will help the executive recover from the coffee room discussion around that event. By recover, I am referring to employees not wanting to be fully engaged. Employees will go the extra mile for bosses they trust and respect.

Data from one survey showed that, "inadequate resources, poor planning, bad ideas, and unforeseen external events account for less than a third of the failures. More than seventy percent resulted from poor organizational health, manifested in symptoms, such as negative employee attitudes and unproductive management behavior."[25]

A great example of exemplary team behavior and leadership can be easily described in *Lessons From The Geese*[26], which I have seen quoted often over many years.

Fact 1: As each bird flaps its wings, it creates an uplift draft for the following bird. By flying in a V formation, the whole flock adds a greater flying range than if one bird flew alone.
Lesson 1: People who share a common direction and sense of community can get where they are going more easily because they are traveling on the strength of one another.
Winning teams already understand it's how well you perform together that matters. It's that common sense of direction, purpose and community that provides synergy.

Fact 2: Whenever a goose falls out of formation, it feels the drag of trying to fly alone and quickly gets back into formation to take advantage of the lifting power of the bird in front.
Lesson 2: Stay in formation, accept help when we need it and give help when it is needed.
Don't be afraid to ask for or accept help. That's why it's called a team.

Fact 3: When the lead goose gets tired, it rotates back into the formation and another goose goes in the point position.
Lesson 3: Share the task of leadership and do not resent the leader.
Know when to step up and step back. We all have different skills and abilities to help with difficult tasks.

Fact 4: The geese in formation honk from behind to encourage those up front to keep up that speed.
Lesson 4: We need to make sure that our honking is encouraging and not something else.
Encourage your team members when they have a tough challenge; be positive.

Enablers for Successful Change and Sustainable Continuous Improvement

Fact 5: When a goose gets sick, is wounded, or is shot down, two geese drop out of formation to help protect it. They stay with their disabled companion until it is able to fly again or dies.

Lesson 5: If we have as much sense as geese, we will stand by one another in difficult times.

If a team member is struggling, help them. Focus on core values.

What a simple and beautiful reminder of what to do.

I selected these five truisms from a larger list.[27] They make a lot of sense and reinforce some key items to remember.

- "Confidence comes from success, knowledge comes from failure.
- If you are miserable, quit and do something else; if you're still miserable, it's you.
- Success is based on current behavior, not past performance.
- People won't perform for those they don't respect.
- The workplace is about business, not you."

Figure 4.7 shows that there is a three-way relationship around trust.

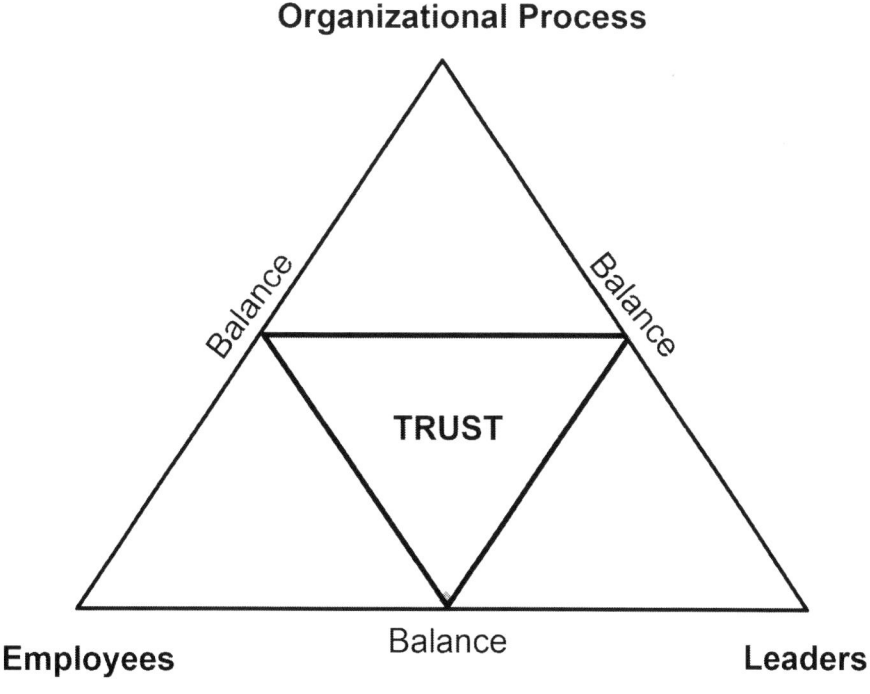

Figure 4.7: Trust relationships

Chapter 4

- Employee must trust the organizational process and leaders.
- Leaders must trust the employees and the organizational process.
- The organizational process must enable employees to function properly regarding what the team members and leaders are capable of and willing to do.

"Since knowledge workers spend half their time on interactions, our research and experience suggest that companies should first explore the productivity barriers that impede these interactions. Armed with a better understanding of the constraints, senior executives can get more bang for their buck by identifying targeted productivity improvement efforts to increase both the efficiency and effectiveness of the interactions between workers."[28]

Focus on work relationships to develop trust and continually improve the workplace. It can best be stated by a sign I saw on a wall at the Nissan battery plant in Smyrna, Tennessee.

> Tell Me – I Forget
> Show Me – I Remember
> Involve Me – I Commit

REFERENCES

1. Keller, Scott and Price, Colin. "Organizational Health: The Ultimate Competitive Advantage." *McKinsey Quarterly*, June, 2011.
2. Adapted from Blache, Klaus. *Success Factors for Implementing Change: A Manufacturing Viewpoint*. Dearborn: Society of Manufacturing Engineers, 1988.
3. Adapted from Deming, Dr. W. Edwards. *Out of the Crisis*. Cambridge: Massachusetts Institute of Technology, 1986; Scherkenbach, William W. *The Deming Route to Quality and Productivity*. Washington, D.C.: Cee Press Books, 1987; and copies distributed at meetings/training with Dr. Deming.
4. Spear, Steven and Bowen, H. Kent. "Decoding the DNA of the Toyota Production System." *Harvard Business Review*, 1999: p. 97.
5. Ibid, p. 98.
6. Swartz, Jon. "Yahoo fires embattled CEO Bartz." *USA Today*, 7 September 2011: p. 1b.
7. Fontelera, Jorina. "Why Having Engaged Employees Matters." *ThomasNet.com*, May 13, 2009: http://news.thomasnet.com/imt/2009/05/13/why-having-engaged-employees-matter-better-business-performance.
8. Krueger, Jerry and Killham, Emily. "At Work Feeling Good Matters." *Gallup*, December 8, 2005: http://www.gallup.com/businessjournal/20311/work-feeling-good-matters.aspx.
9. Ibid, adapted from Gallup survey results.
10. Morris, Tom. *If Aristotle Ran General Motors*. New York City: Henry Holt and Company, Inc., 1997.
11. Ibid.
12. Ibid.
13. Wellman, Joan; Hagan, Pat; and Jeffries, Howard. *Leading the Lean Healthcare Journey: Driving Culture Change to Increase Value*. New York City: Taylor & Francis Group, LLC, 2011.
14. Fox, Tom. "Stephen M.R. Covey's guide to building trust." *The Washington Post*, July 13, 2013: http://www.washingtonpost.com/blogs/on-leadership/wp/2013/07/18/stephen-m-r-coveys-guide-to-building-trust/.

15. Wyatt, Watson. "Connecting Organizational Communication to Financial Performance – 2003/2004 Communication ROI Study." *Institute for Public Relations*, July 12, 2012: http://www.instituteforpr.org/organizational-communication-and-financial-performance/.
16. Sutton, Robert. "Why good bosses tune in to their people." *McKinsey Quarterly*, August, 2010.
17. Power, Brad. "*Keep Your Eye on Process Improvement.*" *Harvard Business Review*, August 18, 2010.
18. Magee, David. *How Toyota Became #1: Leadership Lessons from the World's Greatest Car Company*. New York City: Penguin Group, 2007.
19. Liker, Jeffrey K. *The Toyota Way: 14 Management Principles from The World's Greatest Manufacturer*. New York City: McGraw-Hill, 2004.
20. Thomas, Paul. "Eluding the OpEx Black Hole." *Pharmaceutical Manufacturing*, June 2009: pp. 21-22.
21. Kotter, John. P. "Leading Change." *Harvard Business Review*, January 2007: p. 150.
22. Collins, Jim. *Good to Great*. New York City: HarperCollins Publishers, 2001.
23. Vlasic, Bill. *Once Upon A Car: The Fall and Resurrection of America's Big Three Automakers- GM, Ford and Chrysler*. New York City: Harper Collins Publishers, 2011.
24. Adapted from El-Homsi, Anwar and Slutsky, Jeff. *Corporate Sigma: Optimizing the Health of Your Company with Systems Thinking*. New York City: CRC Press, 2009.
25. Keller, Scott and Price, Colin. "Organizational Health: The ultimate competitive advantage." *McKinsey Quarterly*, June, 2011.
26. Adapted from McNeish, Robert. *Lessons From The Geese*. 1972; http://www.aikentdc.org/Lessons_From_The_Geese.pdf
27. Tobak, Steve. "20 Truisms That Can Change Your Life." *CBS MoneyWatch* 9 December 2010. http://www.cbsnews.com/news/20-business-truisms-that-can-change-your-life/.
28. Matson, Eric and Prusak, Laurence. "Boosting the productivity of knowledge workers." *McKinsey Quarterly*, September 2010.

Chapter 5
Model for Sustainable Change

"It is not the strongest of the species that survives, nor the most intelligent, but the one most responsive to change."
— Charles Darwin

Life is like riding a bicycle. To keep your balance, you must keep moving."
— Albert Einstein

As global best practices, leveraging of resources and competition become the norm, the ability to quickly implement change is not just expected, but required for success and survival. In addition, the ability to engage the entire workforce is paramount for achieving that success.

To attain and sustain the ability to make numerous small, ongoing improvements and large, complex changes when necessary will largely determine your ability to compete. There are various change models in use today, but many appear to have a common foundation that in some way emulate or stem from Lewin, Gleicher, Beckhard, Harris, and Kotter. If you've found a change model that works for you, keep using it! You're doing better than most. I always say that the best model to use is the one that works for your team culture. Don't force a change model just because a well performing company or competitor is having success with it. However, if your workforce is not as engaged as they could be, or your change projects don't all work out or aren't sustainable, then consider the proposed model from my experiences.

5.1 Dysfunctional Activity Costs

Every organization has processes, both formal and informal, that drive activities for employees to follow. The level to which these processes or standardized work is followed can be attributed to the clarity of roles and responsibilities. Let's assume there is perfect alignment between what the company intended and what the employees actually do, although this is rarely the case. For example, a specific direction may be given at a departmental meeting and everyone nods in agreement or there is just silence, with no

Chapter 5

expressed opposition. However, a few minutes after the meeting breaks up, discussions start around the coffee machines. Employees start saying things like, "I didn't believe him because just last week I saw him……," or "she didn't sound like she meant it," and "the only time they talk like that is when they are taking something away." The variation between the direction given at the meeting and the actual direction taken is one example of the cost of disengaged employees and a dysfunction.

Savall and Zardet refer to this cumulative collection of dysfunction after dysfunction as hidden costs. What is unique about these costs is that no single individual is typically responsible for a specific dysfunction. Although cumulatively, all individuals involved are responsible, Savall and Zardet also identified that: "…these hidden costs cannot be reduced through the action of one individual, yet if one single individual is missing from the improvement action, hidden costs subsist. Therefore, it is futile to seek solutions for improving the firm's efficiency by asking one volunteer or group of volunteers to say what is good for the enterprise as a whole as found, for example, in quality circles. The firm's performance results from an efficient combination of the behavior of *all* company actors. Improvement must stem from a coordinated series of actions throughout the firm."[1]

The key enabler for doing this is an engaged workforce. A few facts about dysfunction activity costs are:

- The more dysfunctions you have, the more time is needed to deal with the dysfunctions, usually resulting in overtime.
- Excess resources are used up to deal with dysfunctions.
- Dysfunctional costs are not counted by the company's financial statement.
- Production is impacted with delays and losses due to dysfunctions.

An example is removing all clerical staff to save head count and money. Higher paid managers are then doing work that they are slow at and it costs the company more for the same work. Also, it takes away time from more important work that managers should be doing. A lack of fair rules causes dysfunction. For example, a top leader says, "We need to cut costs and will no longer pay for business lunches when traveling." When questioned about the policy, the leader replies, "I pay for my own lunch also." What do you think most employees that make just a small percentage of the leader's salary think about that reply? What do you think the cost of dysfunction is versus the cost of a few lunches? If the policies aren't viewed as fair at the lowest level in the organization, there will be costly dysfunction.

Dysfunction also can be caused by forcing common practices too stringently. "Find the right mix of global and local. Be global where possible, local where necessary. Gain an in-depth understanding of what really needs to be localized. Allow for cultural differences and don't assume what works for one country, market, or plant will work in another. The Volkswagen Group's solution was to build an operating model that balances global and local. Thanks to this 'global' approach, the Volkswagen Group enjoyed year-on-year EBIT growth between 2004 and 2008."[2]

As the workforce gets more engaged, it will have a positive impact on dysfunction. These dysfunctional activity costs are driven by the behavior of everyone in an organization, including operators, maintenance, engineering, supervisors, plant managers, hospital directors, doctors, nurses, etc.

Another supporting perspective is from Jim Collins in *Good to Great*. "All companies have a culture, some companies have discipline, but few companies have a *culture of discipline*. When you have disciplined people, you don't need hierarchy. When you have disciplined thought, you don't need bureaucracy. When you have disciplined action, you don't need excessive controls."[3] With such a culture of discipline, where people know what to do and are willing to do it, great performance is a natural outcome.

Still another supporting theory is the flywheel loop in *Good to Great*. When companies became great, "there was no single defining action, no grand program, no one killer innovation, no solitary lucky break, no miracle moment. Rather, the process resembled relentlessly pushing a giant, heavy flywheel in one direction, turn upon turn, building momentum until a point of breakthrough, and beyond."[4] It is about the numerous small contributions of the many that cumulatively result in success. This is similar to having all employees highly engaged at correcting and removing dysfunctions and waste until the organization reaches greatness. Jim Collins points to three things that summarize his Hedgehog Concept. All three need to be present for understanding and making companies great.

1. "What you are deeply passionate about.
2. What you can be the best in the world at.
3. What drives your economic engine."[5]

It takes long-term commitment, discipline, a highly engaged workforce and working on the right thing. "Change is like ketchup. It's tough to first get the stuff started and then you can't stop it."[6]

5.2 What the Best of the Best Companies Do

In my experiences of working with and benchmarking over two hundred facilities of various types and cultures, I have consistently evidenced three winning behaviors that stood out in plants/organizations that were the best of the best in terms of performance and positive employee attitude.

The better plants had utilized most of the tools and techniques used during lean implementation. These included such items as PDCA, standardized work, visual controls, and so on (Figure 5.1). After observing operations, talking with employees and analyzing data from numerous facilities around the globe, I separated the top quartile. Within that top group, I observed three things that were consistently present, but not so much or not at all in the other facilities.

Chapter 5

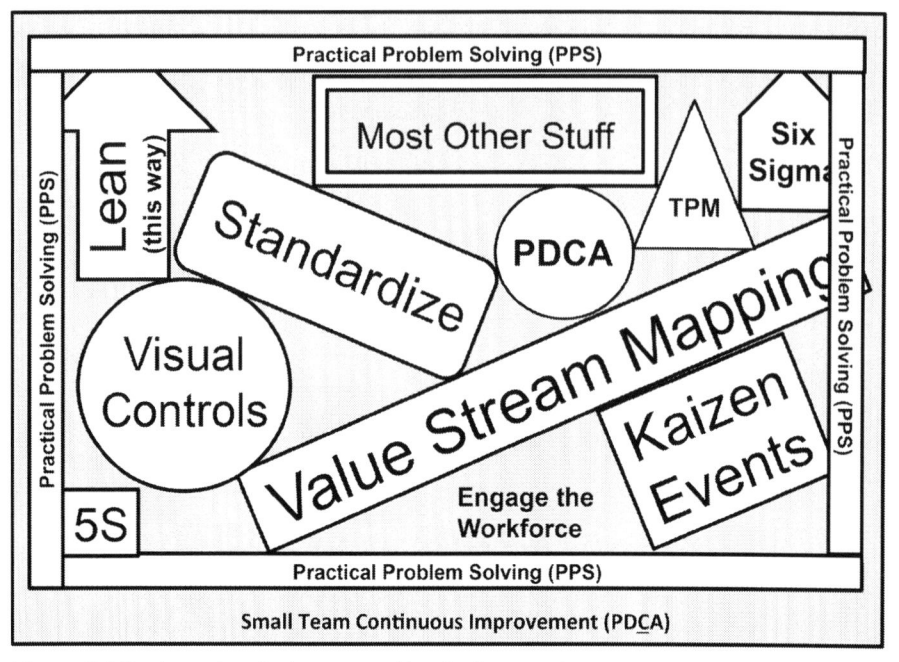

Figure 5.1: Tools and techniques used by the better plants

1. **Small team continuous improvement and engaged employees willing and able to make a difference.**

    This refers to small teams engaged in continuous improvement as the main process to level production and process flow. Many companies will respond with, "We already have that." But what I am referring to is having an active and robust single team process that improves safety, quality, throughput, etc., and is the central and ongoing way of gaining competitive advantage. I tend to see more companies doing things, like counting kaizen events, having elaborate 5S programs, setting goals at one major continuous improvement workshop (every company has their own name for it) that everyone must be involved with, and mandated one hundred percent employee suggestion participation. In the best of the best facilities, the small team continuous improvement process is the driving force and tools, like 5S, large kaizen events, quality campaigns, value stream mapping and so on, are only used when progress has stalled or there is a special need. Then, as soon as feasible, the team focus goes quickly back to the continuous improvement process.

2. **Common practical problem-solving process/tool used by all levels of the organization to change the thinking process.**

    This refers to a form used to respond to any issue of significance in safety, quality and maintenance reliability. Employees go through the steps on the form, including the original problem description (i.e., observed problem); problem definition (i.e., real problem); analysis to find the root cause; containment, if needed; lessons learned; follow-up to confirm long-term fix; and more.

Forms I have worked with are one-page, some two-sided, and are able to contain the input and responses from all the items mentioned and more. There are various problem-solving forms available, with varying levels of problem-solving detail. The type of form I have found to work best has significant detail, when needed, and is an ISO document, so sign off and closure is an audited requirement. You may need to change a few items on the form to satisfy informational and investigative needs in safety, quality and maintenance & reliability. However, the core components of the form remain common. This sounds rigorous, but after using it a few times, it is relatively simple. Also, when everyone in the facility is using the same form/process, it organizes and focuses the discussions/reviews of the issuer. If the form is not introduced at a new facility, then it is important to integrate the currently used terminology for 5 Whys, root cause analysis and related tools and techniques that could be tied to the form. This will minimize potential confusion and align the efforts. It does not have to be an A3 form; it just needs to be comprehensive enough to handle most problems and used by all. Having everyone in the facility using the same process accelerates changing the thinking process to one of problem-solving and continual improvement. Also, when everyone is applying the same process, it helps create and sustain a feeling of unity and teamwork.

3. **Discipline in performing the check (C) in plan-do-check-act (PDCA). Regular checks with positive coaching are done always - no excuses.**

All of the good plants did checks on their processes. However, with closer inspection, some locations had three month old data on a monthly data point, standardized worksheets weren't up-to-date, or over time, less leadership was showing up for the daily process audits. The best facilities were persistent and timely at doing the check in PDCA and mentoring team members.

All the good plants were using the many tools and techniques typically applied in the implementation of lean and reliability (Figure 5.2). However, the best in safety, productivity, quality, delivery and cost exhibited the previously mentioned three winning behaviors. Furthermore, the focus was on improving the big picture, such as overall process, total system, entire facility, versus department. For example, with good data, a group determined it was better to operate at a suboptimal level for a while (i.e., less parts per hour) to maintain level flow for the facility, resulting in less disruptions and higher overall production by the end of the week.

Remember, if you are properly supporting your ongoing, continuous improvement process, many of the special kaizen events would not be necessary. The focus for sustainable continuous improvement should be on improving flow from a systems thinking perspective. Then, selectively use as needed the many improvement tools (e.g., 5S, VSM, RCM, FMEA, kaizen, etc.) to reenergize, accelerate implementation, or give

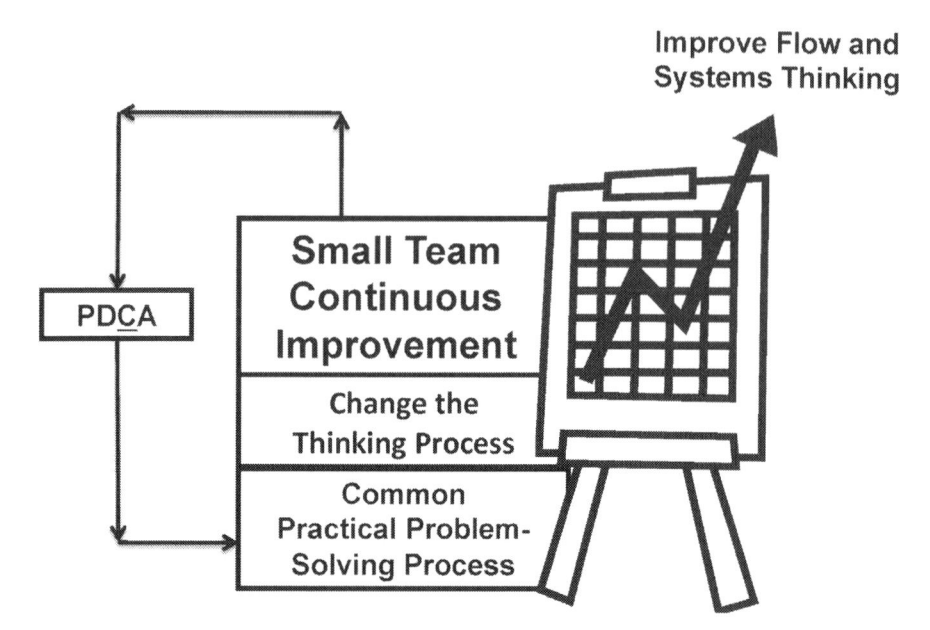

Figure 5.2: Mainstream improvement process in the best plants

attention to a specific improvement effort. However, the mainstream focus always should be on the ongoing, small team continuous improvement process. This appears so simple, yet difficult to implement. Many of the practices at competitors that understand small team continuous improvement are difficult to emulate exactly. That's because where they are today is based on a long time of numerous, small incremental improvements.

So, how important is this? Remember the factor of seven? If the employee/workforce is engaged and there is buy-in to the change, the likelihood of success is seven times higher. It shouldn't be surprising that companies with highly engaged employees do better in productivity and profitability than companies with low employee engagement.

- Twelve percent higher profitability[7]
- Eighteen percent higher productivity[7]
- Organizations with more than four engaged employees for every one actively disengaged have 2.6 times more growth in earnings per share[7]
- Twenty percent less absenteeism[8]
- Eighty percent more like to be top performers[8]
- Engaged employees is the most consistent predictor of business performance[9]
- Nineteen percent higher operating income[10]

Towers Watson focuses on three key components for sustainable engagement.
- **"Engaged** – Feeling attached to the company and willing to exert extra effort on its behalf.
- **Enabled** – Having the tools and resources to be successful.
- **Energized** – Working in an environment that supports one's health and well-being."[9]

Model for Sustainable Change

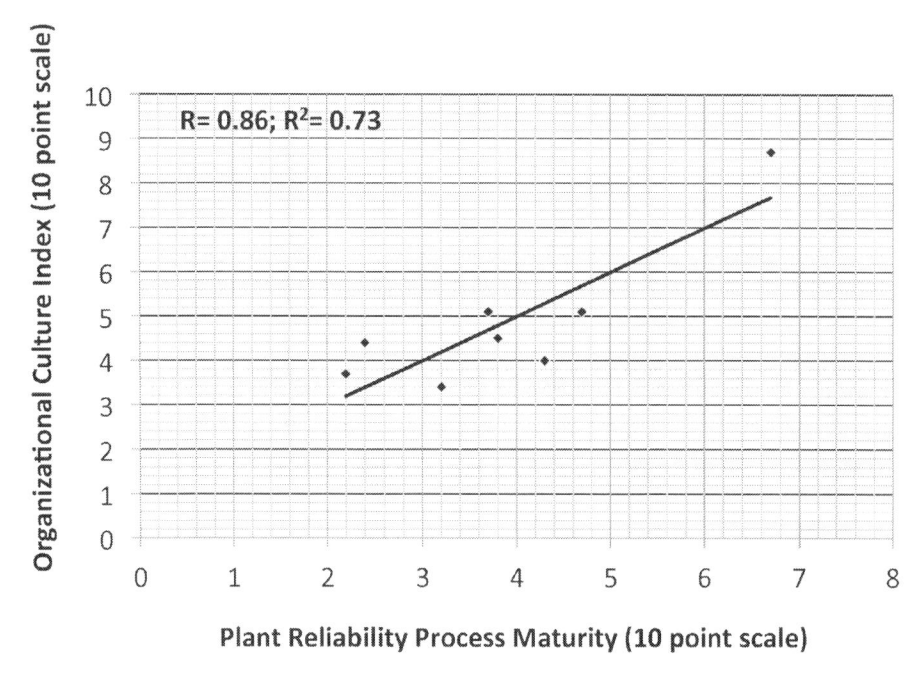

Figure 5.3: Organizational culture and reliability process maturity

Forty percent of employees were highly engaged (scored high on all three components) and twenty-four percent were disengaged (lower on all three components). The remainder of the employees were in-between, with nineteen percent not sustainably engaged (unsupported) and seventeen percent detached.

Figure 5.3 is a plot that shows the relationship between organizational culture and maturity of the reliability process based on an index using multiple variables. Facilities with the highest organizational culture scores also had the most developed reliability process.

5.3 Simplified Sustainable Change Model

The change models of Lewin; Gleicher, Beckhard, Harris, and Kotter shown in Chapter 2 (Figure 2.8) can be aligned with a simplified model for sustainable change (Figure 5.4).

Grasp the Situation

Make sure you understand the situation/problem. Talk to the people closest to the issue at hand. Use the 5 Whys and get a clear description of the task.

Share the Knowledge

Individuals need to understand the vision and reasons for change. Most importantly, they want to know how it is going to impact their life. A force field analysis will reveal most of the issues needing resolution. But, it's still necessary to have a clear vision of the future

Chapter 5

Lewin	Gleicher, Beckhard, Harris	Kotter	
Unfreeze	D = Dissatisfaction V = Vision	Establish a sense of urgency Form a strong coalition Create a vision for change Communicate the new vision and strategy	Grasp the Situation → Ya Gotta Wanna → Share the Knowledge
Transition	F = First Concrete Step	Empower team members to act on the vision Create short-term wins to grow support Consolidate improvements and use the momentum to continue	Doable First Step → PDCA
Refreeze	$\Delta = D \times V \times F > R$ R = Resistance to Change	Institutionalize the change	STANDARDIZE → COACH & CALIBRATE → EXPERIENCE

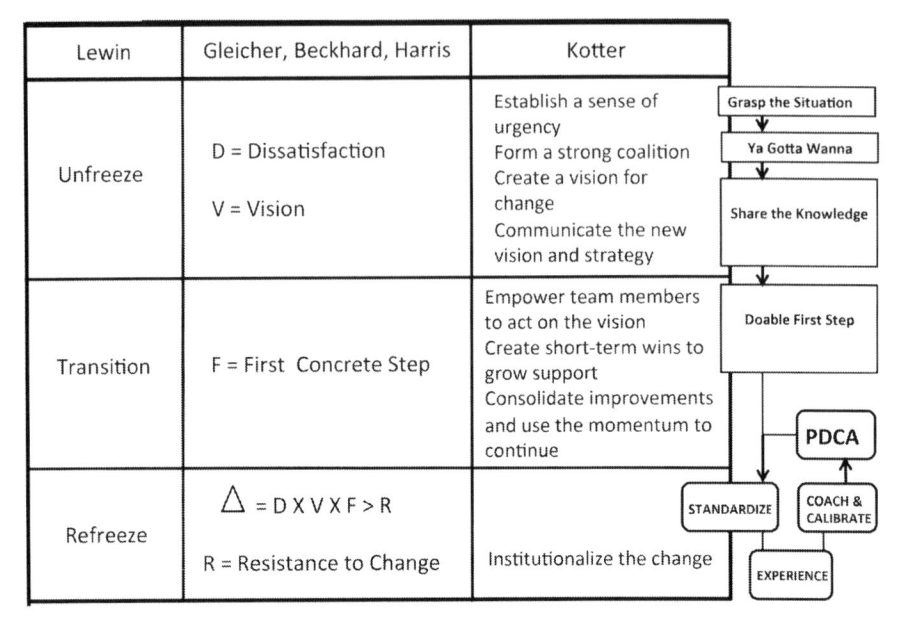

Figure 5.4: Simplified model for sustainable change

state. Employees must feel a sufficient level of confidence by knowing where they end up is more desirable than today.

Ya Gotta Wanna

You need to understand how the change impacts the team members involved to be able to deal with the causes of resistance. Just as you need to decide whether or not to support a change, so does each team member.

Doable First Step

The initial steps toward change must appear to be attainable to assure early wins. This will help build confidence and momentum toward the change. As the team members empowered to act on implementing the change see positive results, enthusiasm to accomplish additional steps will grow. After several small successes, bigger steps will appear more doable.

Standardize

This is a critical step for two reasons. First, the standardized work enabling the future state needs to be followed to assure best practices and the ensuing results. Second, it's important that everyone has the same detailed vision of the future state, otherwise individuals will be dissatisfied with the outcome, feeling that the change didn't go far enough or it went too far. Defining in detail the standardized work/method of the future state helps to avoid such a situation.

Experience - Coach & Calibrate – PDCA

To help sustain the change, you need to support ongoing continuous improvement to continually make the change better. There are always things related to any change that affect each individual differently. These additional interactions and improvements will help you work through these individual issues and establish further buy-in to the change. Performing the check in PDCA and coaching to establish/maintain the standardized work assures that it stays consistent and relevant. Allowing, nurturing and mentoring continuous improvement is a constant reminder of what each employee needs and that what they are doing is important.

This does not mean that the only coaching that goes on is during the check process of PDCA. Coaching the workforce in a positive way by focusing on improving the process versus finding blame and asking questions that foster learning should go on during all the PDCA steps. The only difference is that during the check step, the coaching focuses on questions to maintain the standardized work or current best practice.

5.4 Managing Complex Change

Managing complex changes require more planning and patience. However, the tools and concepts are similar. In the late 1980s, I was given a copy (similar to Figure 5.5) of *Managing Complex Change*.[11] At least once a year, I see it surface in someone's presentation or article, so it's obviously still a good visual to illustrate what's needed for complex change

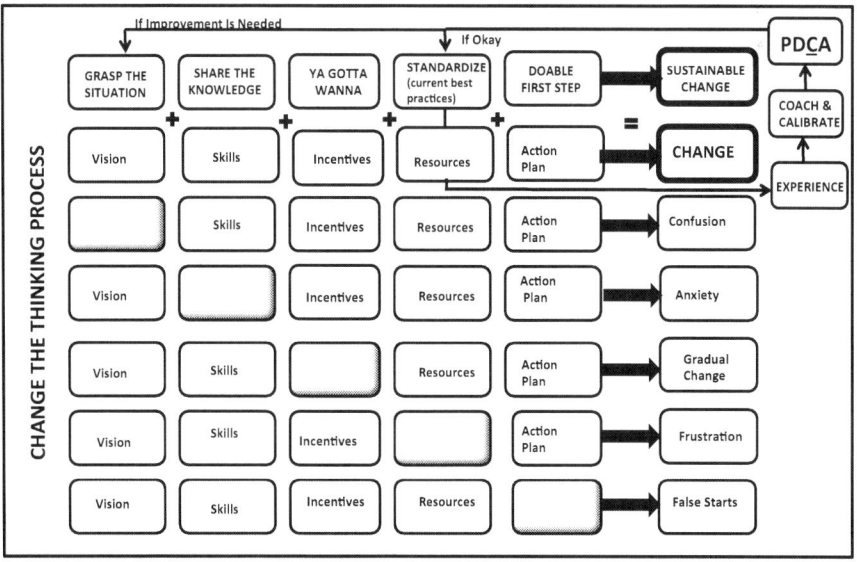

Adapted from Ambrose 1987

Figure 5.5: Managing complex change

Chapter 5

CHANGE STATE	CHANGE STAGE	CHANGE ACTION
CURRENT	1. Willing to Change 2. Wanting to Change	Grasp the Situation Share the Knowledge
TRANSITION	3. What to Change 4. Working the Change	Doable First Step Standardize
FUTURE	5. Why Change	Experience – Coach & Calibrate - PDCA

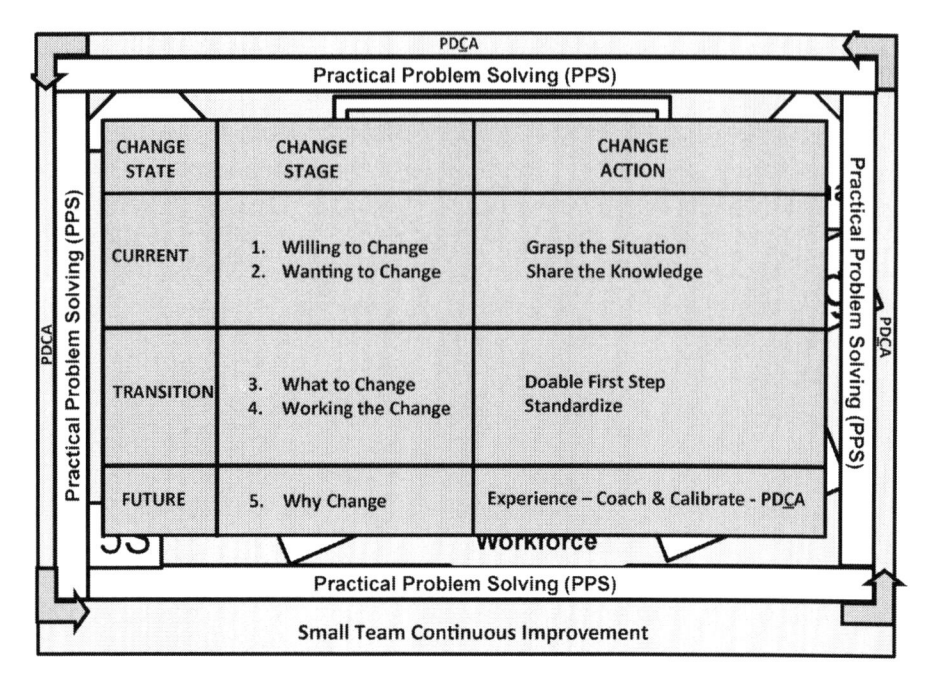

Figure 5.6: Model for sustainable change

and removing possible roadblocks. To work well, complex change needs all the components on the top line of Figure 5.5 present. However, if you don't have a clear vision, it causes confusion. If the workforce lacks the skills to enable the change, it will cause anxiety. If the incentives aren't sufficient or dissatisfaction of the current state isn't high enough, the change will be slow. If there are not enough resources to get the job done, there will be frustration. If there is not a doable action plan, then the team may give up or be focused on the wrong initiative. Of course, having more than one component absent will compound the forces against the change. This matrix can be viewed as a template for a force field analysis for the minimum requirements needed for complex change. In practice, each of the components will be at varying levels of fulfillment, relative to readiness for change.

Figure 5.6 overlays the simplified model for sustainable change described in Chapter 4. To accomplish the action plan, you must grasp the situation to establish the vision, share the knowledge to assure the needed skills, ya gotta wanna satisfy what's in it for me, have a doable first step that is seen as realistic with the available resources, and standardize to enable repeatable tasks.

5.5 Assessing Readiness for Change Scorecard

There are various assessments that can be used to determine readiness for change. These range from a basic force field analysis to a detailed assessment and surveys. The readiness for change scoring chart (Figure 5.7) has worked well. Typically, a score of at

Model for Sustainable Change

Figure 5.7: Change readiness questionnaire

FOR THE AREA IMPACTED BY THE CHANGE, HOW TRUE IS EACH STATEMENT?

	Not at all 0	Seldom > 20%	Some > 40%	Often > 60%	Usually > 80%	Almost All 100 %
Desire to change (Is Dissatisfaction + Incentives + Vision > Status Quo ?)						
Employees have the knowledge and skills needed for change						
Reason for change is clearly understood						
Employees have tools and resources to enable change						
Employees see the initial step toward implementing the change as doable						
Vision (future state, what the future should look like) is the same for all						
The future state detail can be clearly described by all						
Momentum is sufficient to allow the change						
Small team continuous improvement is active						
Systems thinking (overall process) is utilized						
Team members are focused on problem-solving						
Standardized work is used and changed to reflect improvements						
The workforce is disciplined to remove abnormalities and sustain standardized work						
Coaching and mentoring is done at all levels, with focus on process improvement versus finding blame						
It's easy to make small changes within your span of control						
Employees support the change (as discussed informally at the coffee machine, etc.)						
Continuous improvement is a daily practice versus a separate initiative						
The change supports the current team's norms						
To what extent there is agreement on the value of the change						
There is confidence/trust in the team leading the change						
Add the number of checks in each column	0	1	2	3	4	5
Multiply the number of checks times the number shown						
Add the results of each column for a total score						

least sixty is needed for change to be successful, or at least have a chance. The scoring chart should be done individually and then compiled. It should then be discussed as a team to understand the reasons for differences in responses. The maximum score is one hundred. Although it is okay to take averages for the team/department score, I think it's better to make a team selection for each response after active discussion on reasons for the variances.

References

1. Savall, Henri and Zardet, Veronique. *Mastering Hidden Costs and Socio-Economic Performance.* Charlotte: Information Age Publishing, Inc., 2008.
2. IBM. *Capitalizing on Complexity: Insights from the 2010 Global Chief Executive Officer Study.* IBM, 2010, pp. 59-60.
3. Collins, Jim. *Good to Great.* New York City: Harper Business, 2001.
4. Ibid.
5. Ibid, p. 118
6. Idhammer, Christer. Paraphrased comment from the Society for Maintenance and Reliability Professionals (SMRP) Annual Conference, Greensboro, North Carolina, 2011.
7. Robison, Jennifer. "The Economic Crisis: A Leadership Challenge." *Gallup Business Journal* 12 May 2009.
8. Watson Wyatt. 2008-2009 Work Canada Report.
9. Towers Watson. "Global Workforce Study and Global Trends in Employee Attraction, Retention and Engagement." *Towers Watson Sustainable Engaged Newsletter*, October 2014; http://www.towerswatson.com/en-US/Insights/Newsletters/Global/Sustainably-Engaged/2014/global-trends-in-employee-attraction-retention-and-engagement.
10. Irvine, Derek. "Employee Engagement: What It Is and Why You Need It." *Bloomberg Business Week* 8 May 2009, http://www.businessweek.com/bwdaily/dnflash/content/may2009/db2009058_952910.htm.
11. Ambrose, D. *Managing Complex Change.* Pittsburgh: The Enterprise Group, Ltd., 1987.

Chapter 6

Sustaining Change

"Let your practice keep step with your knowledge."
— Chinese Proverb

"To improve is to change; to be perfect is to change often."
— Winston Churchill

6.1 Change the Thinking Process

To change the thinking process, you have to change the actions. A good process for doing this utilizes one page reports, as mentioned earlier in the book, and practical problem-solving forms used by all. If the continuous improvement process is active, team members also know when it's time to make a change. Most have heard the boiled frog phenomenon, where the frog won't jump out of a pot gradually heating up because it doesn't sense the need for change. Don't be like the frog in the boiling pot. An improvement focused thought process is needed for successful, ongoing improvement, total productive maintenance programs and lean implementation.

"You cannot succeed without internalizing the principles of lean throughout all of management and using that thinking to guide the implementation, daily decision-making, problem-solving, managing and coaching. Lean is not about what we see; lean is about how we think."[1]

To make any process take hold, people need to not just understand, but to experience the difference. When setting up a best in class maintenance process at one facility, I started with a shared vision. Then, I took the team, consisting of trades and engineers, to a highly respected plant with a very good maintenance process. The team brought back many ideas and were energized. Less than two years later, we made a return trip to see what else could be learned. It was very quiet on the drive back, so I asked, "What's going on?" Their comments can be summarized as, "We can never be like that again." What I didn't mention to the team, until after the second trip, was that although there were some very good practices to be learned, such as predictive technologies, there were limitations due to their culture, even though it was a good facility. If I would have said this during the

Chapter 6

first trip, it would have been a difficult point to get agreement on when viewing the tools and techniques utilized. Because the visiting team had grown in lean thinking, problem-solving skills, understanding standardized work and implementing an overall continuous improvement culture through their own experiences, they were able to recognize the limitations on their own. Nothing else needed to be said.

It's important to monitor and nurture the dynamics of the teams as they form and mature. Brue Tuckman identified four stages of team development in 1965. In 1977, a fifth was added in conjunction with Mary Ann Jensen. A brief version of the five steps[2,3,4] are:

Stage 1: Forming – meet, uncertainty, first impressions, share information.

Stage 2: Storming – discussions, conflicts, begin trying to work together based on team maturity.

Stage 3: Norming – trust grows, beginning of making decisions with team.

Stage 4: Performing – focused on tasks to achieve the goal, know how to resolve issues without the team leader.

Stage 5: Adjourning – some self-evaluation, capturing lessons learned, celebrate success, develop allies for future support, sadness that it is over.

All stages are necessary and unavoidable for a team to grow. Figure 6.1 illustrates the five stages in relationship to team members' feelings, increasing team autonomy and decreasing team leader input.

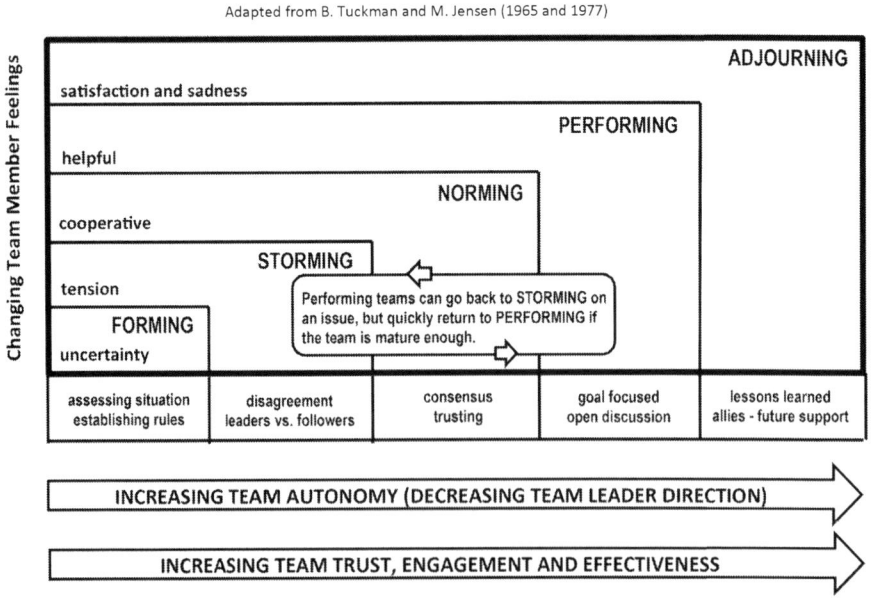

Figure 6.1: Lifecycle of teams relative to team member autonomy, feelings and performance

Note that teams in the performing stage can fall back into the storming stage on an issue. However, if the team is mature enough, they can quickly get back to the performing stage.

I've seen "culture eats strategy for breakfast" and "culture eats strategy for lunch" quotes in many writings and presentations. Although the original sources appear unconfirmed, most link the quotes to Peter Drucker. I'll just say, "Culture eats strategy for breakfast and lunch" because people will follow culture before strategy and culture is more sustainable. I have frequently seen another quote attributed to Peter Drucker that I always tried to rationalize, but eventually decided that it didn't work for me.

"Company cultures are like country cultures. Never try to change one. Try instead to work with what you've got."[5]

Chad Dickerson found up to 128,000 Google results for this quote, supposedly in *The Daily Drucker*. But, he found that the author gave his nephew a copy of *The Daily Drucker* and asked him to list some of his favorite quotes, which is where it came from. So, it's actually a misquote and not in the book. Good job, Chad! We will make you an honorary engineer for this root cause investigation regarding the misquote. The closest that Chad found for the actual text was:

"What these [business] needs require are changes in behavior. But 'changing culture' is not going to produce them. Culture, no matter how defined, is singularly persistent. Nearly 50 years ago, Japan and Germany suffered the worst defeats in recorded history, with their values, their institutions and their culture discredited. But today's Japan and today's Germany are unmistakably Japanese and German in culture, no matter how different this or that behavior. In fact, changing behavior works only if it can be based on the existing 'culture.'"[5]

This is a much clearer and more meaningful understanding of behavior change and culture. The misquote was limited and not that supportive of change. Remember, if you hear, say, or do something often enough, you take it for truth, even if it's not.

Changing the culture is the missing link needed for successful and sustainable outcomes. Reliabilityweb.com's research report *on Asset Management Practices, Investments and Challenges* 2014-2019[6] found that forty percent of respondents selected organizational culture as the biggest obstacle for improving asset performance.

6.2 Big Picture Thinking

Employees need to understand the big picture to help them make better decisions and realize why some decisions that may not seem fair or reasonable from one work unit's perspective are the optimal choice for the facility.

Resistance to change seems to be more of an issue in the United States, where forty-one percent named it "the greatest obstacle to productivity…..the United Kingdom, thirty-two percent, Mexico, thirty-two percent, Brazil, twenty-eight percent and Germany, twenty-five percent."[7] It was also mentioned that in the United States, sixty-four percent of the companies credited the adoption of a lean culture and continuous process improvement for improved productivity. Employees need to know that what they do is meaningful.

6.3 Organizational Learning

We have all come across people who always view everything in a negative manner, while others are always upbeat. You can put these individuals into similar circumstances and one will always see the glass of water half empty and the other will see it as half full. I'm not just referring to managers with good jobs. I'm also referring to the people at the car wash, restaurant, engineering office, hotel, appliance store, etc., who stand out because they want to do their job well and are proud of it. Others don't like their job or circumstance and it's immediately obvious in their attitude.

"Some employees thrive no matter the context. They naturally build vitality and learning into their jobs, and they inspire the people around them."[8] Through research, professors Gretchen Spreitzer and Christine Porath in partnership with The Ross School of Business's Center for Positive Organizational Scholarship decided on the word "thriving." This was based on twelve hundred white- and blue-collar employees being surveyed over seven years with various industries.

"We think of a thriving workforce as one in which employee are not just satisfied and productive, but also engaged in creating the future – the company's and their own. ……people who fit our description of thriving demonstrated sixteen percent better overall performance (as reported by their managers) and one hundred and twenty-five percent less burnout (self-reported) than their peers. They were thirty-two percent more committed to the organization and forty-six percent more satisfied with their jobs. They also missed much less work and reported significantly fewer doctor visits, which meant health care savings and less lost time for the company."[8]

Two components of thriving were identified:

1. Vitality – sense of being passionate, excited and alive; getting energy from knowing they are making a difference.
2. Learning – new knowledge and skills to stem growth and expertise.

What is important is that you need both.

Their research identified four main mechanisms:
1. Providing Decision-Making Discretion: Employees at all levels are energized by being able to make decisions, gaining a greater sense of control and continually learning.
2. Sharing Information: People make better decisions with more knowledge. They need to understand the big picture.
3. Minimizing Incivility: It can be as simple and devastating as having a bad boss. The hidden or dysfunctional costs of reduced performance are enormous. It's about how you are treated, both words and action, compared to what you expect as workplace norms.
4. Offering Performance Feedback: Make it direct and timely to ensure that it's useful.

Sustaining Change

The good thing is all four of these items are capable of being implemented by most organizations to establish a thriving, positive thinking team.

"You might expect optimism to erode under the tide of news about violent conflicts, high unemployment, tornadoes and floods, and all the treats and failures that shape human life. …..the belief that the future will be much better than the past and present is known as optimism bias. Optimists live longer and are healthier."[9]

As individuals, teams, groups and organizations learn, it's important that employees realize that it's okay to say, "I don't know." Learning doesn't mean that you have to know everything. A few years ago, I purchased a new camera from a popular electronics store. The memory card wasn't working, so I returned to the store and found the saleswoman that sold me the camera. I explained that I had problems downloading the pictures. Her reply was, "The memory card needs to be formatted." I explained that I tested it with an old memory card and viewing the pictures worked. So, I said, "It's a problem loading new pictures and I never heard about formatting them from anyone before." She continued to try to convince me that she was correct. About that time, another customer walked by and stated, "I just bought that same camera and you don't need to format anything." The saleswoman suddenly remembered that Nikon had a factory defect on this, but she hadn't seen it for a long time. We tried another camera and it worked. It was obvious from the first few words that she did not know, but would not accept that. She lost my confidence early on in the discussion.

> "It is better to keep your mouth closed and let people think you are a fool than to open it and remove all doubt."
> — Mark Twain

It's okay to say, "I don't know."

6.4 Flexibility

Individuals and organizations need to be more flexible in adapting to what works in today's business climate. For example, the top two chief financial officer (CFO) priorities in a Key Issues Study[10] by The Hackett Group were identified as efficiency and effectiveness of the annual budgeting process (eighty-four percent of respondents) and forecasting performance, including accuracy, cycle time and efficiency (eighty-one percent of respondents). Neal Vorchheimer, senior vice president of finance for Unilever North America, stated: "We used to have what we called an annual plan and we would spend six months putting it together. As soon as the budget was approved, it was out-of-date. So, we decided to do away with it. We're using bottom-up forecasting to come up with the best view of the eight quarters on a rolling basis."[11]

Changing the culture to support such a new approach requires all the same steps, tools and techniques already discussed.

"Some fall apart; others actually thrive with change and fluctuating environments. They face the challenge and regain their equilibrium faster. This is what resilience is about: the ability to bounce back faster than others."[12]

Chapter 6

"The single most important factor in managing change successfully is the degree to which people demonstrate resilience: the ability to absorb high levels of disruptive change while displaying minimal dysfunctional behavior."[13]

In *Managing at the Speed of Change*, Daryl Conner provides the five attributes of resilience.

1. "Positive – Views life as challenging, but opportunity filled
2. Focused – Clear vision of what is to be achieved
3. Flexible – Pliable when responding to uncertainty
4. Organized – Applies structure to help manage ambiguity
5. Proactive – Engages change instead of eroding"[14]

Managing at the Speed of Change details the associated beliefs, behaviors, skills and knowledge to attain each of the five attributes.

Resilience also can be viewed in highly reliable organizations.

"…..basic message is that expectations can get you into trouble unless you create a mindful infrastructure that continually does all of the following:

- Tracks small failures;
- Resists oversimplification;
- Remains sensitive to operations;
- Maintains capabilities for resilience;
- Takes advantage of shifting locations of expertise.

Failure to move toward this type of mindful infrastructure magnifies the damage produced by unexpected events and impairs reliable performance."[15]

Without continuous improvement and being vigilant with maintaining a mindful infrastructure, more problems will find you, unless you find them first.

6.5 Business Plan Deployment

Back in 1991, a study by the National Research Council concluded:

"….the most cost-effective increase in U.S. manufacturing capacity may well be achievable through improved maintenance practices for existing equipment."[16]

This statement is still valid today, except I would change "maintenance" to "reliability and maintenance (R&M)." Why, after all this time, is that conclusion still so? The National Research Council study recognized that a comprehensive approach is necessary, with an emphasis on changing culture. This, of course, is still the challenge.

Sustaining Change

```
Behavior                    Support for the operator
                              Individual
                      (commit to following all safety rules)

                              Team Members
Daily Actions         (speak up if unsafe act is observed
                            and track near misses)

                          Maintenance Department
Objective                (reduce reactive maintenance
                                to 10 percent)

                                 Plant
Plant goal             (zero accidents linked to plant
                           manager compensation)

                               Corporate
           Vision          (an organization where
                            employees are the most
                               important asset)

                              Leadership
```

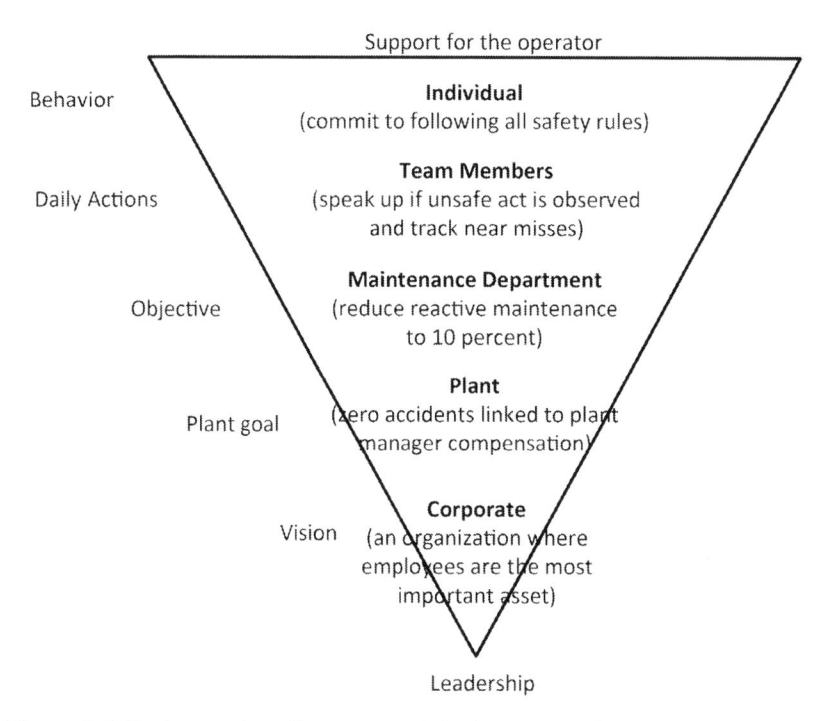

Figure 6.2: Business plan alignment and deployment, safety example

If you are going to set up an R&M process, I would recommend:

1. Instilling a culture that supports problem-solving and continuous improvements.
2. Establishing a robust reliability process that provides data/feedback for improvement decisions.
3. Implementing a maintenance process to support the above recommendations.

In most practices, the order is typically reversed. You already have a long-standing maintenance process. A reliability process may be partially developed or non-existent and the culture is an ongoing process needing work.

To attain facility and organizational goals, there must be a business plan alignment and deployment that is understood at each relevant level. At the corporate level, there must be a vision, plant goals that support the vision, departmental objectives with targets aligned to support the plant goals, team actions aligned to support the departmental objectives and individual behavior needs aligned to support the team. Figure 6.2 is a safety example of a partial business plan alignment and deployment.

Note that it all starts with an individual commitment to follow safety rules, supported by team members watching out for each other (e.g., reporting near misses and corrective follow-up is a good thing), supported by the maintenance department performing mainly

Chapter 6

proactive maintenance since more reactive maintenance is directly linked to more safety issues, supported by plant management, with safety performance linked to compensation and supported by the corporation providing adequate resources to enable the vision. Of course there are numerous goals and objectives that should be visibly tracked on a tracking wall, with some form of PDCA for continuous improvement and progress tracking.

6.5.1 Business Performance and Continuous Improvement

Performance is an action word. It's an action or the result of an action. The improvement can be measured against a baseline or benchmark that depicts your business performance.

However, the biggest challenge for organizations that have made large gains implementing a successful new process is not backsliding to old practices. This could occur from changes in attitude from cumulative issues on the ground floor. However, the more frequent reason is a change in either top leadership or key implementation/leadership at any point from when you are building momentum for the new practice to having completely implemented the changes. The new leader (s) may not agree with the vision, have a more controlling management style, focus more on bottom-line results without regard to people concerns, stop sharing business details, or reduce training to save money and keep a production focus. It wouldn't take long before high performance practices and accompanying results are no longer evident.

Kaplan and Norton, known for the balanced scorecard (BSC), found "that sustaining performance management systems like the BSC requires two components:

1. Having a clearly defined *process* that fits comfortably into the governance cycle of the organization.
2. Establishing an entity (a department or organization) that is responsible for its management and its success."[17]

They refer to the title, office of strategy management (OSM), for the group that "integrates and coordinates activities across functions and business units to align strategy and operations. It keeps the diverse organizational players-executive teams, business units, regional units, support units (e.g., finance, human resources, information technology), theme teams, departments and, ultimately, employees aligned with each other."[18]

Implementation of strategies to the full extent of the goals and objectives can only happen if the organization is aligned from the very top to the very bottom. A key role that such a group can provide is coordination of the best use of resources. There are many initiatives, like lean, TPM, RCA, RCM, FMEA, 5S, safety, Six Sigma, kaizen events and others, that require most of the same resources at the implementation level. So, some resistance is simply because individuals leading a specific process want the resources to support their initiatives of interest. It also takes trades and engineers away from daily production support. This situation is most evident after a large success, like a measurable increase in throughput. Usually, three or more groups are taking credit for it because, at some time during the improvement period, they all had the same resources doing something relative to these throughput improvement initiatives.

6.5.2 Balanced Scorecard Metrics

Having past success in business does not guarantee future success. So, it's important to have indicators of where you are heading and how much progress is being made.

The balanced scorecard is a well-known tool for strategy and performance management. The scorecard was "organized around four distinct perspectives – financial, customer, internal, and innovation and learning. The name reflected the balance provided between short- and long-term objectives, between lagging and leading indicators, and between external and internal performance perspectives."[19]

Each of the four perspectives is populated with objectives, performance measures, targets and improvement actions. When preparing an organization for innovation and learning or learning and growth, the balanced scorecard can be used for performance measurement and strategy alignment. From a change management viewpoint, it is a tool to help align employees' goals with the company's objectives. By having the correct metrics at each organizational level, the desired behavior can be influenced. Rewarding the proper metrics is important because the wrong measurements or use of them can drive bad behavior. Key performance indicators (KPIs) are values used to measure process performance. The best KPIs are relevant and meet three criteria:

"1. The KPIs should encourage the right behavior.
2. They should be difficult to manipulate to 'look good.'
3. They should not require a lot of effort to measure."[20]

The old adages of, "What gets measured gets done" and "If you can't measure it, you can't manage it," apply here. Having data is a way of feeling more in control. Now that you have data, you can understand it. How many metrics do you report on in your organization? Five, ten, thirty, over fifty?

"When there was a single overriding indicator, such as profit or return on investment, it was relatively easy for managers to know what they were supposed to achieve, even if they did not know how to achieve it. In these days of multiple measures, all of which are assumed to be equally important, it is no longer clear to many people where the organization's priorities lie."[21]

Most large companies have over one hundred KPIs, with many having over two hundred KPIs. It's just like when you get blood analysis done by your doctor. Twenty metrics may be compared against normal ranges for a quick review. However, you focus on the vital few for improvement (e.g., blood pressure, cholesterol, etc.). Select the few that will drive the changes you are striving for and focus most of your efforts on them. Work on what matters.

6.5.3 Coach and Calibrate

Positive coaching to guide daily practices back to standardized best practices is an ongoing process needed to attain and sustain a high performing organization. A big part of coaching is demonstrating patience and a willingness to ask questions to allow team members to develop solutions (e.g., growing their problem-solving skills, understanding and buy-in). So, the first step is being able to ask the right questions to grasp the situation without assigning blame. The technical questions around process, equipment standards, work tasks and more can be all asked, but you need to start with a meaningful positive interaction. How you ask questions will lead you to a win-win outcome, agreeing to disagree (i.e., showing respect), or a negative result. When there is a lot of emotion involved in a discussion, it's easy to go down the path of, "I'm right and you're wrong," but it will quickly lead to frustration, regret and no problem resolution, which would probably make the situation worse. With a little practice, you can learn to phrase your questions in a manner conducive to a more positive outcome.

6.6 Choice Map

Marilee Adams's choice map (Figure 6.3) provides a simple, but powerful visual for a thought and question process to enable more positive resolutions.

"Judge Questions Include:

- What's wrong with me?
- Whose fault is it?
- Why are they so stupid?
- How can I prove that I'm right?
- Haven't we been there, done that?
- Why bother?

Results of Judger's Questions:

- A mood of pessimism, stress, and limitation;
- A mind-set that's judgmental, reactive inflexible;
- Relating with 'attack or defensive' behaviors.

Learner Questions Include:

- What do I want?
- What works?
- What are the facts and what can I learn?
- What are my choices?
- What action steps make sense?
- What's possible?

Figure 6.3: Choice map

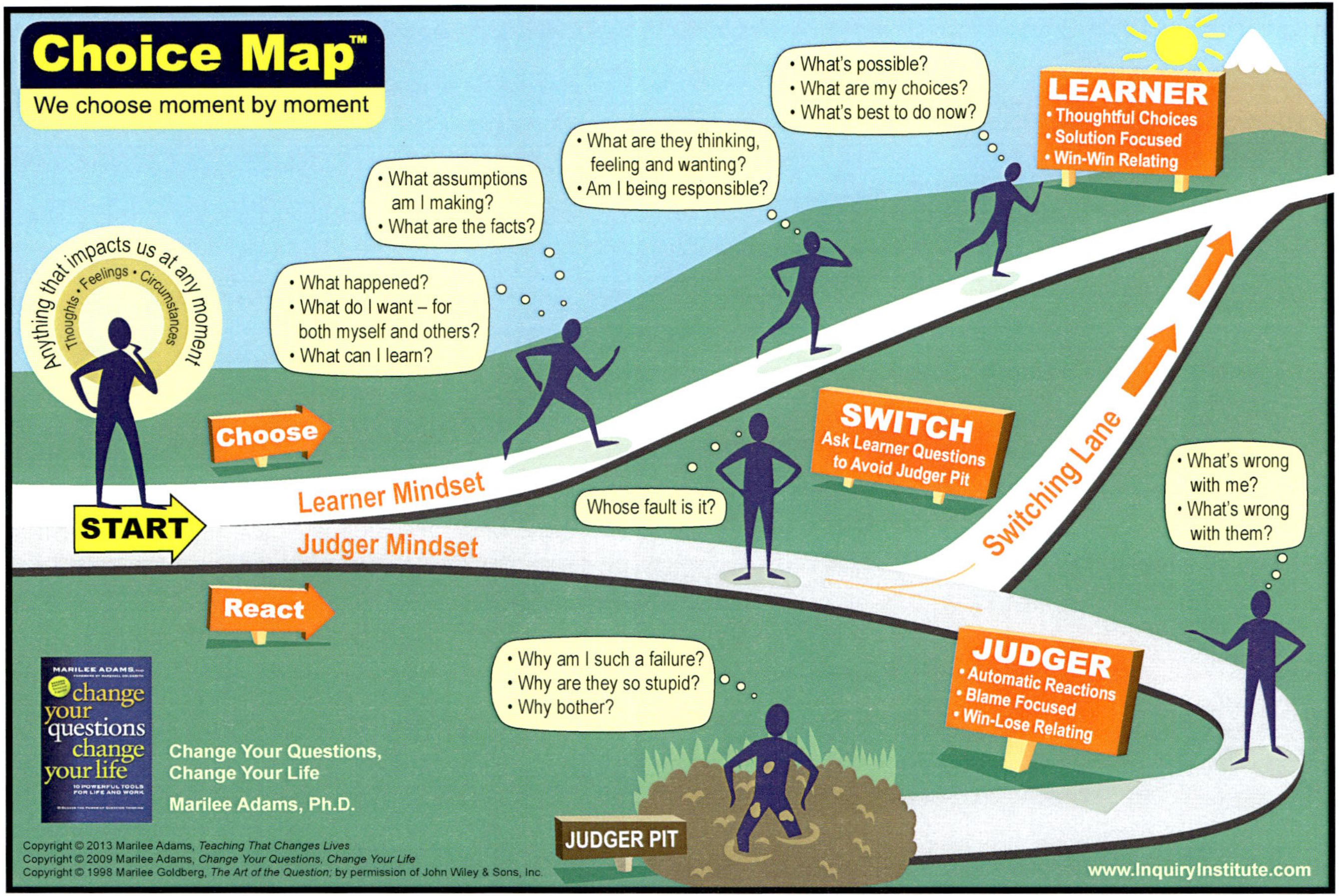

Reproduced with permission of the Inquiry Institute; www.Inquiryinstitute.com; 800-250-7823

Chapter 6

Results of Learner's Questions:
- A mood of optimism, hope and possibilities;
- A mind-set that's thoughtful, understanding, flexible;
- Relating that is connected and collaborative.

We all ask both kinds of questions and we have the capacity to choose which ones we ask moment by moment."[22]

The questions you ask will take you down a judging or learning path, getting the corresponding answers and reactions. You may also find yourself becoming more negative if you slip into the judging mode. If you find yourself going toward the judger pit, then start asking yourself switching questions. Among them are:
- Am I judging?
- Is this how I want to feel?
- Where would I rather be?
- How else can I think about this?
- Am I reacting to assumptions or facts?

Continue asking switching questions until you are back in learner mode.

References

1. Flinchbaugh, James. "Right Tool, Right Problem, Right Thinking." *Assembly Magazine* 6 January 2006.
2. Abudi, Gina. "The Five Stages of Team Development." *The Project Management Hut*. 8 May 2010. 13 December 2014: http://www.pmhut.com/the-five-stages-of-project-team-development.
3. Tuckman, Bruce W. "Developmental Sequence in Small Groups." *Psychological Bulletin*, Vol. 63, No. 6, 1965: p. 63.
4. Tuckman, Bruce W. and Jensen, Mary Ann C. "Stages of Small-Group Development Revisited." *Group & Organization Studies*, Vol. 2, No. 4, 1977: pp. 419-427.
5. Dickerson, Chad. "Why liberal arts education matters: the story of a Drucker (mis-) quote. February 3, 2013: http://blog.chaddickerson.com/2013/02/03/liberal-arts-matter/
6. Reliabilityweb.com. *Asset Management Practices, Investments and Challenges 2014-2019*. http://www.reliabilityweb.com/index.php/articles/asset_management_practices_investments_and_challenges_2014-2019/.
7. Quality Digest. *Worldwide Productivity Movin' Right Along*. October 2005: http://www.qualitydigest.com/oct05/news.shtml#3.
8. Spreitzer, Gretchen and Porath, Christine. "Creating Sustainable Performance." *Harvard Business Review*, January/February 2012.
9. Sharot, Tali. "The Optimism Bias: Those rose-colored glasses? We may be born with them. Why our brains tilt toward the positive." *Time*, June 6, 2011: p. 40 & 46.
10. Banham, Russ. "Let It Roll: Why More Companies are Abandoning Budgets In Favor of Rolling Forecasts." CFO Magazine, May 1, 2011: p. 45.
11. Ibid, p. 44.
12. Carr, David C., Hard, Kelvin J. and Trahant William J. *Managing The Change Process: A Field Book for Change Agents, Consultants, Team Leaders and Reengineering Managers*. New York City: McGraw/Hill, 1996.

13. Conner, Daryl R. *Managing at the Speed of Change*. New York City: Villard Books, 1993.
14. Ibid.
15. Weick, Karl E. and Sutcliffe, Kathleen M. *Managing the Unexpected: Resilient Performance in an Age of Uncertainty*, Second edition. Hoboken: John Wiley & Sons, Inc., 2007.
16. National Research Council. *The Competitive Edge: Research Priorities for U.S. Manufacturing*. Washington, D.C.: National Academies Press, 1991.
17. Kaplan, Robert S. and Norton, David P. "The Office of Strategy Management: Emerging Roles and Responsibilities." *Journal of Management Excellence*, Issue 2, September 2008: p. 17.
18. Ibid, p. 18.
19. Kaplan, Robert S. and Norton, David P. *The Balanced Scorecard: Translating Strategy Into Action*. Cambridge: Harvard Business Review Press, 1996.
20. IDCON. "Maintenance Key Performance (KPIs)." *IDCON Reliability Tips*. October 2007.
21. Neely, Andy and Austin, Rob. "Measuring performance: The operations perspective," Part I in *Business Performance Measurement: Theory and Practice*, edited by Andy Neely. Cambridge: Cambridge University Press, 2002.
22. Adams, Marilee. *Change Your Questions, Change Your Life: 10 Powerful Tools for Life and Work (Inquiry Institute Library)*. Oakland: Berrett-Koehler Publishers, 2004.

Chapter 7
It's Up to You

"I have not failed 10,000 times. I have not failed once. I have succeeded in proving that those 10,000 ways will not work. When I have eliminated the ways that will not work, I will find the way that will work."
— Thomas Edison

"With regard to excellence, it is not enough to know, but we must try to have and use it."
— Aristotle

7.1 Making It Work for You

We all have different levels of optimism, genetic makeup and activities or paths that we choose.

"Studies show that fifty percent of individual differences in happiness are determined by genes, ten percent by life circumstances and forty percent by our intentional activities."[1]

So, focus on the forty percent that you can control and make the most of your situation. I remember ten to fifteen years ago a common phrase was, "Have a good day." I always say, "Make it a good day," because we should all take control of our circumstances toward a positive outcome.

"Too many patients, when they are diagnosed with an illness or an injury, do not follow through with their treatment. They don't take their medication conscientiously and they don't change their habits, as recommended. As a result, they are soon back in the doctor's office or the emergency room."[2]

Whether it's a medical treatment or a methodology at work, you need to follow your standardized work plan. Practice it and follow the plan in real settings that emulate what you want to be successful in. I remember when I had basketball practice and every day we practiced free throws. However, it was always near the end of practice and after running the length of the court at least ten times. The reasoning was that it's more difficult to make free throws when you are breathing hard from strenuous running. Most of the important free throws are at the end of a close game when you are more tired, so that is how you should practice them.

Chapter 7

Likewise, you need to get out on the plant floor and practice improving how you want to function in your workplace every day. When implementing lean, reliability, maintainability and other continuous improvement tools, you need to stay the course, while at the same time demonstrate empathy, listening skills and flexibility. For example, when implementing 5S in one plant, several trades employees did not like the visual aid of colored tape around the wastebaskets to show where they should be stored. The employees saw it as childish and resisted a few items like that, but not the 5S concept in general. We decided to place an "X" on the floor underneath the wastebaskets to bring attention to when they are out of place. It's important to work through issues like this so the needed discipline and standardized work are followed. You can't partially do it and expect success. Take the time to change people's behavior. You should not put a time limit on it.

It's also necessary to get accountability to enable many of the needed tools and techniques. Too many groups still associate blame with accountability. Of course, there are times when blame is appropriate, such as blatant safety violations, signing off on maintenance checks without really checking, poor workmanship by taking shortcuts, etc. The main reason for accountability should be to support problem-solving and continuous improvement. Airlines use fingerprints to sign off on work performed because the potential consequences of not following standardized work are high. That level of accountability is not needed for most industries, but the foundation of knowing that each employee is capable and willing to do his or her job to the standardized work is a cornerstone of ongoing continuous improvement. Culture is the willingness to do what's needed to perform and continually improve one's job in support of company goals. What people do when they think that no one is watching is a true measure of your culture.

When implementing lean manufacturing concepts, there are differences in plant floor applications, depending on whether the business is high or low volume, or customized/job shop or flow shop. When instilling an ongoing improvement process, the same opportunities apply in all types of businesses. I read a business article titled, "Is your business a 'mensch'? It parallels many of the items discussed in this book. In Yiddish, the word *mensch* is the highest praise a person can give another person. In German, it translates to human being.

Business and personal qualities to aspire toward that are depicted in the article are:

1. Always do the right thing.
2. Say what you mean, mean what you say.
3. Be good to people.
4. Be dependable.
5. Be a mensch yourself.

"Bringing the mensch mentality to your company means thinking about your business as a 'collective of character,' a group of people behaving and working to the highest possible standard with intentions and actions beyond reproach. Earn that reputation and great things are sure to follow."[3]

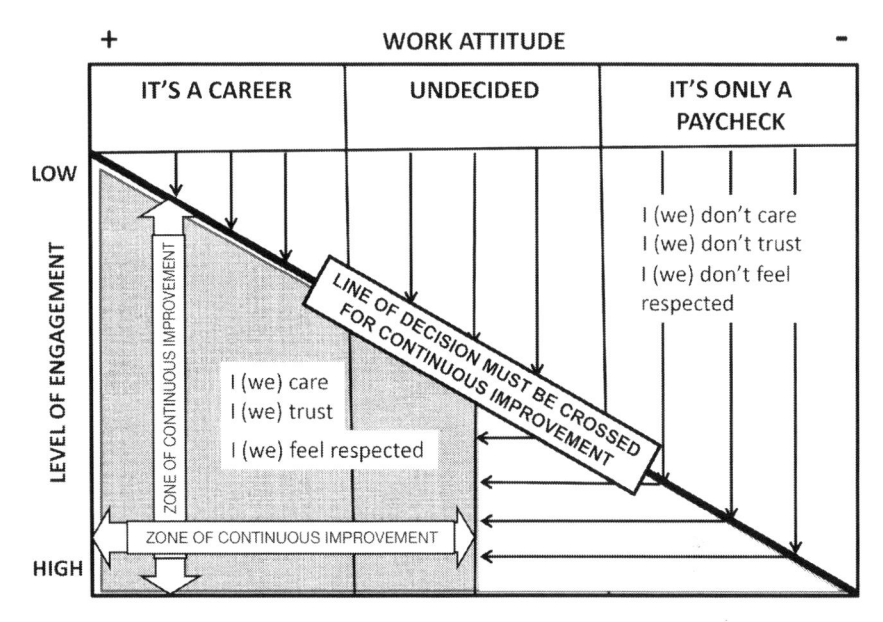

Figure 7.1: Zone of continuous improvement

It starts by understanding the thinking of individual team members, the collective group and the entire facility. Figure 7.1 shows the zone of continuous improvement for individuals, groups and plants. Each must ask:

- Do I (we) care?
- Do I (we) trust?
- Do I (we) feel respected?

You need to assess how many individuals are above and below the line of decision before deciding on the proper steps toward continuous improvement. Start by moving some of the undecided and disgruntled that are engaged to the zone of continuous improvement. If enough individuals or groups are in the zone of continuous improvement, then the entire group/facility can make significant progress. Use the tools and techniques, like force field analysis and the matrix for complex change to assess and engage the workforce.

To improve your organizational culture, you first need to believe yourself that a robust, small team continuous improvement process is the path to success. Otherwise, your daily actions and responses will not align with your spoken words. Some managers believe, but aren't willing to take the time needed for change due to short-term financial pressures. Also, their stay in one location is typically shorter than the time required to instill a new culture. You need to be able to explain the vision of what will improve and why it's important to recruit followers. This is relevant at all levels and projects. There is an increasing amount of data that supports the operational benefits of improving culture,

Chapter 7

similar to that already presented in earlier chapters, but still not a lot of it. Furthermore, when it comes to people, there is more variability in outcome. If you believe, do. To some, this may be called an axiom, which is an assumption without proof. Merriam-Webster defines axiom as "a rule or principle that many people accept as true." It also can be defined as "a starting point of reasoning" or "a premise so obvious that over time it is accepted as truth." It starts with you.

> *"Perfection is not attainable, but if we chase perfection, we can catch excellence."*
> — Vince Lombardi, Head Coach, Green Bay Packers

7.2 Do Something

Remember to go look and see. Get out on the plant floor to grasp the situation. When you need meetings, keep them organized, focused and brief.

The three evils of meetings are:

- "Meet, but don't discuss.
- Discuss, but don't decide.
- Decide, but don't do."

— Takeshi Kawabe, student of Taiichi Ohno

The best practices that you are doing today will, at best, represent only average performance tomorrow. Go and do something to get started. Take another step forward in your travels toward continuous improvement.

"The earth travels some two and a half million kilometers every day around the sun, eight times faster than that around the center of the Milky Way galaxy, and, perhaps, twice faster still as the Milky Way falls toward the Virgo cluster of galaxies. We have always been space travelers."[4]

So, just take a few more steps.

It's important to continually improve just to stay even with the competition. A robust continuous improvement process can help get the team through the change much faster. Figure 7.2 shows that the time spent resisting, rationalizing and instilling the change will be accelerated.

Physicists will tell you that everything in the universe goes from an orderly to a disorderly state. The same can be said for organizations, businesses, departments and teams in the absence of continuous improvement.

It's Up to You

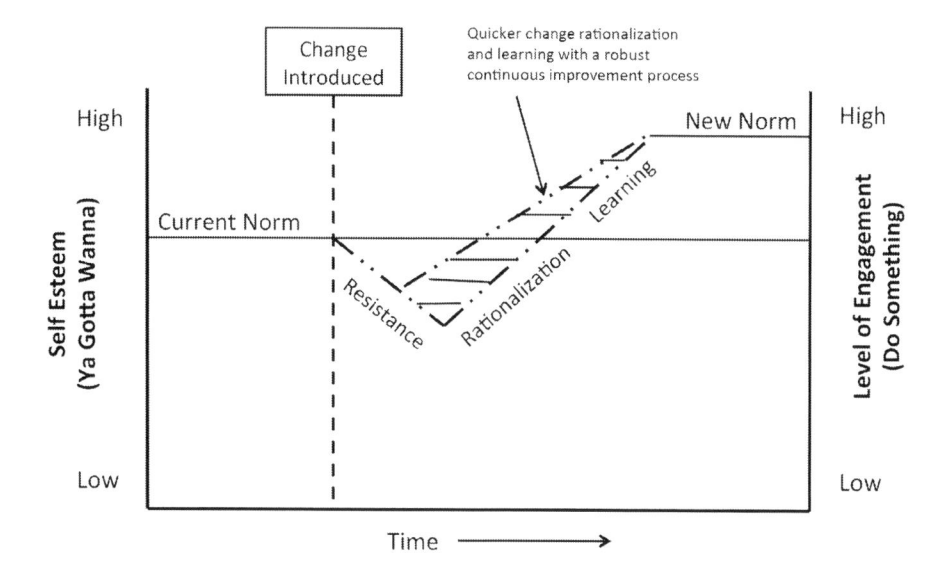

Figure 7.2: Change benefits of a robust continuous improvement process

Adapted from Carnall, 1986

> *"A wise man who has seen everything is not the equal of one who has done one thing with his hands.*
> — "Chinese Proverb

Everyone has ideas on how to make things better, but fear of being judged or failing often stops innovation and implementation. Also, it's lower risk to rationalize doing nothing. When you do decide to take action, work on the main task (s) as long as possible. Multitasking is not as effective or efficient, although it has the appearance of getting more done. Working on several things simultaneously may be more interesting, temporarily rewarding and, at times, necessary. But, it's been shown that "participants who completed tasks in parallel took up to thirty percent longer and made twice as many errors as those who completed the same tasks in sequence."[5]

Remember to listen and be open to learning. I really enjoy the old story of the Zen master and the teacup. A man of prominence came to the Zen master asking in a demanding tone to be taught about Zen. The Zen master suggested that they first discuss it over a cup of tea and served his visitor. He poured the cup full and kept on pouring. The visitor could watch no more and said, "It is already full. No more will go in." Like this cup, the Zen master said, "You are full and nothing more can be added. You must first empty your cup."[6]

In other words, be open to learning, no matter what your role is in the organization.

Chapter 7

7.3 Ya Gotta Wanna

I observed "Ya Gotta Wanna" on some team boards in an assembly plant in the early 1980s and never forgot it.

> *"Nothing in this world can take the place of persistence. Talent will not; nothing is more common than unsuccessful men with talent. Genius will not; unrewarded genius is almost a proverb. Education will not; the world is full of educated derelicts. Persistence and determination alone are omnipotent. The slogan 'Press On!' has solved and always will solve the problems of the human race.*
> — "Calvin Coolidge

Persistence, not giving up, "stick-to-it-iveness," as I like to say, will overcome many naysayers and much organizational resistance. Listen, observe and learn.

> *"Smart people learn from their own mistakes. Wise people learn from other people's mistakes."*
> — Author Unknown

There are always two choices: do nothing or do something. Realize that doing nothing – which often is risk avoidance – is just as significant of a choice. Understand clearly the consequences of both. Throughout your continuous improvement journey, you will always have two choices. It reminds me of a German song I heard several years ago while working in Europe. Its German title is, "Alles hat ein Ende nur die Wurst hat zwei." This translates to, "Everything has an end, only the hot dog has two."

I started this book's Preface with a hot dog story, so it's only fitting that I conclude with one. With this metaphor, every time you need to make a choice, think about the hot dog and remember that you always have two choices. You always have the opportunity to make a difference.

REFERENCES

1. Lyubomirsky, Sonja. *The How of Happiness: A New Approach to Getting the Life You Want*. London: Penguin Press, 2008. and https://en.wikipedia.org/wiki/Sonja_Lyubomirsky
2. Roth, William F. Comprehensive *Healthcare for the U.S.: An Idealized Model*. Boca Raton: CRC Press, 2010.
3. Hess, Michael. "Is your business a 'mensch'?" *CBS Money Watch*, 8 October 2012.
4. Sagan, Carl. *Cosmos*. New York City: Ballantine Books, 1985.
5. Asplund, Christopher L.; Dux, Paul E.; Ivanoff, Jason; and Rene Marois. "Isolation of a Central Bottleneck of Information Processing with Time-Resolved fMRI." *Neuron*, Volume 52, Number 6, 2006: pp. 1109-1120.
6. Adapted from how the author heard the story and https://en.wikipedia.org/wiki/101_Zen_Stories.

Appendix A

Appendix B

Date:
List Team Members:

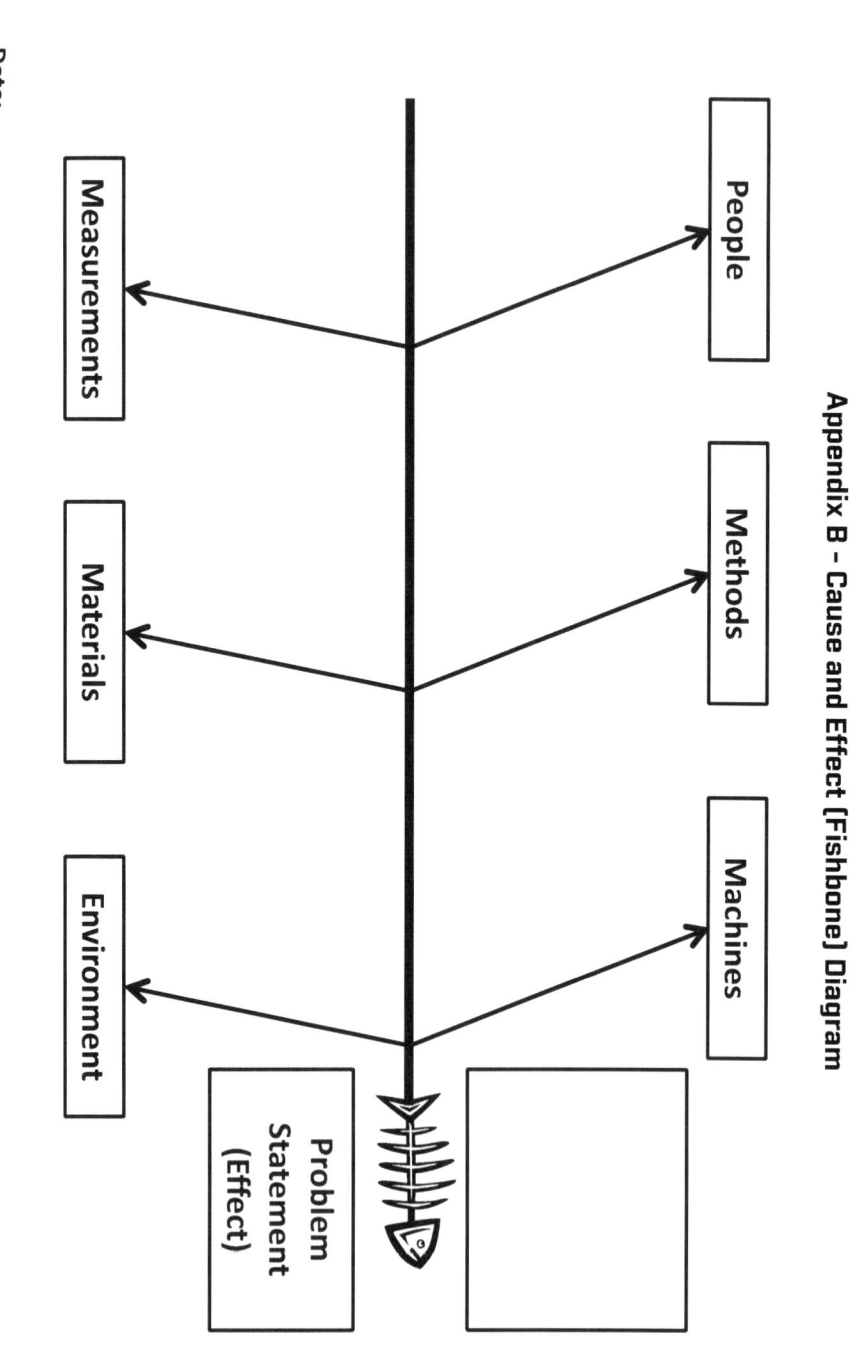

Appendix B - Cause and Effect (Fishbone) Diagram

- People
- Measurements
- Methods
- Materials
- Machines
- Environment

Problem Statement (Effect)

Appendix C (page 1)

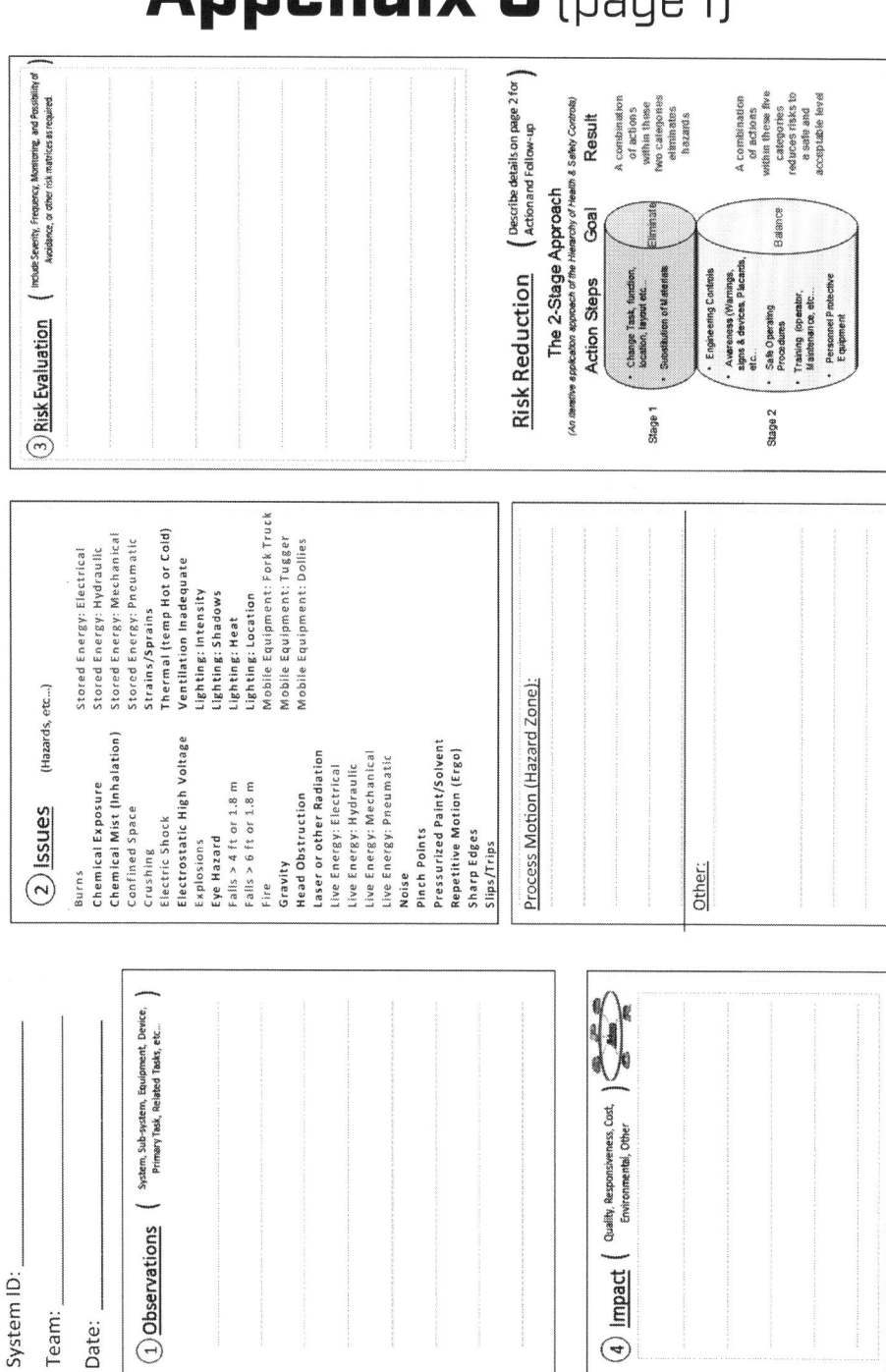

Appendix C: Risk Assessment Worksheet

System ID: _____
Team: _____
Date: _____

① Observations
(System, Sub-system, Equipment, Device, Primary Task, Related Tasks, etc...)

_____
_____
_____
_____
_____
_____

② Issues *(Hazards, etc...)*

Burns	Stored Energy: Electrical
Chemical Exposure	Stored Energy: Hydraulic
Chemical Mist (Inhalation)	Stored Energy: Mechanical
Confined Space	Stored Energy: Pneumatic
Crushing	Strains/Sprains
Electric Shock	Thermal (temp Hot or Cold)
Electrostatic High Voltage	Ventilation Inadequate
Explosions	Lighting: Intensity
Eye Hazard	Lighting: Shadows
Falls > 4 ft or 1.8 m	Lighting: Heat
Falls > 6 ft or 1.8 m	Lighting: Location
Fire	Mobile Equipment: Fork Truck
Gravity	Mobile Equipment: Tugger
Head Obstruction	Mobile Equipment: Dollies
Laser or other Radiation	
Live Energy: Electrical	
Live Energy: Hydraulic	
Live Energy: Mechanical	
Live Energy: Pneumatic	
Noise	
Pinch Points	
Pressurized Paint/Solvent	
Repetitive Motion (Ergo)	
Sharp Edges	
Slips/Trips	

Process Motion (Hazard Zone):
_____
_____
_____

Other:
_____
_____
_____

③ Risk Evaluation
(Include Severity, Frequency, Monitoring, and Possibility of Avoidance, or other risk matrices as required)

_____
_____
_____
_____
_____

Risk Reduction
(An iterative application approach of the Hierarchy of Health & Safety Controls)

The 2-Stage Approach *(Describe details on page 2 for Action and Follow-up)*

Action Steps | **Goal** | **Result**

Stage 1
- Change Task, function, location, layout etc.
- Substitution of materials

Eliminate — A combination of actions within these two categories eliminates hazards

Stage 2
- Engineering Controls
- Awareness (Warnings, signs & devices, Placards etc.
- Safe Operating Procedures
- Training, operator, Maintenance, etc.
- Personnel Protective Equipment

Balance — A combination of actions within these five categories reduces risks to a safe and acceptable level

④ Impact
(Quality, Responsiveness, Cost, Environmental, Other)

_____
_____
_____
_____
_____

141

Appendix C (page 2)

Appendix C: Risk Assessment Worksheet

Step ⑤ 2-Stage Details

List of Actions Required to Eliminate or Mitigate Risks — Responsibility — Est. Date

Due Diligence Matrix - To assure that all possible "Hierarchy of Control" combinations have been considered

Hierarchy of Health & Safety Control	Possible "Action Combinations" to Achieve Safe and Acceptable Risks - 34 total "Action Combinations" possible		
	Stage 1	Stage 2	
Action Combination # -->	1 2 3	4 5 6 7 8 9 10 11 12 13 14 15 16 17 18 19 20 21 22 23 24 25 26 27 28 29 30 31 32 33 34	
☐ Elimination by Change	✓ ✓		
☐ Elimination by Substitution	✓ ✓		
☐ Engineering Controls		✓ ✓ ✓ ✓ ✓ ✓ ✓ ✓ ✓ ✓ ✓ ✓ ✓ ✓ ✓	
☐ Awareness Devices		✓✓ ✓✓ ✓✓ ✓✓ ✓✓ ✓✓ ✓✓ ✓✓	
☐ Safe Operating Procedures		✓✓✓✓ ✓✓✓✓ ✓✓✓✓ ✓✓✓✓	
☐ Training		✓✓✓✓✓✓✓✓ ✓✓✓✓✓✓✓✓	
☐ Personnel Protective Equipment		✓✓✓✓✓✓✓✓✓✓✓✓✓✓✓✓	

Action Combination # _____

Has a Safe and Acceptable Risk been Achieved? → Yes → Assessment Complete

Revise Action List Requirements ← No

Uptime® Elements

Technical Activities

REM Reliability Engineering for Maintenance
- Ca – criticality analysis
- Rsd – reliability strategy development
- Re – reliability engineering
- Rca – root cause analysis
- Cp – capital project management
- Rcd – reliability centered design

ACM Asset Condition Management
- Aci – asset condition information
- Vib – vibration analysis
- Fa – fluid analysis
- Ut – ultrasound testing
- Ir – infrared thermal imaging
- Mt – motor testing
- Ab – alignment and balancing
- Ndt – non destructive testing
- Lu – machinery lubrication

WEM Work Execution Management
- Pm – preventive maintenance
- Ps – planning and scheduling
- Odr – operator driven reliability
- Mro – mro-spares management
- De – defect elimination
- Cmms – computerized maintenance management system

Leadership

LER Leadership for Reliability
- Es – executive sponsorship
- Opx – operational excellence
- Hcm – human capital management
- Cbl – competency based learning
- Int – integrity
- Rj – reliability journey

Business Processes

AM Asset Management
- Sp – strategy and plans
- Cr – corporate responsibility
- Samp – strategic asset management plan
- Ri – risk management
- Ak – asset knowledge
- Alm – asset lifecycle management
- Dm – decision making
- Pi – performance indicators
- Ci – continuous improvement

A Reliability Framework and Asset Management System™

Reliabilityweb.com's Asset Management Timeline

Business Needs Analysis → Design → Create/Acquire → Operate / Maintain / Modify/Upgrade → Dispose/Renew → Residual Liabilities

Asset Lifecycle

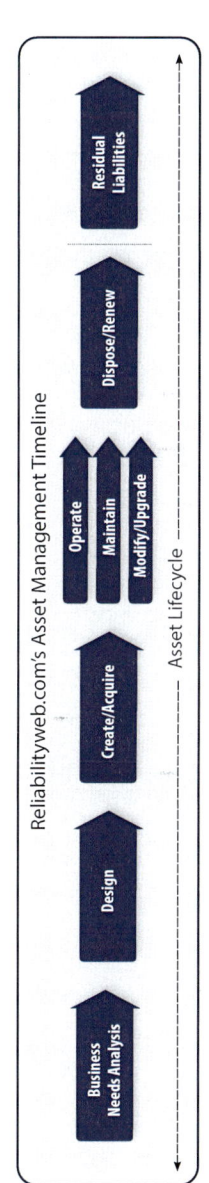

Copyright 2016-2021 Reliabilityweb, Inc. All rights reserved. No part of this graphic may be reproduced or transmitted in any form or by any means without the prior express written consent of Reliabilityweb, Inc. Reliabilityweb.com®, Uptime® and A Reliability Framework and Asset Management System™ are trademarks and registered trademarks of Reliabilityweb, Inc. in the U.S.A. and several other countries.

reliabilityweb.com • maintenance.org • reliabilityleadership.com

Reliabilityweb.com® and Uptime® Magazine Mission: **To make the people we serve safer and more successful.** One way we support this mission is to suggest a reliability system for asset performance management as pictured above. Our use of the Uptime Elements is designed to assist you in categorizing and organizing your own Body of Knowledge (BoK) whether it be through training, articles, books or webinars. Our hope is to make YOU safer and more successful.

ABOUT RELIABILITYWEB.COM

Created in 1999, Reliabilityweb.com provides educational information and peer-to-peer networking opportunities that enable safe and effective reliability and asset management for organizations around the world.

ACTIVITIES INCLUDE:

Reliabilityweb.com® (www.reliabilityweb.com) includes educational articles, tips, video presentations, an industry event calendar and industry news. Updates are available through free email subscriptions and RSS feeds. **Confiabilidad.net** is a mirror site that is available in Spanish at www.confiabilidad.net.

Uptime® Magazine (www.uptimemagazine.com) is a monthly magazine launched in 2005 that is highly prized by the reliability and asset management community.

Reliability Leadership Institute® Conferences and Training Events (www.reliabilityleadership.com) offer events that range from unique, focused-training workshops and seminars to small focused conferences to large industry-wide events, including the International Maintenance Conference (IMC), MaximoWorld and The RELIABILITY Conference™ (TRC).

MRO-Zone Bookstore (www.mro-zone.com) is an online bookstore offering a reliability and asset management focused library of books, DVDs and CDs published by Reliabilityweb.com.

Association of Asset Management Professionals (www.maintenance.org) is a member organization and online community that encourages professional development and certification and supports information exchange and learning with 50,000+ members worldwide.

A Word About Social Good

Reliabilityweb.com is mission-driven to deliver value and social good to the reliability and asset management communities. *Doing good work and making profit is not inconsistent*, and as a result of Reliabilityweb.com's mission-driven focus, financial stability and success has been the outcome. For over a decade, Reliabilityweb.com's positive contributions and commitment to the reliability and asset management communities have been unmatched.

Other Causes

Reliabilityweb.com has financially contributed to include industry associations, such as SMRP, AFE, STLE, ASME and ASTM, and community charities, including the Salvation Army, American Red Cross, Wounded Warrior Project, Paralyzed Veterans of America and the Autism Society of America. In addition, we are proud supporters of our U.S. Troops and first responders who protect our freedoms and way of life. That is only possible by being a for-profit company that pays taxes.

I hope you will get involved with and explore the many resources that are available to you through the Reliabilityweb.com network.

Warmest regards,
Terrence O'Hanlon
CEO, Reliabilityweb.com

Reliabilityweb.com®, Uptime®, The RELIABILITY Conference™, MaximoWorld and Reliability Leadership Institute® are the trademarks or registered trademarks of Reliabilityweb.com and its affiliates in the USA and in several other countries.